0079206

D1686090

LOW LIFE AND MORAL IMPROVEMENT IN MID-VICTORIAN ENGLAND

Low Life and Moral Improvement in Mid-Victorian England

Liverpool through the journalism of Hugh Shimmin

Edited by
John K. Walton and Alastair Wilcox

Leicester University Press
(a division of Pinter Publishers)
Leicester, London and New York

© Introduction and notes © John K. Walton and Alastair Wilcox, 1991

First published in Great Britain in 1991 by Leicester University Press
(a division of Pinter Publishers Ltd)

Editorial offices
Fielding Johnson Building, University of Leicester
University Road, Leicester, LE1 7RH

Trade and other enquiries
25 Floral Street, London, WC2E 9DS

British Library Cataloguing in Publication Data
A CIP cataloguing record for this book is available
from the British Library

ISBN 0 7185 1351 7

For enquiries in North America please contact
PO Box 197, Irvington, NY 10533

Library of Congress Cataloging-in-Publication Data
Shimmin, Hugh, d. 1879.
   Low life and moral improvement in mid-Victorian England:
Liverpool through the journalism of Hugh Shimmin/edited by John K.
Walton and Alastair Wilcox.
      p.   cm.
   Includes bibliographical references and index.
   ISBN 0–7185–1351–7
   1. Liverpool (England) – Social conditions. 2. Liverpool
(England) – Social life and customs. 3. Liverpool (England) – Moral
conditions. 4. England – Social conditions – 19th century.
I. Walton, John K. II. Wilcox, Alastair. III. Title.
HN398.L5S56 1991   90-24901
306'.09427'53–dc20   CIP

SB 2795 /37.50. 6.91

Typeset by Mayhew Typesetting, Bristol, England
Printed and bound in Great Britain by Billings and Sons Ltd, Worcester

Contents

Preface

This project originated in a seminar discussion on the M.A. course in Modern Social History at the University of Lancaster, when the authors discovered a shared interest in Hugh Shimmin. Its purpose is to make Shimmin's work more widely available in a form which makes it accessible to students while whetting the appetite for further research. The introduction offers some biographical, contextual and comparative comment on Shimmin and his writings, and the notes provide elucidation and basic bibliographical guidance. Otherwise, Shimmin is left to speak for himself, impeded only by any distortions we may have imposed by our criteria for selecting from the large supply of available material. We hope that our supporting material will help readers to approach Shimmin in an informed and critical way, without feeling that our opinions and interpretations have been imposed upon them. The editors' thanks go to Jenny Smith, for typing – and commenting on – a substantial proportion of the Shimmin text with characteristic verve and efficiency; to Gill Parsons, for 'tasting' the Manchester *Free Lance* and reporting – correctly – that it would be useful; and to Marilyn Dale, for her tolerance of the sociable by-products of Alastair Wilcox's research trips to Liverpool. Alastair Wilcox would also like to thank his brother Nigel, who first introduced him to the works of Hugh Shimmin. Our thanks also to the members of the Centre for Social History seminar at Lancaster for valuable comment on an early version of the introduction. The mistakes are our own. It only remains to add that we have followed Hugh Shimmin's idiosyncrasies of grammar, spelling and punctuation faithfully.

J.K.W.
A.W.
Lancaster and Freckleton, 11 August 1990

Introduction

Hugh Shimmin was a prolific, idiosyncratic and opinionated journalist whose work covered a wide range of themes and social issues in the Liverpool of the 1850s and 1860s. He had a great deal to say about such contentious matters as housing conditions and sanitary reform, poverty and philanthropy, working-class leisure and family life, and (usually implicitly) the workings of class relations and the social structure. He tackled these questions in the context of a city which was second only to London in mid-Victorian Britain in terms of size, commercial opulence and social pathology. His work poses problems of interpretation and evaluation for social historians, but it deserves to be better known and more widely used than is currently the case.

Shimmin's work is often footnoted but rarely discussed, even by historians whose main interest lies in Victorian Liverpool and Merseyside. Margaret Simey's examination of charitable effort in nineteenth-century Liverpool, published forty years ago, contains extended discussions of the influence of Shimmin and his newspaper, the Porcupine, on attitudes and policy in this regard,[1] but subsequent commentators have been slow to follow her example.[2] This is partly a matter of the distinctive trajectory of Liverpool's historiography. Historians' main concerns have lain with trade and transport, especially the slave trade, the docks, the business history of shipping lines, and the development of links between the port and its hinterland.[3] Or they have focused on politics and local government, through the twin lenses of sectarianism and the municipal dimension of sanitary reform.[4] Or they have approached the lives and preoccupations of ordinary Liverpudlians more closely through basically (but not entirely) statistical studies of migration, demography and social structure, making sophisticated use of the census enumerators' books through computer-assisted analysis.[5] Or again they have charted the struggles of the emerging labour movement, especially under the difficult circumstances of the waterfront, and with special reference to anarcho-syndicalism and the great transport strike of 1911.[6] In almost all these themes the Irish have been close to the centre of the stage; but in none of them has a sustained attempt been made

to present the Liverpool working class, or a significant fragment of
it, in all the phases of its existence: at home, at work, at play, at
prayer, and in its relations with its 'betters'. There is nothing on
Liverpool to approach, for example, the thematic range of Gareth
Stedman-Jones's work on the East End of London.[7] The agenda of
research has been set in such a way as to drive Hugh Shimmin's
writings to the margins, in striking contrast to the importance of
Henry Mayhew to the social history of working-class London or of
Engels to that of Manchester and the 'cotton district'. Thus, and
only thus, is it possible for a recent 'economic and social history of
Merseyside' to make no reference to Shimmin in the text, to cite
none of his writings in the bibliography, and to pay more attention
to trade and transport, narrowly conceived, than to the ways of life
and standards of living of the people at large.[8] A better understanding of Hugh Shimmin and his work is a useful first step
towards a much-needed new social history of Liverpool itself.

Shimmin's writings have been most readily available through a
reprint edition of his *Liverpool Life*, which began as a series of
articles for the *Liverpool Mercury* in 1856 and achieved local
notoriety for its portrayal of the complex pattern of intersecting
social circles which made up a distinctive Liverpool 'underworld' of
vice, crime, blood sports, gambling, drink and squalor. Even within
Liverpool Life there is more to Shimmin's range than this. His first
volume includes a paean of praise to the Corporation's Cornwallis
Street baths for their promotion of cleanliness and rational recreation, and in similar vein the second volume describes the Free
Library and Museum, and a reformatory, and goes on to discuss
the 'social condition of the people' and their homes, and the nature
and limitations of attempts at reform through religious agencies.[9]
These themes are taken up more strongly in Shimmin's later work,
for during the 1860s, especially, he emerged as an expert on Liverpool's courts and alleys, and the sanitary and social problems
associated with them. He also emerged as a chronicler of working-
class home life, with a fund of illustrative stories drawn more or
less from experience, and a horror of statistics and abstract
formulae. He was also a fiercely satirical commentator on the Liverpool political scene, above all at local government level. All these
facets of Shimmin need to be considered if his influence is to be
evaluated and his value as an historical source assessed. He must
not be treated as Mayhew (most obviously) has been, with some
texts and themes picked out for special treatment and tendentious
interpretation while others are allowed to languish unread and
undiscussed.[10]

Shimmin was in a position to know whereof he spoke, although
he was much closer to some kinds of experience than to others, and

his discourse poses plenty of problems for the critical historian. A brief outline of his life will do much to aid understanding of his work. He liked to present himself as the archetypal self-made man: his life reads, and was made to read, as a text on self-help. As the *Liverpool Daily Post* obituarist commented, 'Few men beginning life in so humble a sphere have occupied such a prominent position as Hugh Shimmin.'[11] And the *Liberal Review* stated that his life 'taken as a whole may profitably be studied by those who are about to enter upon the battle of life'.[12]

Shimmin's origins are obscure in more than just the sense of being humble. But if we treat his novel *Harry Birkett* as a kind of romanticised autobiography, in outline at least, we pick up his story in Whitehaven (which is undoubtedly the 'Poebeck' of the book) as a young child in about 1825. His father was a Manxman, but his formative years were passed in west Cumberland. In his early teens he went with his father, a stonemason with a recurrent drink problem, to work on the rebuilding of a great house about sixty miles from Whitehaven. 'Hazel-hall', as Shimmin called it, may well have been Holker Hall, which was being rebuilt at about that time; and Shimmin's romantic claim to have met his future wife at this time finds circumstantial support from his wife's birthplace being listed in the census enumerators' books as Haverthwaite, which is a few miles short of Holker on the line of the direct route from Whitehaven across the fells. This fits in exactly with the story line of *Harry Birkett*.[13]

If we continue to follow the plot of the novel, Shimmin's father seems to have left 'Hazel-hall', where his son continued working; and he is next heard of as a repair and maintenance worker on the docks at 'Riverside', which is undoubtedly Liverpool. Shimmin and his beloved mother soon moved to join him, taking a sailing ship from Whitehaven. They found the errant father stupefied by drink in a pub near his low lodgings, and made some attempt to reestablish family life. It is at this point that the plot of *Harry Birkett* can be reinforced by Liverpool sources, including especially Shimmin's obituaries, and a more reliable picture can be pieced together.[14]

Soon after his arrival in Liverpool Shimmin was apprenticed to a bookbinder; in the fifth year of his apprenticeship his father, who had never been a reliable provider, died, plunging the family into even deeper poverty than before. Shimmin became the main support of his mother and the younger children. He made a little extra by collecting rents for the landlord, which must have been a hazardous task, and help was forthcoming from religious contacts and associates of the family. But soon after completing his apprenticeship he was put in charge of the workshop, and although this excited the envy of those who saw him as a 'boss's man' and resented his rejection of the drinking customs which prevailed among most of the work force, it put his future and that of his family on a firm footing.[15]

Harry Birkett gives us several insights into Shimmin's character and background. He was clearly familiar with the stresses and problems of working-class life. From an early age he seems to have been accustomed to bringing his father home from the pub or the beerhouse, especially on pay day; and his attitudes to drink are firmly rooted in experience of what havoc it could play with working-class living standards. The squalor of slum living, and the inadequacies of working-class dwellings in both Whitehaven and Liverpool, are also clearly portrayed from bitter experience. Conditions in Whitehaven, incidentally, could be every bit as bad as in the worst parts of Liverpool, as Robert Rawlinson's report to the Board of Health was to point out in 1849: 'Few persons would believe the human wretchedness that exists in Whitehaven, without making an inspection . . . Many of [the] rooms are swarming with vermin; disease and fever prevail throughout.' And the Manx quarter was said to be the worst of all.[16]

Shimmin also knew at first hand about the pressures among neighbours towards a sociability which encouraged gambling and communal drinking as well as offering solace and mutual assistance. Those who opted out of this mode of existence were shunned as stand-offish and cultivating airs and graces. Shimmin's mother seems to have suffered in this way, finding compensation in the Primitive Methodists and later in the temperance movement. Religious influences were clearly very important in Shimmin's own life. In Liverpool a customer at the bookbinder's guided him into attendance at Meanly Lane School and thence to Paradise Street Chapel. This Unitarian chapel had been reinvigorated by the dynamic preacher James Martineau, and the Liverpool Unitarians also had a Domestic Mission, set up to reach out to the city's poor, under the influence of the American movement begun by Dr Tuckerman. Contact with the Unitarians will have brought Shimmin into some sort of relationship, however distant, with Liverpool's most influential merchant families, in a tolerant questioning, philanthropic atmosphere. He was also closely involved with the Wesleyans, and these highly respectable contacts, along with a preference for books and a quiet life at home, seem to have kept him away from the temptations which beset adolescent life in Liverpool, and of whose existence he was well aware.[17]

Harry Birkett also continually stresses the importance of self-improvement through steady application to study, and Shimmin himself became an eager pursuer of skills and knowledge outside working hours. To the last days of his life he would proudly show his friends the treasured copy of the moralistic, improving *Life of Dr Franklin* which his early patron had given him on completion of his first six months' school attendance. But perhaps the crucial formative influence was his joining the Mechanics' Institute, after saving assiduously in order to afford the fees. This helped him to expand his range of reading. Carlyle's *Chartism* and *Past and Present* were early texts, and Dickens became a strong influence on his approach and style, as the frequent quotations in his texts make abundantly clear. And through the Mechanics' Institute he came into contact with a separate organisation sharing the premises, the Mental Improvement Society. Attracted by chance in 1845 to a debate on 'Whether trade unions have been beneficial to the working man', he became embroiled in the argument on the trade union side. Though members were allegedly surprised by his 'crude and wild' ideas, sprinkled with some raw Carlyle quotations, the young Shimmin succeeded in joining the society. He then contributed to its magazine, and the vigorous response he evoked proved a central influence on his future career, pushing him strongly towards journalism, and he commented that the episode had changed the course of his life. Membership of the society also brought Shimmin into teaching in their pioneering evening ragged schools.[18]

Membership of the Mechanics' Institute also led Shimmin to a consciousness of his comparatively humble status, as he became aware of the low quality of his clothing and encountered the snobbish hostility of some of the members. This is an interesting sidelight on the Mechanics' Institute itself, and it also engendered an aggressively hostile stance towards empty middle-class pretension, whether in dress, religion or philanthropy. Shimmin may have been an advocate of working hard and steadily in your station, and trying to gain advancement by winning approval for a modest demeanour and work well done, but his sense of personal worth continued to be based on character rather than show. Throughout his work runs a continuing sense of working-class identity; and perhaps throughout his life, too. As one obituary noted:

He was, in short, in appearance rather rough; and he never apparently took any pains to be otherwise. His clothes were generally badly cut, of no particular shape and no special pattern, and looked as if they had been carelessly huddled on. In some respects his appearance was eminently characteristic. He bore the stamp of a self-made man who had not the time or had not thought it worth his while to acquire any of those arts and social graces upon which fine gentlemen pride themselves.[19]

This apparently calculated unpretentiousness in dress was part of a more general mode of self-presentation, which could make Shimmin seem physically unprepossessing and even intimidating:

> At first sight he seemed to be the very opposite of what one would expect an intellectual man devoted to literary pursuits to be. He was above the middle height, stout . . . and his gait was lumbering and awkward. His face was broad and chubby and rather of the sensual order, conveying the idea that the owner of it was a man who was accustomed to enjoy himself, and experienced a keen delight in purely animal pleasures . . . There was . . . a general sense of power surrounding him. He seemed a strong man both mentally and physically. His small eyes set deep in his head were bright and piercing; his brow was full and square.[20]

In some ways he looked not unlike one of the Liverpool 'roughs' described in his own *Liverpool Sketches*, with their 'big heads, broad flat faces and thick necks'.[21] This may help to explain how Shimmin managed to go where he went, see what he did and escape unscathed when gathering the more picaresque material for *Liverpool Life*. There is, indeed, evidence that he became a welcome visitor to some parts of the slums. At his funeral, enduring the drizzle at the Anfield cemetery, were:

> . . . a number of persons, principally women in poor and tattered garments who had probably trudged some miles in [sic] their wretched abodes to supply in their attendance a mute but touching expression of gratitude for private bounties from one whom their poor homes can know no more.[22]

While Shimmin in person remained rough-and-ready and even unkempt, he prospered modestly in business. He was able to buy the bookbinding business in which he had risen to foreman for £70, and eventually he became owner as well as editor of the *Porcupine*, a periodical which he came almost to personify. He eventually left a little over £5,000, after twenty years or so of rubbing shoulders, sometimes rather uneasily, with Liverpool's leading citizens. He ascribed a great deal of his success to his family, and especially to his mother and his wife. Shimmin's mother is visibly the heroine of *Harry Birkett*, with her selfless, loving self-discipline, generosity and powers of endurance and forgiveness. There were also fond memories of his father when sober, which were articulated in an early public lecture on 'Working men's wives' which he delivered in 1858. Here he idealises the cult of home, fireside and family, and brings the memory of his father into the charmed circle:

> I know what it is to see the radiant smile of the father disperse the gloom which was settling on the face of a watchful tender-hearted mother; and I will never forget the glee with which the little hands used to be clapped to welcome father home.[23]

The lecture goes on to outline the perils faced by the working-class family, especially the threat of drink; but here, as elsewhere, Shimmin is every bit as alert to the dangers of female failings as to those of men, and the drunken or slatternly wife is repeatedly the butt of his attacks. Fittingly, in this context, he was always at pains to praise the good humour and good management of his own wife. His childless but apparently very happy marriage reinforced a characteristic sentimentality towards children, which was shown not only in his writings but also in subscriptions and support for the Seaman's Orphanage and Myrtle Street Children's Infirmary. Above all, his wife's thrift had enabled him to raise the purchase price of his master's bookbinding business: she had relieved his depression at the prospect of losing a marvellous opportunity by handing him a savings book containing exactly the right amount. This was clearly an often repeated tale, and Shimmin made no bones about his dependence on his wife's domestic competence. This confirmed his view of the working man's wife as either the pillar of the family, by her support, encouragement and skills, or its subverter, by slatternly, disorganised conduct which drove the husband to the pub and the children into the street. Others shared this perception, of course: thus George Melly, the Liverpool merchant, banker and Liberal politician, lecturing on 'ignorant wives who do not know their duty to their husbands and who bring up uneducated and dirty children'.[24] For Shimmin unwashed crockery and random piles of washing were tell-tale signs of domestic inefficiency, which were likely to show a preference for smoking, drinking and gossip with neighbours rather than household duties, and would probably coexist with financial mismanagement. The harvest would be morally stunted children, and girls who failed to acquire the skills and frame of mind to become proper mothers, just as they invariably made bad domestic servants. So Shimmin drew lessons from his own family life, and was not slow to apply them in examining and censuring the conduct of others from his own position of thrifty and fairly comfortable domestic respectability.

Shimmin's writing career began with two occasional pieces, on fortune-tellers and on policing, which appeared in the *Liverpool Mercury*. Another early piece was a description of a trip to the Lake District, which found an outlet in the *Liverpool Albion*; and he subsequently wrote at greater length in this vein, publishing (under the pseudonym 'Harry Hardknot') a book called *Rambles in the Lake District*. Lyrical descriptions of mountains and waterfalls in *Harry Birkett* suggest that attachment to the Lake District went back to Whitehaven days, and Shimmin continued to find solace there until the end of his life.[25] But there was a moral dimension to *Rambles*. Such excursions were to be taken seriously: travellers who spent the night drinking at the inn would not be among those who awoke to get the full benefit of the scenery and exercise. And readers were gently cautioned not to envy the denizens of the elegant and spacious houses of the wealthy, and urged not to make comparisons between these abodes and their own.[26] Fell walking was certainly a serious pursuit: it was a matter of character-building. Harry Birkett's chief benefactor, in one of the homilies which pervade the book, tells the hero, 'As the pedestrian with his first mountain . . . so the working man with the saving of his first pound.'[27] Even on holiday, high seriousness of purpose was never far from Shimmin's mind.

This was all very well, but it did not catch on to any great extent. The turning point in Shimmin's journalistic career came in 1855–56, when he wrote the series of articles in the *Liverpool Mercury* which was soon afterwards published in book form as *Liverpool Life: its Pleasures, Practices and Pastimes*. The descriptions of back-street amusements, drinking dives, music halls, popular blood sports, and dens of iniquity and vice in general, stirred up a considerable controversy. Critics urged that it was better to leave these pleasures and practices unmentioned than to risk corrupting additional people by making their existence known. So the book of *Liverpool Life* featured at its masthead on the title page the legend 'Publicity the true cure of social evils', and included an appendix of supportive letters from the Rev. Harcus of Toxteth Chapel, the chaplain of the borough gaol and, best of all, the great merchant aristocrat and philanthropist William Rathbone.[28] The book's success may well have owed as much to prurient curiosity as to a concerned pursuit of social inquiry, but it certainly made Hugh Shimmin a name to be reckoned with. Meanwhile, during 1857, he wrote a series of satirical portraits of Liverpool town councillors, which also appeared in the *Mercury*; and in 1866 this also came out in book form, as *Pen and Ink Sketches of Liverpool Town Councillors*. The seal was set on these achievements when in 1860 Shimmin became editor of the new satirical weekly, *Porcupine*, which provided a platform for his views, a vehicle for his crusades, and an outlet for his sense of humour. In the paper's own obituary of Shimmin it described itself thus:

The *Porcupine* developed a new feature in local journalism. The 'freelance' style of criticism on all subjects which was from the first adopted, and the miscellaneous range of its writing, enlisted contributors of all ranks and conditions, and of all opinions. Perhaps no journal in this or any other town has had in its time so many contributors.[29]

Shimmin's own politics were undoctrinaire Liberal, though he moved to the right as he grew older and (it was uncharitably suggested) as he mixed more with civic bigwigs. In later years his religious outlook also shifted as he left Nonconformity and became 'a firm adherent of the Church of England and an admirer of its liturgies'. But in the *Porcupine* years what most engrossed his attention, and made him best known, was his campaigns on housing and sanitary issues. As the obituarist put it:

Though not a scientific man, in the ordinary sense of the term, Mr Shimmin, from personal observation, from reading, and from intercourse with advanced students of sanitary science, had accumulated a vast store of knowledge on that and kindred subjects, and through the pages of *Porcupine*, by his cogent arguments and powerful illustrations, was able to give an immense impetus to sanitary reform in Liverpool.[30]

This was indeed Shimmin's main claim to fame, and his exposures of conditions in the back streets and courts made a major contribution to the Liverpool Sanitary Amendment Act of 1864. But all were fair game for his arrows, fellow Nonconformist Liberals not excluded. Welsh builders and landlords for providing houses without water, tenants for preferring houses without water, landlords for providing squalid accommodation, tenants for making it squalid, Jewish moneylenders, Methodist moneylenders and Church of England clergy were all castigated. Only the Roman Catholics and the Irish escaped the torrent of criticism. Admittedly, Shimmin was readier to criticise than to propose solutions, and he fell into self-contradiction too readily on occasions. Children were seen as helpless victims of environment and circumstance, but despite these disabilities they were subjected to the severest censure when as adults they acted upon the conditioning they had received. At times, too, Shimmin was the victim of his own over-exuberance. His vitriolic temper was combined with a boisterous sense of humour. His impetuosity embroiled him in a semi-official ecclesiastical hearing when he rashly accused a minister of stealing the sermons he preached. By his skilful use of mimicry and parody he reduced the proceedings to farce, and came away unscathed. But he was less fortunate when he accused mercantile companies of insurance frauds in a sequel to his piece on 'Ocean Thuggism' on 23 October 1869. He lost the ensuing libel case and was committed to Kirkdale prison; but such was his popularity that not only was a public subscription raised to cover his legal costs, but he was also allowed to serve his sentence in the chaplain's quarters. Petitions in his support were signed by large numbers of eminent Liverpudlians. He had enemies too, of course, and when his storm-tossed career came to an end a sympathetic speech on his death was interrupted in the council chambers by cries of 'No, no!'[31]

Shimmin was clearly a larger-than-life figure, with a wide range of controversial opinions and insights to offer. The stage on which

he strode was also constructed on the grand scale; and to set Shimmin's journalism properly in context we need to say more about the
city in which it was set.

Liverpool in the 1850s and 1860s was Britain's second city, with
a population of about 444,000 within the borough boundary in
1861. It was above all a commercial centre, whose key economic
activities involved supplying and servicing the needs of merchants
and merchant seamen, loading and unloading vessels, transporting
their cargoes to and from the port's extensive hinterland, and
providing administrative and professional services to oil and drive
the wheels of commerce. Manufacturing industry had shrivelled
after a promising period in the late eighteenth century, and most of
it involved the processing of imports like tobacco and sugar. Ship-
building was migrating across the river to Birkenhead, although
there remained plenty of relatively well paid work for ship repairers
and assorted foundrymen and metalworkers. As befitted a town
which continued to grow rapidly and to extend its already magnificent array of docks (which also needed to be repaired and maintained), building workers were very much in evidence, and it was
in these trades that Liverpool's main concentrations of skilled
manual workers were to be found. Nor should we forget the growing demand for clerical workers, in commerce, banking, insurance
offices and a burgeoning variety of administrative spheres. This
work was not well paid, except for a privileged minority of super-
visors and men in positions of responsibility, but it offered more
security than the casual sectors of dock labouring, transport and
building. But the labour market of central Liverpool was visibly
dominated by an insecure world of casual labour and intermittent,
unpredictable earnings. Work on the waterfront might pay well for
short periods, but only a minority of dockers could look forward
to regular employment which generated a regular and predictable
weekly wage. Most remained dependent on catching the foreman's
eye, and for the majority of working-class Liverpudlians life was of
necessity a hand-to-mouth existence, with no real chance of saving
or insuring against contingencies. The poverty of central Liverpool
was endemic and notorious.[32]

Matters were made more difficult by the limited availability of
regular waged work for women and children. The 1851 census
found that 36 per cent of adult females were in paid employment,
as against a national figure of 45 per cent. Moreover, women
accounted for well over half the adult population of the city: there
were 109 women to every hundred men between the ages of fifteen
and forty-five at the censuses of 1851 and 1861, and the ratio
increased steadily in the older age groups. Nearly three-quarters of
Liverpool's wage-earning women were in the generally ill paid

sectors of domestic service and dressmaking. Admittedly, some women's employment was not recorded in the official figures. The armies of prostitutes, regular and casual, to whom Hugh Shimmin paid sustained attention were not allowed to feature in the census returns, and large numbers of barmaids and other workers in the entertainment districts around the docks and the city centre will also have escaped attention. Part-time charwomen probably slipped through the net as well. For a later period Lambertz and Ayers's oral interviews uncovered a hidden female economy in Liverpool which certainly had its antecedents in Shimmin's time. Women augmented inadequate family incomes by chopping and selling kindling, taking in washing (and sometimes pawning it to cover the regular mid-week cash-flow crisis), keeping small shops in front rooms and cellars, and lending money at exorbitant interest to those who were even worse off than themselves. A lot of this economic activity was hidden from husbands, and was therefore unlikely to have reached the ears of the census taker. So women earned money in Liverpool in a wider range of ways and to a greater extent, than the official statistics might suggest. Even so, the sum of their efforts added up to only a marginal alleviation of family poverty which was all too often extremely severe, even by the standards of the time.[33]

Liverpool also had an unusually youthful population: those under twenty years old accounted for a remarkably constant 43 or 44 per cent of the townspeople in all the mid-Victorian censuses. But the local economy generated few reputable opportunities for children and teenagers. Thus fewer than one in five of Liverpool's under-twenties were recorded as 'occupied' in the 1851 census. In this respect Liverpool, along with several other ports and dockyard towns, was firmly in the bottom cohort of 'principal towns'. These low rates of juvenile employment coexisted with patchy school attendance figures. The 1851 survey found a comparatively respectable level of day school attendance, but a very low figure for Sunday schools. Literacy levels, as measured by signatures and marks on marriage registers, were actually slightly higher than the national figure. But they were swollen by large numbers of literate migrants from elsewhere, and the relatively optimistic general indices conceal the experience of tens of thousands of children in the poorer areas who never went to school at all. This problem was, if anything, worsening during the 1850s and 1860s, helping to account for the unusually slow improvement in Liverpool's literacy statistics during this time, although the Irish refugees from the Famine of the mid-1840s also played their part.[34]

Contemporaries assumed that the devil would find work for idle young hands. Hugh Shimmin's preoccupation with the dangerous lives of the children of the streets, who haunted the markets, the docks, the landing stages and some of the 'low' places of entertainment, both reflected and encouraged this set of expectations. Contemporaries blamed the unemployed and unschooled young for crime and vandalism on a grand scale, and there was talk of an army of juvenile thieves, twelve thousand strong, taught and manipulated by two thousand Faginesque puppet-masters.[35]

But this was only one distinctive feature of crime in Liverpool. The city had developed a spectacular reputation for insecurity of life and property. Philip Waller speaks of 'omnipresent brutality': not just on the waterfront and in the slum districts, but pervading all levels of the city's life. The ubiquity of drink and drunkenness helped to explain the high incidence of stabbings and assaults; and Shimmin's concentration on the drink issue again reflected contemporary concern as well as reinforcing it. Drink played its part in the sectarian violence of popular politics, as processions led to riots on the great rival anniversaries of St Patrick's Day and the battle of the Boyne. These set-piece confrontations between Protestant and Catholic, which also had ethnic and territorial dimensions, reinforced Liverpool's image of chronic urban violence; but it had plenty of more mundane sustenance in the daily life of the town centre and the waterfront.[36]

Contemporaries were divided about how far the most concentrated manifestations of crime and depravity in the central slums should be ascribed to individual moral failings and how far to social arrangements. Shimmin was ambivalent on this central issue, and his internal contradictions, as they are likely to seem to us, responded to continuing debate and uncertainty. Poverty and its treatment brought the same issues into focus. In Liverpool, as in London, charitable impulses were fuelled in large part by a realisation that some were poor through no fault of their own. But this frame of mind coexisted with resentment of the cost of poor relief, leading to strong concern for accountability and control over expenditure, and a fear that designing elements among the 'undeserving' poor would be able to play the system. These latter attitudes predominated. The full writ of the New Poor Law did not run in Liverpool, after successful resistance by civic leaders in the early 1840s; but the Select Vestry ran a notoriously tight ship, and Shimmin himself baulked at the treatment given to some of the honest poor, reiterating the often stressed comparison between conditions experienced in prisons and in workhouses. The central dilemma of social policy in this regard was well illustrated in 1879 by Silas Hocking's best-seller *Her Benny*, which was set in Liverpool. It bathed the honest, earnestly religious, quiescent poor in a romantic evangelical light while emphasising the depravity which surrounded the struggling street children who were the central characters. The book's success indicates the extent to which this tortured frame of mind was characteristic. There was a great deal of overlap between Hocking's attitudes and those of Shimmin.[37]

The inadequacies of Liverpool's working-class housing also contributed to the town's unenviable reputation for awesome social problems. Conditions began to worsen rapidly from the late eighteenth century. A combination of high land values, rapid immigration, low and unreliable working-class incomes, and the need for casual workers to live close to the places where they were hired, generated a dangerous imbalance between housing supply and demand. The response of builders and developers was the creation of warrens of tightly packed back-to-back courts, whose damp cellars were pressed into occupation as living quarters for the poorest of the poor, and whose sanitary arrangements were desperately inadequate, especially under the overcrowded conditions of multiple occupancy which soon prevailed. Working-class housing on this model proliferated over the half-century or so after 1780, and despite subsequent denunciations by Medical Officers and sanitary reformers, and municipal attempts at intervention and amelioration, the legacy of this uncontrolled, market-led speculative development still predominated in much of central Liverpool, around Vauxhall and Scotland wards, and in south Toxteth, in the mid-Victorian years. By this time the central slums had generated a distinctive way of life of their own. There was a great deal of movement within them, but very little migration out of them, as most newer housing was either too expensive or too distant even for the more secure and better paid of the waterfront workers. Conditions within these tightly packed working-class districts varied street by street, and even court by court, as neighbourly consensus set varying standards and sanitary systems, and pollution levels differed over small areas. But the overall impression of overwhelming squalor, and of the need to struggle against impossible odds to maintain the most basic standards of human decency, was in no way misleading.[38]

Under these conditions the very high death rates which prevailed in central Liverpool are not to be wondered at. At a time when the national death rate hovered around 22 per thousand, that for the borough of Liverpool averaged just under 30 per thousand over the five years 1856–60, but then rose again to more than 33 per thousand over the decade 1861–70. The figures for the parish of Liverpool, the oldest part of the borough, were worse still, climbing to an *average* of nearly 40 per thousand during 1866–70. These were stratospheric figures, even by the standards of the time. Infant mortality levels were even more inflated. During the 1850s the death rate for under-ones in Liverpool parish averaged 283 per thousand. In the next decade it topped 300 per thousand. The under-fives accounted for nearly half of all the deaths in the parish in the 1850s. The averages were boosted by epidemic years, as in the cholera visitations of 1854 and 1866, although nothing in the mid-Victorian years matched the terrible typhus epidemic of 1847, whose carnage extended into respectable residential areas and lived long in local memories. And within Liverpool, of course, some wards and streets offered much better chances of survival than others. Thus in 1871 Vauxhall ward, a favourite stamping-ground of Shimmin's, had a death rate of over 43 per thousand, while the Rodney Street area, with it surviving big houses and middle-class residents, was close to the national norm at 23·4. By this time such contrasts had become the small change of social statisticians and the informed reading public. Perhaps 40 per cent of the deaths, on the untrustworthy contemporary definitions, came from infectious diseases with strong environmental associations; and among older people consumption was a major cause of death. The Corporation's efforts to alleviate the situation included a pioneering venture into municipal housing in 1869, as well as the more usual paraphernalia of bye-laws, sanitary regulations, public baths, controls over lodging houses, and a controversial municipal water supply from distant Rivington Pike. But its efforts were limited by technological uncertainty, fear of expense, and undue respect for the rights of property-owners in the abstract and of influential individual owners of slum property in the all too intimidating flesh. It remained almost impossible to keep pace with the deepening social and environmental problems of inner Liverpool; and as part of the extended discussion of ways and means, rights and wrongs, it fell to Hugh Shimmin to transmute the arid statistics into recognisable human experiences, and to lend a new and compelling conviction to the perception and transmission of Liverpool's image as the 'Black Spot on the Mersey'.[39]

Disease and immorality were seldom far apart in the minds of mid-Victorian social commentators, at least when they discussed these phenomena in the setting of the urban slums. Crime and immorality were perceived to be as contagious as typhus, and they were seen as being nurtured by the same conditions. Spiritual neglect and moral atrophy were the almost inevitable companions of poverty and squalor. The domestic inspections carried out under the Liverpool Sanitary Amendment Act of 1864 brought scarifying revelations about overcrowding which had inescapable overtones of sexual promiscuity and incest, with cases of adult daughters sharing beds with their parents and adult brothers and sisters occupying the same bed. Shimmin also hinted at this private relationship between poverty and immorality; and in the public sphere he was not alone in repeatedly emphasising the unwashed conditions of the clothes and bodies of drunken and disreputable haunters of beerhouses and vaults. Cleanliness connoted godliness and physical well-being; filth was inseparable from immorality as well as disease.[40]

Central to all the prevailing images of Liverpool's social problems in the 1850s and 1860s was the uniquely strong Irish presence in the town, which coloured social pathology and popular politics in ways which had no real parallels outside Belfast and Glasgow. It would, indeed, be dangerous to draw these comparisons too simply.[41] The Irish as a major element in Liverpool life long antedated the Famine migration of the mid- and late 1840s, but their numbers were greatly augmented at this time, and so was the scale and intensity of hostility towards them. The 1841 census found nearly 50,000 Irish-born people in Liverpool, accounting for more than one in six of the population. Ten years later there were well over 80,000, and the proportion was approaching one in four. Thereafter, the number of Irish-born stabilised, beginning a gentle decline in the 1860s; but the ethnically Irish population, including the Liverpool-born children of Irish parents, brought up in an expatriate Irish culture, was much more numerous and resilient. The Famine migrants gravitated disproportionately to the existing areas of Irish concentration, especially in the northern dockland districts around impoverished Vauxhall and Exchange wards, where nearly half the inhabitants were Irish-born in 1851. They were visibly and audibly distinctive, and they were ready scapegoats for social ills. They were already being blamed for inflating the poor rates and contributing more than their fair share of theft, violence, drunkenness and vice in the 1830s, and subsequent developments reinforced this stereotype while adding further dimensions involving the carrying of disease and the exacerbation of existing slum conditions through filthy practices and anti-social habits. They were also accused of undercutting local labour in the ceaseless competition for work. On top of this, the overwhelming majority of the poorest Irish had some sort of attachment to the Roman Catholic Church, although we should remember that Liverpool's Irish also included a significant Ulster Protestant contingent who made their own contribution to the cocktail of religious, nationalistic and political conflict which was being vigorously stirred in the middle decades of the nineteenth century. As convenient recipients of blame for social ills, as a stigmatised social grouping with a distinctive culture and way of life, and as by no means passive participants in the popular politics of the pub, the street and the procession, Liverpool's Irish poor were an essential ingredient not only of the life of the town itself but also of the image it presented to the outside world.[42]

Shimmin had remarkably little to say about the Liverpool Irish as a group. He was tolerant towards Irish and Catholics alike, and did not join in the legion of Medical Officers, editorial writers, Tory politicians and Protestant demagogues in denouncing the evil influence of this much maligned minority. He was a little more interested, indeed, in the Liverpool Welsh, who were every bit as distinctive, and arguably as important in the life of the town, as their noisier and more controversial counterparts from across the Irish Sea. Like the Irish, the Welsh were marked out from their neighbours by language and religion. In mid-Victorian times many migrants from North Wales were still at best uncertain in their use of English, and they were insulated from the rest of Liverpool society by a network of Calvinistic Methodist chapels, with associated cultural and financial institutions, in which worship was through the medium of Welsh. They were also pulled together by the Welsh stranglehold on the Liverpool building industry and associated trades in raw materials, especially timber and roofing slate. Their religion helped to draw them towards the temperance movement, and in the mid-Victorian years they were already escaping from the dockside slums and colonising the new terraced houses which their compatriots were building in Everton. The Welsh did not endear themselves to the locals, many of whom disliked their exclusive ways and tendency to insider dealing; but, helped no doubt by their much smaller numbers, they never became scapegoats or objects of vilification and controversy in the way that the Irish did. But they deserve a higher profile than they are sometimes given in historical writing on Liverpool.[43]

As befitted a seaport at the hub of the world economy of the mid-Victorian years, Liverpool played host to a variety of other immigrant groupings, from the inconspicuous (and often very successful) Scots to Jews, Germans, Italians and Chinese. And, as Shimmin's forays into dockland places of entertainment demonstrated, its passing trade embraced seamen of every conceivable nation. In its most famous and (to outsiders) most familiar guise, it was a world city, offering a unique combination of the glamorous, the exotic, the seedy, the horrific and the dangerous. It therefore came to attract a great deal of attention from beyond its own boundaries.[44]

Liverpool was second only to London as the 'shock city' of the mid-Victorian years. Asa Briggs used the phrase to describe the impact of Manchester on perceptions of the new world of factory industry in the 1830s and 1840s; and the power of this version of 'the shock of the new' was certainly enough to attract an impressive array of foreign observers trying to see into the future, journalists and novelists in search of copy and colour, and earnest social analysts pursuing understanding of current social conditions and propounding systems for their improvement. Thus Manchester called forth extended comment from Engels and de Tocqueville, Dickens and Disraeli. It was at the forefront of discussion whenever social problems and political threats were in the limelight. It was fascinating – a 'great human exploit' – and frightening, grim and exciting. If this was the future, then how, if at all, was the old world going to cope with it?[45]

After the mid-nineteenth century this smoky mantle of problem and portent was passing from Manchester's shoulders. The state of the factory districts became less threatening and less newsworthy as Chartism faded, the Corn Laws were repealed and the Ten Hours legislation took the steam of indignation out of the Factory Movement. Manchester and its satellite towns had stabilised. The apparent threat of revolution had visibly receded, in this quarter at least. The focus of media concern shifted towards the problems of London and its East End, of large-scale commerce, casual and sweated labour, overcrowded tenements and cellar dwellings, costermongers and street arabs, crime and prostitution. The spotlight shifted from the 'factory slaves' and the exhausted mothers toiling at their remorseless machines, to fall on the sweated needlewoman in her garret, and the filthy half-starved waif struggling for a bare survival in the gutter. The dark fascination of the waterfront displaced the living hell of the factory. As Stedman Jones showed in *Outcast London*, the metropolis became the most threatening concentration of poverty, crime, filth, violence, moral corruption, disease and political unrest in mid-Victorian Britain. And, unlike Manchester and the textile districts, it was all dangerously close to the greatest concentrations of property, fashion and, above all, power and government. This changing agenda of fears and concern was helped on its way by the writings of Henry Mayhew, but it brought together a large number of articulate and committed writers during the 1850s and 1860s, from George Godwin to James Greenwood. It all added up to an important transition in the perception and popular propagation of hopes and fears, dreams and nightmares.[46]

Liverpool became the provincial exemplar of the themes which were being worked out in the literature of London, although it has never attracted the attention from historians that its importance merits. The emphasis lay more with casual work than the sweated trades, as befitted the different balance of Liverpool's economy; but the moral and physical threat presented by the dockland slums was all the more arresting because Liverpool, too, had opulence closely juxtaposed against its squalor. And Liverpool was also a 'great human exploit': a triumph of human ingenuity against unsatisfactory

natural resources. Its docks were among the greatest wonders of
Western civilisation, and contemporary visitors made free with
adjectives like 'stupendous' and 'cyclopean'. By the 1850s the Albert
Dock and its adjoining miles of waterfront were compulsory sights
for tourists and foreign travellers; and many of the latter, especially
the Americans, made their first landing there anyway. It was not
difficult for such visitors to penetrate the adjoining slums, however
superficially, and mark the contrast between public opulence and
private squalor for themselves. Thus the French academic Hippolyte
Taine, fresh from marvelling at the magnitude of the docks and the
vulgarity of St George's Hall:

At six o'clock we made our way back through the poor quarters of the
city. What a spectacle! . . . Every stairway swarms with children, five or
six to a step, the eldest nursing the baby; their faces are pale, their hair
whitish and tousled, the rags they wear are full of holes, they have neither
shoes nor stockings and they are all vilely dirty . . . What rooms! A thread-
bare strip of oilcloth on the floor, sometimes a big sea-shell or one or two
plaster ornaments; the old, idiot grandmother crouches in a corner; the
wife is engaged in trying to mend some wretched rags of clothes; the
children tumble over each other. The smell is that of an old-clothes shop
full of rotting rags . . . Livid, bearded old women came out of gin-shops;
their reeling gait, dismal eyes and fixed idiot grin are indescribable. They
look as if their features had been slowly corroded by vitriol . . .
Rembrandt's beggars were happier and better off in their picturesque
hovels. And I have not seen the Irish quarter! The Irish flock to this town,
there are said to be a hundred thousand here, and their quarter is the
nethermost circle of Hell.[47]

Not quite, as it turns out: there are rumours of even worse things
in Belfast. But Taine seems to have been even more shocked by the
Leeds Street area of Liverpool than he was by equivalent districts
of London's East End. Nathaniel Hawthorne, the American
novelist, was similarly affected during his years as American consul
in Liverpool during the mid-1850s. He was immediately fascinated
by nearby Tithebarn Street:

I never saw . . . nor imagined . . . what squalor there is in the inhabitants
of these streets as seen along the sidewalks. Women with young figures,
but old and wrinkled countenances; young girls without any maiden
neatness and trimness, barefooted, with dirty legs. Women of all ages, even
elderly, go along with great, bare, ugly feet, many have baskets and other
burthens on their heads. All along the street, with their wares at the edge
of the sidewalk and their own seats fairly in the carriageway, you see
women with fruit to sell, or combs and cheap jewelry, or coarse crockery,
or oysters, or the devil knows what, and sometimes the woman is sewing
meanwhile.[48]

This was an early reaction; but further experience confirmed these perceptions. He wrote succinctly to a friend:

Liverpool is a most detestable place of residence . . . smoky, noisy, dirty, pestilential . . . The streets swarm with beggars by day and by night. You never saw the like, and I pray that you may never see it in America.[49]

Hawthorne also noted the prevalence of spirit vaults and the close connection between poverty and drink. When his comments on Liverpool were published they gave offence to some of the leading citizens whose hospitality Hawthorne had enjoyed; but this does not make them any the less convincing. And his perceptions, like those of Taine, are confirmed and developed by local observers who went beyond the thoroughfares and behind the frontages. Shimmin was only the most articulate and assertive of a group of such people.

Hawthorne and Taine are representatives of an important type of social observer and commentator: the well educated, articulate visitor from outside the local culture, with plenty of scope for comparison with other places but only superficial understanding of what they are observing. As we see, they offer vivid impressions in quotable prose, but they make no attempt to go beyond describing external appearances, with no attempt to explain the circumstances, and still less to prescribe alternatives. But at least they went beyond the respectable streets and did more than politely reproduce the preferred perceptions of their hosts. Frederick Olmsted, the future designer of New York's Central Park, did rather better than this. He, too, emphasised the beggars, the poverty and the 'very frequent, and often splendid' liquor shops. But he noticed distinctions and nuances which give his work additional interest. For example, there were exceptions to the general appearance of poverty among working-class men, who were distinctively 'thin, meagre, and pale', with a 'stupid, hopeless, state-prison-for-life sort of expression'; but the better fed and more cheerful specimens were usually in the uniform or livery which betokened regular employment and predictable pay: 'railroad hands, servants, and soldiers'. Or there are Olmsted's remarks on the 'sailors' wives', prostitutes who undertook to look after sailors during their time on shore: he was 'surprised at [their] quietness and decency . . . they were plainly and generally neatly dressed, and talked quietly and in kind tones to each other, and I heard no loud profanity or ribaldry at all'. These detached, morally cool observations might serve as something of a corrective to some of Shimmin's outraged rhetoric about the women of the streets. Similarly, the women of the fish market are praised for being 'nice and neat' despite the nature of their work. And he talked to labourers, as well as observing them from a safe distance. With all its inevitable limitations, Olmsted's work shows how helpful an observer from another culture, with

few preconceptions and an enquiring mind, can be in illuminating
social conditions on the basis of a brief but busily observant
visit.[50]

Several other *genres* of urban social description were emerging in
the 1830s and 1840s (especially), and proliferating in the mid-
Victorian years. They provide an important qualitative dimension
to set alongside, and sometimes correct, the quantitative evidence
which can be made to look so misleadingly 'scientific'. Some, of
course, incorporate statistical material of their own, and almost all
make 'quantitative' statements at some point. Their tone ranges
from the clinically proto-social-scientific to the anecdotally
sentimental, from the detached to the highly charged moralistic
evangelical – though these are not inevitably, or even always,
opposite poles. Liverpool had its fair share of unofficial social
commentators, and they offer a useful range of comparative
perspectives from which to view the work of Hugh Shimmin.

The most exhaustive compilation of evidence about the living
standards of working-class Liverpudlians was John Finch junior's
astonishingly thorough presentation of the condition of Vauxhall
ward, which was prepared for the Liverpool Anti-Monopoly
Association in 1842. Finch sought ammunition to bring to bear
against the Corn Laws and other obstacles to Free Trade, and his
survey was conducted at perhaps the lowest point of the worst
depression in the notoriously difficult 1830s and 1840s. Finch's
statement of his mode of proceeding is worth quoting:

Six of the most intelligent working men that could be met with, were
employed in collecting information from every occupant in the ward.
Working men were chosen in preference to persons of a more wealthy
class; as, it was considered, the latter might have been more easily deceived
by simulated distress. They were appointed to different districts, and gave
in their returns daily, with the name of each occupant, and the particulars
now published. They were instructed to state plainly the object of the
inquiry; not to give or promise to give present relief; and where the information communicated was doubtful, or apparently incorrect, to omit it.
Cross inquiries were afterwards instituted, to check the information first
obtained.[51]

Two of the six men had helped with the 1841 census enumeration,
and each of them supplied an impressively well expressed letter at
the end of the pamphlet, offering impressions and descriptions to
put flesh on the bones of the statistical tables, derived from their
labours, which formed the main body of the report.

Finch's informants obtained an almost complete breakdown of
the occupations of male household heads, although households
headed by women were classified solely on the basis of gender.
They secured information on regularity of employment from 4,814

of the 5,973 families, and on family earnings from 4,387. Very full information was also obtained on birthplaces, migration patterns, length of residence, quality of accommodation, and tenurial arrangements. Whatever speculative reservations we might have about the actual (as opposed to the prescribed) conduct of the survey, this comes across as a remarkable response rate, even though, as Finch remarked, 'the difficulty in obtaining information increased as the inquiry became more inquisitorial'.[52] Among the arresting findings of the survey were that, of the 2,126 families who were found to be 'indigent', 1,052 supported themselves by 'promiscuous charity, pawning, and crime', which apparently included prostitution, 1,017 were kept afloat by 'savings, credit, relations and casual employment' and only fifty-seven by 'parish relief, with other assistance'.[53] Subjective though these and other categories obviously were, they provide a useful approach to the understanding of living standards and survival strategies among the poorer quarters of Liverpool. None of the mid-Victorian surveys approaches Finch's methodological sophistication, and his work deserves to be better known. It provides a statistical foundation which is entirely absent from Shimmin's work, and its techniques are closer to the work of subsequent 'social scientists' than are those used by Mayhew in his much praised *Morning Chronicle* phase as careful researcher and critic of orthodox political economy.[54]

Finch's work built on his father's experience in conducting a survey of forty or fifty houses in Preston Street at the end of 1832, in collaboration with Joseph Livesey. The results of this small survey were published in the *Liverpool Mercury*, which was also to be the first publisher of the articles which became Shimmin's *Liverpool Life*. House-to-house visiting was undertaken, with 'a well disposed workman' acting as intermediary; but the presentation was descriptive and impressionistic rather than statistical. A memorable portrayal of abject poverty resulted, perhaps the most significant comment being the one ascribed to Livesey, to the effect that he had never seen hand-loom weavers 'half so miserable' as the inhabitants of this part of Vauxhall ward. This is a reminder, among many others, that the concentration of historians on conditions in the textile districts rather than the seaports has left us with a lopsided picture of working-class living standards in this controversy-ridden period; and redressing the balance offers small comfort to the 'optimists' in the long-running 'standard of living controversy'.[55]

Finch senior took a broad and not unsympathetic view of the causes of these dismal conditions, blaming 'ignorance, want of employment, low wages and intemperance'; but, despite Finch's background as an Owenite socialist, the remedies he prescribed were directed more against drink than the other evils.[56] Finch junior, on the other hand, regarded obstacles to free trade as constituting the great overarching evil, with prime responsibility for the high prices and intermittent employment which he identified as the more immediate reasons for the misery.[57]

A statistical mode of inquiry was subsequently adopted by the Rev. Abraham Hume, first vicar of the new ecclesiastical district covering Vauxhall in 1847. He was swift in attempting to get to know his teeming parish, and was soon brought to dismay if not despair by the low level of religious observance and the difficulty of improving it. In 1848 he produced a voluminous statistical table covering nearly 3,000 families, inquiring into means of support, religious affiliation and attendance, education, reading material, extent of sickness and country of origin. Hume did most of the survey work himself, with the assistance of students from the theological college at Birkenhead. As Hume lamented:

At the time when this table was compiled, there was neither church nor chapel service in the district; 9,099 admitted that they attended no place of worship [out of 13,028]; . . . and there were 2,092 children of suitable ages receiving no education.

Ten years later Hume produced a survey of the incidence of pauperism, indigence, crime and immorality in relation to the distribution of churches in Liverpool as a whole. His evidence was drawn from the relieving officers and the police, and he plotted his findings street by street on a map with different hatching to show different degrees of poverty and depravity, partly anticipating the system which Charles Booth, who must have known Hume's work, was to adopt for his enormous London survey. Hume realised that his characterisations of streets were somewhat arbitrary, and that in any case a street, in itself, was a very crude statistical unit; but he nevertheless generated a lot of evidence, in this survey and the previous one, which has value in its own right as well as contributing to the history of social surveys and statistical thought. His own concern involved the more effective provision of churches and clergy; the redistribution of charity and manpower from rich parishes to poor ones instead of each parish being an island; increased educational provision, preferably with a vocational flavour, but also inculcating cleanliness and godliness; and a more general participation by the middle classes in the charitable and missionary work of the Churches.[58]

Shimmin was not very interested in this statistical work. He clearly preferred the approach taken by another religious commentator, the Rev. Hugh Stowell Brown, who sought to reach a working-class audience through the medium of the popular address

on practical rather than theological lines. His famous Sunday afternoon lectures in the Concert Hall attracted up to 2,000 working
men at a time to hear humorous, direct commentaries on such
topics as gambling, credit, spending patterns, Sunday leisure and
working-class dwellings. But he remained confused and uncertain
about the roots of the miseries of the slums. Like Shimmin, he was
unable to understand how the degraded artisan who had lost all
hope and self-respect could be found cheek by jowl with a family
of similar status whose clean and orderly dwelling defied the
squalor of its surroundings. At one point he concluded:

To a certain extent, or perhaps . . . to some extent which is not very
certain it is true that the house makes the people . . . Yet if in some cases
the houses make the people, in others the people make the house and much
more frequently the latter than the former.[59]

Denunciation of slum landlords was accompanied with exhortations
to action which took the social and political system as given and
urged improvement through the hard work and elbow grease of
individuals:

Contentment is a lesson often inculcated upon the poor, but I wish that in
one sense they were discontented; I wish that they felt an unspeakable
repugnance to the filthy habitations in which they are huddled together. I
would say – Don't be discontented with the constitution for there's not a
better under the sun; don't be discontented with work, for work is the wise
and benevolent ordinance of God; don't think of agitating for the Charter,
for Socialism, Communism, and all that nonsense, but be discontented with
dirt, and darkness, and foul air and bad smells, and undrained streets, and
jerry-built houses, and set to work resolutely to free yourselves from this
wretchedness.[60]

Thus was the problem of the slums reduced from systems to
specifics, and the responsibility for improvement placed at the door
of working-class people themselves. There was no hint of any
organised working-class pressure group for public health improvement, and perhaps Stowell Brown's advice would have been
differently phrased if there had been. His hope was that artisans
would spend more of their wages on rent to escape the degrading
physical conditions of slum property, and the moral contagion of
other slum dwellers. His sentiments were echoed by, among others,
the Liverpool merchant, banker and Liberal politician George
Melly, and his assumptions were congruent with the economic
orthodoxy which underpinned all approaches to housing reform in
mid-Victorian Liverpool, including Melly's own essays in 'five per
cent philanthropy' and even the Corporation's pioneering municipal
dwellings.[61]

The tendency to view Liverpool's urban pathology as many

subdivided and specific problems, rather than as one grand overarching paradigm, was reflected in a general suspicion of theoretical
thinkers, in which Shimmin shared to the full; but always excluding
the theorists whose systems lay behind the unchallengeable edifice
of orthodox political economy. The refusal of broad analysis for
the multiplication of specifics is perhaps best exemplified by the
Morning Chronicle correspondent, Charles Mackay, who
contributed the Birmingham and Liverpool material for the great
social survey of Britain which that newspaper organised in 1849.
Thus Mackay expatiated at length on the unprotected nature of the
docks and the cargoes in transit which they contained, as a prime
cause of high levels of crime, especially juvenile crime:

Sacks of meal, corn, beans, rice and coffee – all equally tempting to
dishonest poverty – invite young thieves to learn their unhappy trade at the
expense of the merchants of Liverpool and Manchester.[62]

And he erected a monumental thesis about the roots of the
maritime culture of drink, vice and depravity around the Liverpool
docks, ascribing it above all to the prohibition on the use of fire
and lights aboard ships berthed in the docks, which drove the
sailors out to the beerhouses in search of warmth, comfort, and
sociability.[63] In each case the idea, the information and the argument all carry conviction, but modes of explanation are diverted
from the general and abstract to the specific and concrete.
    Mackay was, of course, a colleague in the enterprise that
produced Henry Mayhew's detailed work on the economy of the
East End of London, which was hailed by E. P. Thompson and
Eileen Yeo as as much a pioneering work of serious sociology as
a sustained piece of investigative journalism. This perception does
not command universal assent, as there are alternative visions of
Mayhew as ideologue, careless journalist who was too readily
imposed upon by his interviewees, and mere articulator of the
artisan consciousness of the beleaguered craft workers of the East
End.[64] But Mayhew deserves to be taken more seriously than his
colleagues as a systematic, painstaking analyst of social problems.
It is therefore arresting to find Iain Taylor bracketing Shimmin with
Mayhew – and singling him out, implicitly, above all the other
commentators on Liverpool life. Taylor describes Shimmin's
'Mysteries of the Courts' series in *Porcupine* as 'a series of articles
which must rate alongside those of Mayhew as pioneers of
sociological journalism'.[65] The comparison is explicitly based on
Shimmin's work on housing conditions, and it seems to refer to
Mayhew's *Morning Chronicle* work rather than his later essays in
more popular and titillating fact-gathering on street folk and
criminals; but it helps to set the stage for an evaluation of

Shimmin's work as compared with his contemporaries.

Shimmin's journalism does not really bear sustained comparison with the Mayhew of Thompson and Yeo's *Unknown Mayhew*. He does not analyse wages, working conditions and labour relations in the same systematic way: indeed, he has very little to say about work as opposed to leisure and domesticity. His descriptions of housing, and of the workings of the housing system, contain more critical analysis, firmly grounded in experience and personal inquiry, than the rest of his work; and Taylor is no doubt correct to single this material out. But here, as elsewhere, the description is stronger than the analysis, and it would be very difficult to identify Shimmin as a critical and innovative theoretician in the way that Thompson and Yeo, and Samuel, have tried to do for Mayhew. We learn a lot from perusing Shimmin on housing conditions, but we do not have our consciousness raised to new heights of comprehension.

Where Shimmin does stand comparison with Mayhew, perhaps, is as a colourful re-creator of alternative modes of thought and existence which would otherwise have been lost to us because of the inarticulacy of the subjects. Even where his strictures about stigmatised behaviour are at their most severe, he succeeds in conveying an understanding of, even in some sense an empathy with, the actions he reports. He tries, in his domestic scenes especially, to come to terms with the outlook, thought processes, problems and pressures experienced by the people he describes. In the generic stories, the fictions with pretensions to being drawn from life (such as 'How Jem Burns bought a new hat'), and in numerous reconstructed or invented dialogues, he uses his own experience of slum life to convey its preoccupations and values. He is at his most distant and censorious when reporting on 'low life' entertainments, and this may reflect a failure to come to terms with them in his youth. Mayhew's dialogues may sometimes seem more convincing than Shimmin's, the speech more direct and less filtered through the rearranging mind of the observer; but Shimmin is more convincing on mind sets and value systems below artisan level. He seldom speaks of his Liverpool slum dwellers as if they are a race apart, as Mayhew notoriously does with the street people; and he displays a sustained commitment to understanding, and to conveying that understanding to his middle-class readership, even when understanding stops a long way short of forgiveness.[66]

All this suggests that a better basis of comparison lies between Shimmin and those observers from *within* the working class who tried to interpret the ideas and beliefs, habits and customs of working people to a more elevated audience. Shimmin behaved so unpretentiously, and so clearly continued to identify with what he saw as the best qualities of working people, that this frame of reference has some plausibility. Shimmin is as credible a presenter of the working class at large as Thomas Wright, the oft-cited 'hero of a thousand footnotes'. Wright's life history is obscure, but his status as the 'journeyman engineer' of his by-line may have been somewhat equivocal by the time of his writings, and his insights into the 'inner life of workshops', valuable though they seem, may have been more retrospective than current in tone. In many respects Wright and Shimmin are complementary. Wright is good on the culture of the workplace – or of a certain kind of workplace – and on the political outlooks and organisations of skilled labour. Shimmin is weak on these themes, but stronger than Wright on family and neighbourhood life, and especially about the ideas and expectations of those who fell below and outside the charmed circle of the skilled and apprenticed sectors of the work force. Both are strong on entertainment, though Wright does not share Shimmin's emphasis on low life and social pathology. What the two have in common, however, is a clearly conveyed, if not directly articulated, message that each has only one foot in the class about which he is writing. These are fringe people, semi-detached observers, a little too bookish and individualistic to be fully part of the culture they describe. This is a general, and perhaps an inescapable, problem of the genre; but it should not blind us to the fact that a lot of Shimmin's value to historians comes from his combination of working-class background and materially comfortable but culturally insecure current standing in the middle ranks.[67]

A Liverpool parallel for these years can be found, in a small way, in the cabinetmaker James Hopkinson, who set up as a furniture dealer in the town in 1851. Hopkinson was the son of a grocer and house proprietor, but had served an apprenticeship to cabinet-making, and spent several years working as a journeyman in various towns. His autobiography reveals an earnest but not censorious Baptist, with a variety of interests ranging from antiquity to fishing and herbalism. His comments on Liverpool life give interesting insights into trade matters, especially the business methods of the Liverpool Welsh; and they also reinforce other evidence on the importance of drink in Liverpool working-class culture, the role of petty trading (including a graphic description of the rag market), the high accident rate on the docks and the suffering it entailed, and the distinctive use of the pawnshop by female Irish fish and sand hawkers to supply the trading capital for their little businesses. Hopkinson's autobiography was written for himself and his family rather than as a tract or piece of journalism for public consumption, but it comes from the same amphibious social position as a great deal of writing about the urban working class and lower orders in this period. His background is more secure than Shimmin's and his life – and writing – is private rather than public; but their perspectives have a lot in common, despite Hopkinson's unwillingness to moralise about lives other than his own. It is not until the next generations, with the autobiographies of James Sexton the dockers' union leader and Pat O'Mara, 'the Liverpool Irish slummy', that we encounter directly voices from below this stratum on the frontiers between the skilled working class and the petty bourgeoisie; and this problem of vantage point needs always to be borne in mind.[68]

The voices of both Hopkinson and Shimmin are also distinctively Nonconformist in religion, despite Shimmin's transfer of affections to the Church of England in later life; and Shimmin's writing, at least, often features a kind of evangelical prurience which occurs elsewhere in reformers' accounts of the disreputable behaviour of the lower orders. Traces of it can be found, for example, in another neglected depicter of provincial low life, James Burnley, whose descriptions of Bradford's music halls, rat pits and drinking dens in the late 1870s run parallel to Shimmin's Liverpool exposures. But Burnley was much less heavy-handed in dispensing moral condemnation, and the same applies to the 'How Manchester is Amused' series in *Porcupine*'s Manchester counterpart, the *Free Lance*, which also covered similar ground. These sketches were written from the point of view of a detached and even dispassionate, though critical, outside observer, and they are strong on social description (especially audience composition) without sharing Shimmin's determination to root out and describe every dimension of immorality (as far as the conventions of his time would permit). *Free Lance*'s description of the races at Old Trafford and Castle Irwell is tame compared with Shimmin's lurid and titillating account of Aintree, but we cannot know (without further research) whether the contrast reflects the deeper infamy of Liverpool racegoers or a less single-minded pursuit of evil-doing on the part of the Manchester journalist. Shimmin's work on low life is close to an extreme pole of protesting puritanical prurience, and it is tempting to suggest that the three things shared some kind of affinity, and that those in Liverpool who paraded their doubts about the motives of Shimmin and his readers may not have been completely in error.[69]

Above all, Shimmin was adept at detailed, informed, evocative description. He eschewed statistics: the Victorian statistical movement might as well not have happened, and he looked upon Social Science congresses and those who gave papers at them with Olympian disdain. They were mere theorists, out of touch with the ideas, behaviour and living conditions of those whose ills they proposed to palliate. He painted word pictures of occasions, streets, individuals; and at times he preferred to add immediacy and aid identification by using invented episodes and dialogue to get his message across. This was a common device: Thomas Wright, for example, used it a great deal. As befits his focus on the concrete and the personal, he can be sentimental, querulous and sanctimonious; but he can also conjure up images which remain, flickering but surprisingly three-dimensional, in the mind's inner eye. This makes his work attractive (if sometimes annoying); it also makes it dangerous. We must resist the real temptation to quote extensively and uncritically from the Shimmin *oeuvre*, however seductive it may at times appear. So we need, finally, to address the problems raised by Shimmin's methods and agenda, and to evaluate his work as a source for the study not only of mid-Victorian Liverpool but also of key issues in urban history on a much wider stage.

Outside the fields of housing and public health history, Shimmin is best known for his portrayals of Liverpool low life. He plumbs the depths of the most squalid and dingy places of amusement, and presents these writings as factual, documentary recountings of what he observed. The descriptions carry conviction in their circumstantial detail, and they are valuable for their analysis of those present in terms of age, sex and occupation – a virtue which Shimmin shares with the surveys of 'How Manchester is Amused' in the *Free Lance*. It is remarkable how confident such observers were in their ability to identify occupations at a glance, presumably by the characteristic garb, demeanour and ingrained grime of the trade. He is anxious to convey his knowledge of the distinctive slang of such subcultures as the betting and dog-fighting fraternities. But some aspects of this work must give us pause for thought. Was Shimmin really able to penetrate the furtive and visibly disreputable ranks of the dog fanciers to attend the dog fight which is described in chapter 5? If so, was he really able to sit quietly through the proceedings? In other places, after all, he was apparently identified as an outsider of dangerously superior and probably censorious demeanour; and we see behaviour being modified to adjust for his presence as particularly obscene songs are proscribed. How much of this is *really* first-hand observation; and are the episodes really narratives of a single night or sequence of events? Or are they conflations and confections, running different and perhaps disparate happenings together for maximum effect? We also have to consider the problem – generic in this kind of literature, but also in the mid-Victorian novel – of where Shimmin defined the thresholds of offensiveness and obscenity. Swearing, from 'damn' upwards, was proscribed; but we have no way of knowing just what it was about the comic songs and jokes that provoked wrath and self-censorship, though sexual allusion and innuendo were obviously well to the fore. But when so much is veiled, and so much is indirectly expressed, it is frustratingly difficult to recover the actual content and tone of what is going on.[70] When Shimmin deals with working-class domestic life he tends to operate more overtly through 'faction', the pointed and probably apocryphal anecdote or story-with-a-moral. To be convincing, this way of presenting things has to impress us with the writer's ability to get under the skin and empathise with the thought processes of those whose lives he is re-creating. We have seen that *Harry Birkett* and the other evidence on Shimmin's formative years encourage us to believe that he knew poverty and the slum culture of the docklands at first hand. But this must be qualified by awareness of the extent to which Shimmin is distanced from his subjects by his values and morality. He can *describe* the binge-and-bust life style in which people with insufficient incomes indulge in drunken and gluttonous weekends, only to starve themselves and their children through the rest of the week until the coming of the next pay packet. And he can tell us about the unceasing pressure to drink and gamble as part and parcel of the mutually supportive but sometimes exploitative camaraderie of the slums. But he cannot convey an understanding of the frames of mind in which such behaviour might seem preferable to an unending grind of thrift, deferred gratification and nothing to look forward to. In a setting of predominant casual labour, low wages (usually), ever-present threats from disease and injury, and little real prospect of personal advancement or even security, with little visible reward from education or self-improvement, laziness readily triumphed over cleanliness and immediate physical enjoyment over planning for the future. Shimmin's tendency to blame the victim rather than the system for important aspects of the culture of poverty offers an unduly unsympathetic portrayal of working-class domestic life, and expresses his inability to remember or come to terms with the elements of patronage, personality and sheer good fortune which marked and underlay his own emergence from the depths.[71]

In terms of social prescription Shimmin was a stern individualist, seeing each adult as bearing responsibility for the family's own destiny, and setting great store by individual autonomy and independence. This does not prevent him from displaying humanity towards the honest, thrifty and respectable poor, but he is scornful towards those who are duped by disreputable trickery, and he is suspicious of attempts to explain bad living conditions in environmental terms. The depravity and inadequacies of individuals lie at the centre of his explanatory universe, and the corrective role of local government should be to intervene against the worst abuses in public health and housing provision, and above all to discourage,

and where appropriate to suppress, public and commercial temptations to drunkenness and vice. Above all, indeed, drink is at the
core of Shimmin's analysis of social pathology: a view in which he
was, of course, far from being alone. He would have endorsed
Dickens's description of the owner of a Liverpool singing saloon:
'Mr Licensed Victualler . . . a sharp and watchful man, with tight
lips and a complete edition of Cocker's arithmetic in each eye.'[72]
Such people, along with the proprietors of dancing saloons (in
which Shimmin can see nothing but the slippery slope to frivolity,
immorality, bad servants and bad wives) and gambling dens, were
the kings of Shimmin's demonology. They, and slum landlords who
opposed housing improvement, were the exploiters, rather than the
employers, whose role is noticeably absent from Shimmin's pages.

Shimmin was also at one with many contemporaries in linking
filth, disease, immorality and political sedition in a circle of
mutually reinforcing connected links. Characteristically, too, his
preferred routes out of the morass involve rational recreations,
education, and opportunities for self-help through mutual aid. They
extend to municipal provision of enabling amenities, in such forms
as Rivington water and Cornwallis Street public baths. They
endorse the activities of the Co-op, too; although, significantly, this
classic mid-Victorian mutual aid organisation made little headway
in Liverpool, with its low wages and unpredictable incomes, until
the Edwardian years and beyond.[73]

Anything that enabled people to build skills and character and
shape their own destiny was grist to Shimmin's mill; but within this
framework he says surprisingly little about the temperance movement *as such*, or about the transforming power of religion. Indeed,
much of what he writes about organised religion and its activities
is quite sceptical about its positive power for good, and the
hypocrisy of those who attend as a matter of respectability or in
instrumental pursuit of material benefits is a recurring theme.
Again, it is individuals that count, in spite of the structural faults
of the organisations they join. And we hear practically nothing
about the friendly societies and the trade unions, those great
bastions of working-class mutuality against a hostile world. Like
the Co-op, and for similar reasons, they were unusually thin on the
ground in Liverpool.[74]

There are further telling omissions in Shimmin. As well as
neglecting the trade unions, he does not talk about work and
labour relations. This is a startling omission which greatly reduces
the all-round value of Shimmin as a depictor of working-class life
as a whole. Shimmin clearly did not have access to the wider
culture of work, whether in the craft workshop or on the docks,
beyond his own limited experience of a bookbinding workshop.

And he makes no mention of the sectarian conflicts which divided Liverpool so bitterly in these years, with regular outbreaks of violence on the great religious and patriotic processional days. This refusal to engage with a dominant topic of popular concern probably reflects Shimmin's own religious position. Until his later years he was detached from the Church of England, which contained the most virulent strains of anti-Catholic prejudice and propaganda in this period; and he was friendly enough with the Roman Catholics to make an annual visit to the Jesuits at Stonyhurst, and to argue for the provision of separate Roman Catholic services in the workhouse. He was opposed to sectarian divisions in education, which had been a red-hot political issue in Liverpool since the mid-1830s; and he was no friend to anti-Irish bigotry. Indeed, he mocked the Orange Order and its peculiar ways in several sharp little asides. His politics were those of personality and municipality, and he set aside and scorned the great sectarian divide which dominated the political outlook of so many of his contemporaries.[75]

Shimmin's sidestepping of issues which mattered so much to so many of his fellow townspeople illustrates the individuality of his position. In many ways, despite the clubbable aspects of his personality, he was a quirky social misfit. And much of his work is destructive rather than constructive. It attacks a wide range of targets: indeed, hardly anyone escapes unscathed. But he has little positive to offer in solving problems; and certainly nothing original. His preoccupation with the cultivation of individual responsibility, with the need to provide role models and good examples, and with the need to 'connect' across class barriers, are the small change of debate on defusing the threat of Chartism in the 1840s, although the nature of their target has changed somewhat.[76]

The value of Shimmin's contribution lies more in description than in analysis or prescription. Here is where he has a distinctive voice and a usefully idiosyncratic line of vision. He might be dismissed as a prurient voyeur on the strength of *Liverpool Life*, and this guiltily audience-pleasing side of his work cannot be ignored. But even when he is describing the most disreputable activities there is far more to him than this: he provides a well informed qualitative dimension alongside the quantitative studies, and he brings within our purview phases of Liverpool life, and interpretation of Liverpool attitudes, which would otherwise remain concealed from the historian's gaze. Admittedly, he offers us some Liverpools at the expense of others, and at times his prose can descend to the banal and the emptily didactic, especially when he is describing worthy ventures like the Co-op. Even here, however, he is seldom less than informative. Although he has his ups and downs, Hugh Shimmin emerges as one of the most stimulating of the qualitative social observers of mid-Victorian England. Moreover, he deals with a neglected and difficult agenda. We need to know much more about the texture of working-class attitudes and behaviour in places other than the metropolis and the 'cotton towns', and Shimmin's work is an important contribution towards eventually restoring balance to the historiography. Reprints of other pieces of provincial social description, appropriately set in context and annotated, would take us further down the road to a more comprehensive and representative understanding of the varieties of town life in a rapidly urbanising and diversifying nation.[77]

Notes

1. M. B. Simey, _Charitable effort in Liverpool in the nineteenth century_ (Liverpool: Liverpool University Press, 1951), pp. 53–61, 82–4.
2. But see the very useful thesis by L. Feehan, 'Charitable effort, statutory authorities and the poor in Liverpool, _c._ 1850–1914', Ph.D. thesis, Liverpool University, 1988.
3. See especially S. Marriner, _The economic and social development of Merseyside_ (London: Croom Helm, 1982).
4. Easily the best and widest-ranging contribution in this idiom is P. J. Waller, _Democracy and sectarianism: a political and social history of Liverpool, 1868–1939_ (Liverpool: Liverpool University Press, 1981). For sectarianism see also the lively P. Ingram, 'Sectarianism in the north west of England, with special reference to class relationships in the city of Liverpool, 1846–1914', Ph.D. thesis, C.N.A.A. (Lancashire Polytechnic), 1988; F. Neal, _Sectarian violence: the Liverpool experience, 1819–1914_ (Manchester: Manchester University Press, 1988). On municipal government, B. D. White, _A history of the Corporation of Liverpool, 1835–1914_ (Liverpool: Liverpool University Press, 1951); F. Vigier, _Changes and apathy: Liverpool and Manchester during the industrial revolution_ (Cambridge, Mass.: M.I.T. Press, 1970); and on housing, C. Pooley and S. Irish, _The development of Corporation housing in Liverpool, 1869–1945_ (Lancaster: Centre for North West Regional Studies, 1984).
5. See especially the work of Colin Pooley, particularly 'Choice and constraint in the nineteenth-century city: a basis for residential differentiation', in R. J. Johnston and C. Pooley, eds., _Nineteenth-century cities_ (London: Croom Helm, 1982).
6. Joan Smith, 'Labour tradition in Glasgow and Liverpool', _History Workshop Journal_ (1984), vol. 17, pp. 32–56, and references cited there; P. L. F. Garner, 'Policing the Liverpool general transport strike of 1911', M.A. dissertation, Lancaster University, 1984.
7. G. Stedman Jones, _Outcast London_ (London: Peregrine Books, 1976); 'Working-class culture and working-class politics in London, 1870–1914: notes on the remaking of a working class', _Journal of Social History_ 7 (1973–4), pp. 460–507.

 8. Marriner, 1982.
 9. H. Shimmin, *Liverpool Life* (Liverpool: Egerton Smith, 1857), I, chapter 8 (chapter 28 of this volume); II, chapters 8–13 (chapters 11–13 are chapters 11, 19 and 30 of this volume).
10. K. Williams, *From pauperism to poverty* (London: Routledge & Kegan Paul, 1981), pp. 237–9. This criticism is largely met, with regard to Mayhew, by A. Humpherys, *Travels into the poor man's country: the work of Henry Mayhew* (Firle: Caliban Books, 1977), which Williams does not cite. As regards Shimmin, our agenda has been affected by uncertainty as to which of the *Porcupine* contributions came from Shimmin himself. The journal attracted a wide range of contributors, and we have not included any *Porcupine* items which were not published in Shimmin's name or ascribed to him at the time. This may mean that we have given too little weight to Shimmin's writings on charity, its problems and its abuses, for writings on this theme in a decidedly Shimminian idiom were a regular feature of *Porcupine*, as Simey points out.
11. *Liverpool Daily Post*, 13 January 1879.
12. *Liberal Review*, 18 January 1879.
13. *Harry Birkett; the story of a man who helped himself. By the author of 'Town Life',* etc. (London, 1860), pp. 43–4, 64, chapters 9–11; N. Pevsner, *The buildings of England: north Lancashire* (London: Penguin, 1969), pp. 144–5.
14. Ibid., chapters 14–18.
15. *Porcupine*, 18 January 1879, and see above, nn. 11 and 12; *Harry Birkett*, chapters 20, 26 and *passim*.
16. R. Rawlinson, *Supplement to the report to the General Board of Health on . . . the town of Whitehaven* (London: H.M.S.O., 1849).
17. See above, nn. 11, 12, 15; A. Holt, *Walking together: a study in Liverpool Nonconformity, 1688–1938* (London: Allen & Unwin, 1938), p. 193; *Harry Birkett*, pp. 27–8, 104.
18. See above, nn. 11, 12, 15; *Harry Birkett*, pp. 284–7. Dickens wrote his own sketch of Liverpool low life: see 'Poor Mercantile Jack', in his *The uncommercial traveller* (The Oxford Illustrated Dickens, 1978 edition), pp. 40–51. This deals with merchant seamen and the traps laid for them by predators in the Liverpool underworld, and was written *c.* 1860. Dickens was taken around by the police, and his lurid descriptions include a very strong hint at a case of male child prostitution.
19. *Liberal Review*, 18 January 1879.
20. Ibid.
21. H. Shimmin, *Liverpool sketches* (Liverpool, 1863), p. 122.
22. *Liverpool Daily Post*, 16 January 1879.
23. H. Shimmin, *Working men's wives* (Liverpool, 1858), p. 3.
24. G. Melly, *Stray leaves* (Liverpool, n.d.), vol. 2.
25. *Liverpool life*, collection of original cuttings, Liverpool library, H390.SHI; *Liverpool Daily Albion*, 13 January 1879, 15 January 1879; and above, nn. 11, 12, 15, 19.
26. 'Harry Hardknot', *Rambles in the Lake District* (Liverpool and

London, 1857).
27. *Harry Birkett*, p. 290.
28. Shimmin, 1857, II, pp. 107–11.
29. *Porcupine*, 18 January 1879.
30. Ibid.
31. *Liverpool Daily Post*, 13 January 1879.
32. Marriner, 1982; I. C. Taylor, '"Black Spot on the Mersey": a study of environment and society in eighteenth- and nineteenth-century Liverpool', Ph.D. thesis, Liverpool University, 1976; G. Anderson, *Victorian clerks* (Manchester: Manchester University Press, 1976).
33. Taylor, 1976; A. T. McCabe, 'The standard of living in Liverpool and Merseyside, 1850–1875', M.Litt. thesis, Lancaster University, 1975, p. 13; P. Ayers and J. Lambertz, 'Marriage relations, money and domestic violence in working-class Liverpool, 1919–39', in J. Lewis, ed., *Labour and love* (Oxford: Blackwell, 1986); and cf. E. Higgs, 'Women, occupations and work in nineteenth-century censuses', *History Workshop Journal* 23 (spring 1987), pp. 59–80.
34. McCabe, 1975, p. 14; W. B. Stephens, *Education, literacy and society, 1830–70: the geography of diversity in provincial England* (Manchester: Manchester University Press, 1987), pp. 87–98, 321, 327.
35. W. R. Cockcroft, 'The Liverpool police force, 1836–1902', in S. P. Bell, ed., *Victorian Lancashire* (Newton Abbot: David & Charles, 1974), pp. 150–68; E. C. Midwinter, *Old Liverpool* (Newton Abbot: David & Charles, 1971), chapter 3.
36. Waller, 1981, pp. 24, 170; Cockcroft, 1974; Ingram, 1988; Neal, 1988; Midwinter, 1971.
37. Waller, 1981, pp. 168–70; Feehan, 1988; S. K. Hocking, *Her Benny: a tale of Victorian Liverpool* (Liverpool: Gallery Press edition, 1988); Midwinter, 1971, chapter 4; E. C. Midwinter, *Social Administration in Lancashire 1830–60* (Manchester: Manchester University Press, 1969), chapter 4.
38. Pooley, 1982; I. C. Taylor, 'The insanitary housing question and tenement dwellings in nineteenth-century Liverpool', in A. Sutcliffe, ed., *Multi-storey living* (London: Croom Helm, 1974), pp. 41–87; J. H. Treble, 'Liverpool working-class housing, 1801–51', in S. D. Chapman, ed., *The history of working-class housing* (Newton Abbot: David & Charles, 1971); T. A. Roberts, 'The Welsh influence on the building industry in Victorian Liverpool', in M. Doughty, ed., *Building the industrial city* (Leicester: Leicester University Press, 1986); McCabe, 1975, chapter 3.
39. A. T. McCabe, 'The standard of living on Merseyside, 1850–75', in Bell, 1974, pp. 128–33; McCabe, 1975, chapter 2 and p. 72; Waller, 1981, pp. 83–4.
40. See especially C. Hamlin's piece on sanitary improvements in large towns, *Victorian Studies* 32 (1988–9). Gerry Kearns of the Department of Geography, Liverpool University, is currently working on this theme. For graphic Liverpool material to set chapters 11–13, 19 and 23–4 in context see McCabe, 1975, pp. 68–9; J. H. Treble, *Urban*

poverty in Britain (London: Batsford, 1979), pp. 173–6; Waller, 1981, p. 107.
41. Cf. Smith, 1984; T. Gallagher, *Glasgow: the uneasy peace* (Manchester: Manchester University Press, 1987); H. Patterson, *Class conflict and sectarianism* (Belfast: Blackstaff Press, 1980).
42. Taylor, 1976, table 1.3; C. Pooley, 'The residential segregation of migrant communities in mid-Victorian Liverpool', *Institute of British Geographers*, new series, 2 (1977), pp. 364–82; W. J. Lowe, 'The Irish in Lancashire, 1846–71: a social history', Ph.D. thesis, Trinity College, Dublin, 1975; J. Papworth, 'The Irish in Liverpool, 1835–71: segregation and dispersal', Ph.D. thesis, Liverpool University, 1981; Ingram, 1988.
43. Roberts, 1986; Waller, 1981, pp. 9–10; R. M. Jones, 'The Liverpool Welsh', in R. M. Jones and D. B. Rees, *Liverpool Welsh and their religion* (Liverpool, 1984), pp. 20–43.
44. Waller, 1981, pp. 119–20; and Dickens, 1978, pp. 45–7, on the black presence ('Dark Jack').
45. A. Briggs, *Victorian cities* (London: Pelican, 1968), p. 96; and see also G. Messinger, *Manchester in the Victorian age* (Manchester: Manchester University Press, 1985).
46. Stedman Jones, 1976, especially chapter 16; E. P. Thompson and E. Yeo, eds., *The unknown Mayhew* (London: Pelican, 1973); G. Godwin, *Town swamps and social bridges* (1859; reprinted with an introduction by A. D. King, Leicester: Leicester University Press, 1971); J. Greenwood, *The seven curses of London* (1869; reprinted with an introduction by Jeffrey Richards, Oxford: Blackwell, 1981); and see P. Keating, *Into unknown England* (London: Fontana, 1976).
47. H. Taine, *Notes on England*, trans. Edward Hyams (London: Thames & Hudson, 1957), pp. 225–6.
48. Quoted by J. O'D. Mays, *Mr Hawthorne goes to England* (Ringwood, Hants.: New Forest Leaves, 1983), p. 59.
49. Ibid., p. 58.
50. F. L. Olmsted (the elder), *Walks and talks of an American farmer in England* (Columbus, Ohio: revised edition, 1859), pp. 36, 40, 43–6, 49–50, 55.
51. John Finch, *Statistics of Vauxhall ward, Liverpool* (1842; reprinted with an introduction by Harold Hikins, Liverpool: Toulouse Press, 1986), pp. 8–9.
52. Ibid., p. 9.
53. Ibid., pp. 12, 36.
54. Thompson and Yeo, 1973, pp. 56–109.
55. P. T. Winskill and J. Thomas, *History of the temperance movement in Liverpool and district* (Liverpool: Joseph Thomas, 1887), pp. 11–13; J. K. Walton, *Lancashire: a social history, 1558–1939* (Manchester: Manchester University Press, 1987), pp. 166–75.
56. Winskill and Thomas, 1887, p. 12; R. B. Rose, 'John Finch, 1784–1857: a Liverpool disciple of Robert Owen', *Historic Society of Lancashire and Cheshire* 109 (1957), pp. 159–84.
57. Finch, 1986, pp. 23–4.

36 *Introduction*

58. A. Hume, *Missions at home* (London, 1850); *The condition of Liverpool: religious and social* (Liverpool, 1858).
59. W. S. Caine, ed., *Hugh Stowell Brown: his autobiography* (1887), p. 208.
60. Ibid., p. 539.
61. Melly, n.d.; Taylor, 1974, pp. 55–74.
62. P. E. Razzell and R. W. Wainwright, ed., *The Victorian working class: selections from letters to the Morning Chronicle* (London: Cass, 1973), p. 269.
63. Ibid., pp. 270–4.
64. Thompson and Yeo, 1973, pp. 9–109; R. Samuel, 'Mayhew and labour historians', *Bulletin of the Society for the Study of Labour History* 26 (1973), pp. 47–52; G. Himmelfarb, 'The culture of poverty', in H. J. Dyos and M. Wolff, eds., *The Victorian city* (London: Routledge, 1973); F. B. Smith, 'Mayhew's convict', *Victorian Studies* 22 (1978–9); K. Williams, 1981, chapter 5; Humpherys, 1977.
65. Taylor, 1974, p. 50.
66. Williams, 1981, p. 265; but note the qualifications which follow.
67. Thomas Wright, *Some habits and customs of the working classes* (London, 1867), *The great unwashed* (London, 1868), *Our new masters* (London, 1873), each reissued by Frank Cass, London, a century later. Wright does discuss family life: see especially *The great unwashed*, chapter 2. For an extended discussion of Wright, A. Reid, 'Intelligent artisans and aristocrats of labour: the essays of Thomas Wright', in J. M. Winter, ed., *The working class in modern British history* (Cambridge: Cambridge University Press, 1983), pp. 171–86.
68. J. Hopkinson, *Memoirs of a Victorian cabinet maker*, ed. J. B. Goodman (New York: Kelley, 1968), pp. 92–112; J. Sexton, *Sir James Sexton, agitator* (London: Faber, 1936); P. O'Mara, *The autobiography of a Liverpool Irish slummy* (London: Martin Hopkinson, 1934).
69. J. Burnley, *Two sides of the Atlantic* (London and Bradford, 1880), Part II; *Free Lance*, especially 22 December 1866, 12 January 1867, 26 January 1867, 9 February 1867, 15 June 1867. Cf. Dickens, 1978, and chapter 3 below. A telling comment on the prevalence of puritanical prurience in Liverpool in the next generation can be found in S. Hodgson, ed., *Ramsey Muir: an autobiography and some essays* (London: Lund Humphries, 1943), p. 25.
70. Cf. S. Marcus, *The other Victorians* (London: Weidenfeld & Nicolson, 1966), pp. 104–5.
71. Cf. E. Ross, 'Survival networks: women's neighbourhood sharing in London before World War I', *History Workshop Journal* 15 (1983), pp. 4–27.
72. Dickens, 1978, p. 45; and see T. Hull, 'The social significance of the public house in the Liverpool economic system, *c.* 1840–1900', M.A. dissertation, Lancaster University, 1979.
73. W. H. Brown, *A century of Liverpool co-operation* (Liverpool, 1929); E. P. Alcock, 'The Liverpool Co-operative Society, 1886–1939: its

growth, aims and social structure', M.A. dissertation, Lancaster University, 1986.
74. Smith, 1984, pp. 47–8.
75. See above, n. 4, and obituaries cited from the Liverpool press in 1879.
76. Much of the work of Dickens, Disraeli, Carlyle and Ruskin can be viewed in this light; and cf. the argument of P. Joyce, *Work, society and politics* (Brighton: Harvester Press, 1980).
77. For the best introduction to the wider context of urban development in these years, P. J. Waller, *Town, city and nation: England 1850–1914* (Oxford: Oxford University Press, 1983).

Part one
Low life: drink and entertainment

1 An hour in a grog shop

There is not one of these – not one – but sows a harvest which mankind *must* reap. Open and unpunished murder in a city's streets would be less guilty in its daily toleration than one such spectacle as this. – *Dickens*

How bitterly cold it is! How keenly the wind swirls through the narrow court! There are no sounds of revelry there now. Doors are shut, windows are stuffed. Here and there a shimmering gleam lights up a snow-rimed window sill. An hour ago, mother and children crouched around the small fire, and footsteps were eagerly listened for. It is Saturday night. Father is expected home with the wages. The remains of the thin candle have sunk in the socket of the iron holder. It is no use applying at 'the little shop' for anything more now; as 'a clean book' cannot be shown. The children, wearied out, fall asleep. Mother throws over them what rags she can muster, and taking her youngest child to her bosom, and covering it as she best can with her tattered shawl, she steals out, gently drawing the door after her, and is now off in search of her husband.

From four houses out of six in this court, on this night, *seven* wives have gone to look for their husbands. The men are ship-smiths. In two instances, for months at a stretch, the weekly earnings of these men amounted to *ninety shillings*! – yes, often have they drawn five pounds a week; and yet they had scarcely a decent article of furniture in their houses, and nothing worthy the name of a bed to lie down upon.

Would you know how this state of things came to pass? Would you cease to theorise for a time, and *stoop* to look at facts? Follow then one of these wives; keep close up with her as she hurries along. Stand behind her as she pushes open the gin-palace door, by pressing the body of her babe against it! Look there! look there at the bright lights, the costly decorations, the beaming visages behind the bar, the steaming mixtures which are handed to the jabbering crowd, and think of the dark court, the dull misery-stricken house; the wife lean and vixenish, the children pallid and ragged. Can you see any connection between these?

One brazen door after another is pushed open – no husband is met with. Crossing Scotland-place you hear this: 'Haven't you found him? I found my chap, and good-humoured enough he was, too, for once. I got more than I expected from him; come and have two pennoth.' With compressed lips, from which bitter curses have just issued, muttering wrathful imprecations, and threatening vengeance, is it surprising that the shipsmith's wife yields to the solicitation of her neighbour? They go to have 'two pennoth'; and in this locality, as in many others, they have not far to go in order to reach a gin shop. Oh! what thanks are due to the magistrates for the kindness and consideration shown in providing these refreshment houses for their humble brethren![1] Oh! what paeans of praise will flow forth from wives driven to desperation, and children driven to crime, in consequence of the facilities afforded to their protectors for dallying with this body- and soul-destroying vice!

'Have a glass, Mary, have a glass; two pennoth is right enough when you can't get more, but have a *glass* now, it'll do you good this cold night. Dick, two glasses of whiskey.'

The young man thus familiarly addressed smilingly complies with the request, and the women toss off the drink before one can see who surrounds them. They have a good deal of talk before they think of going further, and their threats of vengeance are hurled about. At the door they meet a tall, swarthy man, whom they recognise, and elicit from him, after much to do, as the creature is far gone in drink, that 'Bill is tossing for quarts of ale at _____.' Away the women go. It is not far off, come along with them.

At the door of every gin shop which had been passed, stood puny young shivering children, in filth and tatters. 'Please give me a 'apenny', or 'please buy a box of matches', uttered in a drawl, first called attention to these sorrowful and pitiful objects. And no one who felt the weight, worth and influence of home – no one who gazed on the blear eyes, wan faces and stunted forms of children driven by parents to wear out their lives in such a manner – no one who had not torn off rudely the tender silken cords of a mother's love, which had been twined round the heart in infancy and child-hood, and even yet, in vigorous manhood, vibrate when touched – no man, with right conceptions of the duties, obligations, respon-sibilities and hopes of life, could witness such scenes without fully endorsing the burning words of Charles Dickens: – 'There is not one of these – not one – but sows a harvest which mankind *must* reap. Open and unpunished murder in a city's streets would be less guilty in its daily toleration than one such spectacle as this.'

After a slushing tramp, we reach one of the largest, and certainly the most costly vaults in the town, and it is now, every department of it, filled with dirty, ragged, miserable-looking men, women and children. The wife, fired with whiskey, and tightening her shawl around her babe, goes from division to division; at length she sees the object of her search – her husband, the smut of the forge never removed from his face. He is engaged in 'tossing' who pays for all.

'Two out of three, or sudden death', roars the half-maddened mechanic.

'Sudden death', is the reply.

'That's the style – no two ways', says a bystander.

'I'll give you sudden death!' screams out the wife; and a torrent of indescribable abuse is hurled upon her husband and his companions, as if there and then the awful threat were being put into execution. This has the effect of interrupting the lively and profitable game to which many workmen devote some portion of their time and their money on Saturday evenings – tossing for quarts. Of course there are 'sponges' around, who fawn and flatter, in order that they may be permitted to imbibe their share of the quarts; so that what a man spends on drink for himself is a very small proportion to what he squanders on others.

The woman wearies herself in a little while with foul speech and idle threats, and when her volubility subsides, the husband and she become more reconciled. She 'takes a drop of something hot', has some money doled out to her, and in half an hour, or less, she is gone to market – to the shop – to her home and her children. But her husband is still at the bar of the vaults. He has been here two hours; and here we will stay a while with him.

Leaving for a time the smith and his companions lighting their pipes and preparing to dispose of 'another quart', come on into the next compartment. Seven women are here, forming two groups; some have bonnets on and baskets with them, and all are very talkative. The presence of a stranger in nowise disconcerts them, nor interferes with their conversation; on the contrary, they seem to like it, and, as a cigar which we have asked for does not seem to be forthcoming, a very stout woman in a cotton bedgown, loosely worn, her hair matted and twisted about her head, takes up a pint pot and says, 'You luk as if a spot of hot fourpenny ud do you good – here tek a sup.' This calls forth a roar of laughter from the groups, and is joined in heartily by the ruddy-faced waiter with the pork pie hat, who had looked suspiciously on us several times before. Fire of this sort soon exhausts itself, if it be borne coolly, and the women become friendly and very communicative. We soon know who their husbands are, what they earn, what they spend, and what they 'allow for the house'. We are told their peculiarities, their weaknesses, their loves, and likings; and one woman volunteers a statement, that if we wish to hear a good song, we must hear her husband, who is now at the *Goose Club*, where there is a 'free and easy'.

A little girl, without shoes, scarcely any garments on her, comes in with a quart jug destitute of handle. She places the jug on the marble counter, and has to stand on tip-toe to do this. She then places the money beside it, and never utters a word! The women recognise her, and speak very cheeringly to the tattered child, who replies to their questions, and then stares wildly around at the gilded cornices – the panels – the ceiling – the chandeliers – so glittering and bright. In the meantime the waiter has taken away the jug and half filled it – has swept the coppers into the till – and with a shout of 'There you are, Kitty', pushes the jug towards where the child stands, and then proceeds to supply 'four two-pennoths' which are being bawled out for by some men in the next compartment. There was a slight expression of pity on two of the women's faces, as they looked on the child creeping out, shivering with cold, and carrying a pint of ale to its mother!

Through one division after another we roamed for an hour – girls, boys, women, old men, robust villains, slender mechanics, oyster men, stay-lace women, dog fanciers, street musicians, a comic vocalist ready to entertain a group with song or recitation for 'a drink' – all these were met with. Some were drunk and raving, others were in that dangerous state said to be 'ready for anything'; loungers slouched about, leering wistfully at working men, whom they saw draw money from their pockets to pay for drink; and when we reached the smith again, he was being ejected from the place for using abusive language to the barman. None were more active in thrusting the man out than he who had taken his money, supplied him with drink, and thus instigated him to commit a breach of the peace. What oaths these men hurled at each other; and when we saw the smith skulk away from the policeman who had been called in to protect the dandy barman – the thought crossed us, What about this man's wife? What about his children? 'There is not one of these – not one – but sows a harvest which mankind *must* reap. Open and unpunished murder in a city's streets would be less guilty in its daily toleration than one such spectacle as this.'

2   The Free and Easy

The Free and Easy is just now becoming a place of popular and fashionable resort. At one time its supporters consisted of labouring men or mechanics addicted to ballad singing and beer drinking. Such, however, is 'the progress of the age', it has now found favour with expensively educated and well dressed youths, as well as persons of riper years, who mingle, as it is said, with 'good society', sneer at all attempts to improve the manners or amusements of the mass, and yet consider themselves, and wish other people to consider them – gentlemen.

The members of the wealthier class who frequent the Free and Easy cannot be called proud. Their notions of propriety or equality are expansive, and their equanimity is not easily disturbed. It is not in any way disagreeable to them to toss for drink with a baker's apprentice, halve a roasted potatoe with a low buffoon, or stand 'something hot' for a bloated pimp, or a 'shelved pugilist'. It seems to give some of them peculiar pleasure in being permitted to nurse the opera cloak, and dandle the boquet, while the young lady with light hair, weak eyes, bare shoulders, free manners, and an indifferent voice, tells the audience how she felt when in her mountain home, and how she 'poins' to behold it 'agee-en'.

There is much to be regretted when a man of acknowledged ability and high standing in society is seen taking his supper from a small table placed in a lobby, leading to a free concert room. Here he will have the fumes of 'real cavendish'[2] or spurious Havannahs wafted over the chops, steaks, or kidneys. He will listen the while to puerile attempts at smartness, and, perhaps, with some degree of earnestness take part in loose conversation. He will become on friendly terms with the waiter, and learn from him the private history of the vocalists. He will stand at the entrance to the concert room with his glass to his eye, quizzing the poor young girl when she leaves the platform, and smile very wickedly when he sees the difficulty she is having in crushing her way past the rude men who throng the place. He is in the height of his glory as the evening advances, and he is asked by the bland, courteous, simpering, curly-headed host to 'be kind enough to take the chair for a short time', and how he does enjoy the obscene allusions, and filthy innuendoes of the comic vocalist. Yet this is called rational recreation, and 'gentlemen only are admitted!'

It has frequently been remarked that the humbler classes are influenced in their amusements by the example of those above them. As regards the Free and Easy this can hardly be said. It took its rise amongst the working people, had a specific object in view, and unbecoming and objectionable as the object might be, it was better than the novel features which the respectable men are introducing. The working-man's Free and Easy was generally established, or 'got up', by the landlord of a public house, under the pretence of assisting men to save money for a 'goose feast', Christmas dinner, or what was termed 'a jollification' of some sort. The subscription was fixed at threepence or sixpence per week, rules were drawn up, a chairman, secretary, and treasurer appointed, and the matter made to assume a business shape – and a very serious business it often was to a working man. To render the meetings for payment of subscriptions more attractive, the time was spent in smoking, drinking, health proposing, and singing. Here, on a Saturday evening, the workman turned in – he drank beer, sang his song, and listened to others, and withal there was a degree of order and decency observed which is altogether absent from the modern free and easy, more particularly that frequented by 'respectable men'.[3] In order to see what this class of entertainment now consists of, we visited some of both sorts in the month of November, 1857.

The working man's Free and Easy was held in an old-established house. To keep pace with the times, a new front had been put in, but the interior was just what we had seen it twenty years before. Cold as the night was, the room windows were thrown open to allow the smoke to escape, and the singing attracted a crowd round the door. In the street, watercress, pigs' feet, coloured sweets, stay laces, boys' caps and pickled cockles found purchasers. Soldiers – bearded men with medals on their breasts, who swore a deal, and smoked incessantly – were about the door. They had young girls in company, whose dishevelled hair, sunken eyes, violent gesticulation, coarse features, and still coarser speech, proclaimed their character. There was a rendez-vous for recruiting parties close at hand, and young lads, from sixteen to twenty years of age, were hanging about, or sitting on steps, haggard and forlorn, waiting, probably, for their billet, and no doubt longing for the time to arrive when they had passed through the chrysalis state, and should come forth full grown, scarlet-coated warriors and medal men.

On entering the house we were attracted by the singing in a small parlour. Here was a soldier of one of the Highland corps, singing 'the Cameron men', – his earnestness was clearly apparent. The place was thronged with soldiers, recruits, and their female friends. A youth crushed past the entrance, holding up a pair of scissors. He was almost drunk, and had a habit of treading on people's toes, which called forth some terrible curses; but he, laughingly, excused himself by saying, 'Well, you might have seen as I was anxious to let my wench have a bit of my hair, and you might have kept your toes out of the road for once.' This did not seem satisfactory to one of the soldiers, who was fully prepared for an onslaught, but he was calmed down by the Cameron man saying, 'The fellow isn't worth wasting shot on.' The girl, who was said to be 'crying drunk', took the scissors, and wept aloud while removing the dark locks from her soldier laddie. The operation finished, the youth, like Samson of old, seemed shorn of his strength, for he fell on the form crying, 'As may be I'll never see you more, Bess.' The old soldiers enjoyed this scene heartily, saying the only Bess that he would be likely to think of for the next few years would be '*brown* bess' or her smarter sister *Minié*.[4] Whilst one of the warriors was telling of a fight in the trenches, when Captain Vicars was killed, and another begun, in a very doleful manner to tell of 'what he did on Alma's heights',[5] we left them to proceed upstairs, where the Free and Easy was held. It was a long room, with a low ceiling, and was well filled with working men. There was a seat, elevated a little, for the chairman, and plain forms and narrow tables for the commoners. We counted eighty-four persons engaged in smoking and drinking – the majority were from eighteen to twenty-five years of age. A few of the company drank ginger-beer, but the most popular orders appeared to be 'a glass of ale', or a glass of whisky, hot. There was an organ in the room, at which a blind man presided, and the chairman for the evening was addressing the company as we entered.

He was a stout man, who could not have been washed or shaved for a week previous, he was so filthy; but he seemed quite comfortable in his position, and was acknowledged to be 'a good hand at getting up the steam'. If volubility of utterance, plain speaking, and good lungs, had anything to do with the qualifications of his office, he must be pronounced a good chairman. From his remarks, it was inferred that a doleful cast had been given to the proceedings by one of the company singing 'a dirge, and no mistake'. To restore cheerfulness, and give proper tone, the slovenly chairman called upon Mr _____ for one of his 'care-crushing titbits!' and it was hoped that all gentlemen would 'look sharp', give their orders, and keep quiet, while their cares were being crushed by the 'song as is to come'.

The scene in the Free and Easy, whilst the orders are being given, is a very sad spectacle. To witness the anxiety to obtain drink – the avidity with which it is seized on, and reflect on the money thus

squandered, for which these men have given, in most cases, their
hard labour, is terribly suggestive. There were two female waiters
and one male in attendance. The girls, with gay head-dresses and
ribbons streaming from their caps, were very bold, and were treated
by the visitors with much more civility than they deserved. The
chairman was almost out of patience before the orders were
supplied, and called several times for 'order', before it was restored.
Drink and tobacco to satisfy all for a time having been got in, the
man who had been called on for a song, arose, walked to the
organist, whispered to him, and then turned round and faced the
audience. He was received rapturously.

He was a little man, dressed very neatly in black, with a red
round face, dark bright eyes, and a white cravat, and was said to
be a waiter at the _____ Hotel. He twisted himself to represent a
cripple, drew his handkerchief out very slowly, whiped his eyes a
good deal, pretended to cry, made his lips represent cherries,
imitated the crowing of a cock, drew imaginary corks, pretended to
saw down the railing at the side of the organ, imitated the playing
of a Jew's harp, put his arm in a sling, placed a black eye shade
over one eye, and then began to sing 'Good Mr Brown!' The roars
of laughter which greeted this performance were very hearty, and
very loud. Young men kicked the floor, knocked the tables, clapped
their hands, and shouted 'bravo'. Others could do nothing but
laugh, the tears of joy streamed down their cheeks. One old man,
who was a little overcome with liquor, said such fun would 'be the
death of him'. Whilst another old man, who smelled strongly of tar,
and sat smoking without his coat, said, 'S'help me it's a wonder the
cove's not took up to Buckinum Palliss!'

There was nothing particularly humorous in the song, but the
singer by action and grimace, together with the slow time in which
he sang the chorus excited all around him, and the greatest
enthusiasm prevailed. When he had concluded, offers to treat him
were made from all sides, and he yielded to the solicitation of a
stalwart man, who was nursing a piece of beef and some
vegetables. The man pulled the little singer on to the seat, and
called out, 'Let's have a glass of whisky – Irish, hot, and two
pennorth of rum.' When the whisky arrived the comic singer
discovered that he lacked a cigar. This was ordered, and paid for
by the silly fellow. At the request of the chairman a young man
arose and proposed as a sentiment, 'Those in our arms, we love in
our hearts', and notwithstanding the earnestness by which it was
introduced, the sentiment appeared a satire on the mode of enjoyment here adopted. Two young men then sang the duet of 'All's
well', with good taste, and a smith, who was almost 'quite drunk',
sang a nigger song. He appeared in character without having

occasion to black his face. The organist then performed 'The Battle
of Prague', and called upon the audience to notice particularly,
'Trumpets and drums', and 'Horses galloping', which portions he
was said to render with great effect.

We noticed that as the drink begun to tell upon the audience, so
the interest in the singing decreased. The interruptions during the
singing became frequent, men staggered into the room, looking
about them wildly, and then staggered out, not appearing to meet
with the object of their search. The criticism of the singers became
more honest, and if a man failed to do all that was expected, there
were several around quite willing to tell him of his defects. On one
occasion a young man sang 'The Lass of Richmond-hill', and on
leaving the platform was told by a comfortably dressed, clean
mechanic, that before he attempted to sing that song again, he
might find it of some assistance were he to 'put his head in a rat
hole for half an hour!' The young man was certainly a very bad
singer, and for many reasons would do well to keep his head out
of a Free and Easy. We came away.

A great change had taken place in the company below whilst we
had been in the singing room. The recruits and their girls had
departed; their places were filled by working men drunk. The wives
of some of them were at the door, and others went into the room
to try and persuade them to come home. One man swore very
fiercely that he would not stir a foot unless 'Dickey' were brought
to give him a kiss. He could not have lived very far off, as the wife
returned in few minutes with a pretty little boy in his night-clothes,
very clean, and a sweet babe it certainly was. This proved to be
Dickey, who was held up to kiss the drunken, blasphemous father.
The degraded man cried over his child, and, this done, he showed
it to his drunken companions, saying, 'I'll do any mortal thing for
that dickey-bird.' The wife very properly said he 'should keep
sober, that's enough', and away he staggered to his home, having
undergone his preparation for the Sabbath. Such is a Saturday night
at a working man's Free and Easy.

The Free and Easy to which gentlemen (?) resort is in a very
different locality. Shops of an indescribable character surround.
Some of them are fitted up professedly as 'oyster shades',[6] with
small snugs behind, and through the oval windows of these snugs
frail women are seen to look out at every visitor that is vicious or
silly enough to enter. Others profess to sell plaster casts, but the
Graces and infant Samuels are in strong contrast to all around.
Others are supposed to be milliners' establishments, and very few
are brazen-faced enough to declare in broad daylight what they
really are.[7] In any of them little business appears to be transacted
during the day; but, as evening approaches, the cloak is gradually

thrown off, and their character is revealed. You will see standing at the doors, or somewhere within call, stout young men, with bloated faces, Belcher neckties, closely cropped hair, and determined aspect. Within, you may see loosely attired women, the depravity of whose lives no depth of paint or fashion of dress can conceal. They bustle about, preparing the bait to secure what is termed 'queer fish on the loose', that is, gentlemen bent on 'seeing life as it swings in all its charming variety'. The fashionable vaults, 'The Commercial Coffee-rooms', 'The Cockfighting-house', 'The Sparring Academy', the billiard rooms, the rat pits, are all now in active operation and driving a roaring trade. Fast young men and sedate old scoundrels pass in and out of these places; they give and take 'bushels of chaff' before they reach the Free and Easy.

The room where the Free and Easy is now held was celebrated as a 'betting meet' and billiard room. The cellar, which is 'the Tap', has long enjoyed an unenviable reputation for all that is vile; yet this does not prevent gentlemen frequenting it in the evening, when they are said to be 'fresh', that is, half drunk, their sense of decency washed out by liquor. The singing room is opened at eight o'clock, and has of late attracted large audiences. The drink is very costly, is freely indulged in, and songs or recitations are volunteered by visitors, or called for by the company or chairman. Toasts and sentiments are given, occasionally 'a health' is proposed, and the further every song, toast or sentiment is removed from decency, the more it is applauded. There appears to be no restraint, the most unblushing license is permitted, and what makes the matter more lamentable is the fact, that the majority of the visitors appear to belong to that class of life whose education and intelligence might be expected to prevent them descending to such a degrading species of pastime. On one occasion there were thirty-four persons, apparently respectable men, present, and during the singing of one song, (the words and sentiments of which were so grossly indecent they cannot be alluded to), these thirty-four men were convulsed with laughter, and many of them gave utterance to their feelings in the most disgusting language.

It has often been said in defence of such men, 'They were excited with drink, were not themselves, and therefore excusable.' How can they be held excusable on such ground? The judge on the bench admits of no such excuse in palliation of an offence against the laws of the land; and yet men who obtain that which excites and encourages them to transgress the laws of propriety, decency, or public morality, and that, too, in the face of light and knowledge, are to be excused, forsooth. It is the ample means which such viciously disposed men have at their command that enables the proprietors of these filthy resorts to hang out their red lights, and keep their tri-coloured flags flaunting in the face of those who would teach them the better way. Were gentlemen (?) to withdraw their patronage, the flag would be struck, the light extinguished, and the town purified of such vicious virus as the gentlemen's Free and Easy engenders.

3 The free concert room

During one of our rambles on a Saturday evening, we were attracted by an announcement of excellent singing and the word 'Poses' on the lamp over the door of a 'free concert room' in the neighbourhood of Williamson-square.[8] It is between ten and eleven o'clock when we enter. Passing the bar, around which are several disorderly and drunken women, in company with foreign sailors, we ascend a flight of very rickety stairs, which brings us to the concert room. It is a long narrow apartment, in a filthy state; the walls decorated – or rather daubed over – with landscapes in panels and figures on pedestals, done in water colours. There is a stage erected about two feet from the floor: the drop-scene is tattered, and so dirty and torn that we cannot discover what it is intended to represent. The forms for the accommodation of the audience are arranged along each side of the room, leaving a passage down the centre for the waiters. At the back of each seat or form runs a ledge, which is intended to support glasses, pipes and ginger-beer bottles – thus answering the double purpose of a seat for the party in front and a table for the guests behind. There are thirty-eight people present, of various ages and grades in life. Carters, bakers, shoemakers and sailors, preponderate.[9] There is no charge made for admission, but we have to pay threepence for a glass of stale ginger beer, perfectly unpalatable. There is a piano in the room, presided at by a little hunchback, who is smoking a short pipe when is he is not coughing. Seated by him is a gentlemen who plays the violin – when and how he likes. Close by him is a little girl, whose head is studded with curl papers, and a drunken carter who will persist in the interrogation – 'What the _____ to do with your head? When will it burst?'

A bell is rung: the violin player lays down his instrument, passes his fingers through his disordered hair, enters a little door at the side of the stage – the curtain rises, and the fiddler makes his appearance as a vocalist. The name of the song is not stated, and we cannot discover it. He tells us in some sort of rhyme, and in any sort of time, that when a man is single he can do as he likes – a sentiment which is heartily applauded by the audience. He then tells us of some persons that are joined in wedlock's bonds, and enters into minute details as to the misery consequent upon such unions, concluding every verse by the question, 'Now, what did these get married for?' During the singing of one of the verses there is a little interruption, caused by some sailors, who will persist in kissing the bare-necked, lightly dressed girls who have them in tow. The singer pauses. The mistress of the room looks at him, and calls out, 'Why the devil don't you go on?' To this civil question the singer replies, 'If you want the song finishing, come and do it yourself, for I'm _____ if I can work, and I'll be _____ if I do.' Having made this simple and explanatory statement, he jumps over the four footlights, draws from his pocket a dirty short pipe, sits down by the pianist, and begins to smoke. The proprietress of the room retorts on the vilely spoken violinist with great warmth. Speaking at him through the audience, she says, 'That's what you get for paying a fellow beforehand.' 'What's to do?' asks a gentle creature with several dinges[10] on her face. 'Why, he's _____ cheeky now he's got his tin.' 'Oh, let him go to _____,' replies the lovely nymph; 'he's been as drunk as muck this last hour.' In corroboration of this statement we must say that he certainly was drunk – as a fiddler.

The young lady who had waited upon us, and so perseveringly pressed on us the necessity of considering if there was anything else we would like, now came up and said she would 'go on'. Good humour being partially restored between the proprietress and her performers, the young lady passed up the room, entered the door, and in a few moments appeared on the stage, clad in a style something between a Bavarian broom girl and a fishfag. She sang a song, in which she declared herself to be 'a lady's maid – quite a lady's maid'. Her tone was extremely vulgar, and with tune and time she appeared to have no acquaintance. Not meeting with any applause for this performance, she said she would make another vocal effort, and she good-humouredly asked the fiddler to accompany her. He acceded to the request most joyfully, but his cutty pipe, from which the smoke 'so gracefully curled', still kept possession of his mouth. The song was something about a dream – a joyous dream; but as the vocalist scorned to pronounce the words in any dialect we could understand, and as the absence of 'tune and time' on the part of the fiddler rendered 'confusion worse confounded', the mysterious dream was never unravelled. We were considerably relieved when the jargon about the dream ended, and the audience – at least such of them as were conscious, for several were asleep – appeared to be equally delighted. The fiddler jumped upon the stage and said, 'The next performance will be Adam and Eve, in three pictures' – an announcement which the audience heartily applauded. The room was then darkened: the pianist ceased coughing, but still kept on smoking. The notes of the piano where then heard, the curtain rose, and before us was 'Adam and Eve in Paradise'.

The living figures, to use professional language, are in 'skin-tights'. Eve is ill-shaped in body, anything but innocent in face, short-necked, and lascivious-looking. Her hair is long, dark, and thrown carelessly and not without grace over her shoulders. She has a garland of fig leaves, or something to represent that, round her loins; in other respects (except the 'skin-tights') she is nude. Adam is fine in form, but in face flushed and fuddled-looking. It would be humiliating to think that these are anything but indecent caricatures of the 'parents of all living'. Adam is the incarnation of indelicacy: Eve, that of indecorous and dissolute carnality. Coarseness is their distinguishing characteristic. Both are naked; they know it, but neither of them is ashamed. The first *tableau* represents Adam's expression of surprise at the sight of Eve. The figures are turned round before the audience, so that all the 'points' may be more clearly seen. Loose, ribald, and indecent jests proceed from the audience as the classical picture rotates.

The second *tableau* represents Eve's astonishment at beholding Adam. Eve now looks temptingly at her partner, and holds out an apple towards him. Adam, as one of the sailors says, only looks 'sheepish' at his tempter. In the next *tableau* Adam seizes the apple, but has no sooner done so than 'the voice of the Lord' is heard in distant thunder, and they both crouch down in dismay at the displeasure they have awakened. After the figures have made the usual circle, the curtain falls, but rises again in a few minutes to show us what one of the attendants calls 'The Consummation of Bliss'. Adam and Eve are still in the garden. Adam is smiling, and sitting on a bank of roses. Eve is lolling across him in the most voluptuous manner. The wicked leers which pass from eye to eye amongst the audience; the chuckle of delight which issues from many of the nymphs around; the long and loud applause which accompanies this exhibition of man's want of moral tone, and woman's total deprivation of moral purity, proclaim with trumpet tongue that the scene is as vicious as it is indecent – as profane as it is immoral.

Eve soon leaves the scene where bliss is consummated, steps out of the garden into the room, condescends to sit near to and drink with a sailor 'half seas over', and obligingly informs him that they *do* 'The Morning and Evening Star', 'The Graces', and other beautiful pictures, *when there is a good company in the room*!

The room was again lighted, and a little boy, said to be only seven years of age, made his appearance upon the stage to perform a clog dance – à la Juba. The lad was very active, and appeared unusually confident for his years. The clog dance finished, he retired for a moment or two, and came on again to give a grotesque dance, interspersed with posturing. Poor little fellow! what amusement can there be in looking at this child going through his performances – twisting his young limbs, and straining all his joints? His posturing at an end, he left the stage to act the part of a beggar. With cap in hand he went round the room soliciting coppers from the persons assembled. Whatever he gets – it can't be much – is hard earned in the devil's workshop. We observed that little drink was consumed in the room. The hints we received from the girls, the arrangements, and the class of entertainments, indicated that the proprietor did not rely alone upon the sale of liquor for money-making. As we were leaving the concert room we passed into a room on the left, where we saw most indecent behaviour. At the bottom of the stairs, attracted by music, we turned into a large room on the right, where we found fifteen abandoned women of the most degraded class. Some of them were dancing the polka with Spanish sailors, who gesticulated a great deal, and smoked a great deal more. The tars had no jackets, but they had on red flannel shirts, long leather boots, into which the legs of their trousers were crammed. Those not indulging in the polka were sitting round the room engaged with girls. After a careful survey of the place and the people we retired, encountering at the door as we departed one of the 'invisible blues',[11] and a great number of loose girls.

Being still desirous of seeing more of the *licensed* preparations for the coming Sabbath, we entered another 'free concert room'. The place differs considerably from the last described, the walls not being daubed or decorated; but there is a similar stage, and a similar arrangement of forms constructed for drinking as well as for sitting purposes. The company are not so numerous, nor are the persons so 'respectable'. There is a small bar in this room, attended by a good-looking, athletic young man, who is particularly active in carrying off the empty glasses and in refilling them as required. We counted twenty-five persons, evidently all from the lowest class in society. There were only five females present, but they did not appear to be of the most degraded class. Standing for a moment or two at the top of the stairs, we looked round the room, considering where we should sit, and were then accosted by a young girl in Highland male costume, who asked us to 'step forward'. We accepted the invitation, and were conducted to the end of the room, which was partitioned off from the common forms. Here we might repose on hair-cushioned seats, lounge on the sofa, or loll on an easy chair. We observe now that the 'Highland youth' has very short kilts, with legs much exposed and not very straight, is fluent in speech and light and flippant in manner – a sort of caricature

of a taciturn 'braw John Highlandman'. We were informed that the
part of the room where we were seated was devoted to 'respectable
people'. It was decorated with a few engravings and prints, framed.
A model of a first-class man-of-war, in a glass case, attracted the
attention of a young sailor, who, on referring to the craft with a
scrutinising air, said, 'Well, I'm blowed if he's got his davits out'.
There was no indication of a 'concert' but the melancholy tones of
an indifferent violin, the performer on which appeared to be 'done
up', or, as a vocalist afterwards informed us, 'drunk', and 'knocked
off his pins'. We asked the lady if there was to be any singing, and
she replied, 'I'm going to favour the company in two twos'. She
immediately tossed off some liquor of an amber colour which she
had in a glass before her, walked up the room, and stepped on to
the stage, which was only elevated about a foot from the floor, and
had not the accommodation of a side door. She sang a song with
a chorus that was taken up by the whole of the company, and
appeared to give great satisfaction. The burden of it was, 'Hurra,
hurra, cigars and *co*-niac.' We afterwards learned from the singer
that it was 'a very good song, the chorus of a jolly, flowing
character, the melody extremely simple and expressive, and
sounded remarkably well at sea', where she had the pleasure of
singing it very often 'to the great gratification of Captain Shrimper,
of the Great Sea Snake – a crack ship that sailed well with the wind
close on the quarter!' The nautical lady again jumped on the stage,
carrying with her a piece of music. The regular pianist had received
his wages, and, we were told, had gone on the spree; but 'another
gentleman' took his place at the instrument to accompany the lady
in the song, 'The Standard Bearer'. The vocalism was wretched,
and a slight hiss was heard. The lady 'looked daggers', and as she
left the stage cast a glance at one side, and said, 'I'm very much
obliged to you: I'm sure it becomes you very well; but it just shows
what your eddication has been.' The master of the room, a smartly
dressed young man, of gentlemanly deportment, who had accidently
come in, inquired what was the matter. 'Some one hissed when I
was singing "The Standard Bearer", and I was never hissed before
in my life', said the vocalist, now almost affected to tears. One of
the audience, a gentleman with 'an open countenance', said, 'If you
mean to say that it was any of us three, you are most _____
mistaken; and all I say is, that whoever it was it is a _____ shame.'
The lady replied that she did not allude to any person in particular,
but she distinctly heard a hiss. The master of the room allayed the
excitement of the audience, and her professional sisters, with the
assistance of some fire water, contrived to allay that of the lady.

   In a short time harmony was again restored, and the Highland
youth, in a consolatory tone, addressing the vocalist, said, 'I never

heard you sing so well. I was just saying to Mr Nozzle (a nigger singer with blackened face, striped shirt, tight trousers, and top boots), Doesn't she sing that "Standard Bearer" charmingly and with feeling? and he said, "Stunning, Maria".' The lady then turned and addressed herself to us. She lamented the little interruption, but it showed what *low* people are capable of, and would do. She then began to be communicative, and informed us that her five years' residence in America had given her a high opinion of the great republic and a thorough contempt for England. She would rather live on one meal a day in America than eat four meals of roast beef and plum pudding in her native country. No later than that day she had been speaking to a captain, who, it was very likely, would take her to the land of freedom, and she would then be glad to leave this country to its fate! What a dread alternative! During this confidential confab the lady kept sipping at a glass, and it soon became evident that her eyes were getting very glossy. The black, with a chuckle, said 'her squinters' told that she was getting 'sloppy', an opinion which appeared to be entertained by the whole of the performers, who assembled in a cluster at the end of the room devoted to the 'respectables'.

The tete-a-tete with the lady was disturbed by a young man, one of the audience, who jumped upon the stage, pulled off his ragged jacket, and in his shirt sleeves began to dance, having previously given directions to the fiddler what tune he was to play. The agility of the youth in what we were told was 'step dancing' was great, and with his heavy shoes he beat time in an excellent manner. He continued 'shaking himself up' and beating time in a variety of ways for about a quarter of an hour, when one of the ladies, seeing signs of impatience amongst the audience, called out to the youth to 'drop it'. This brought the dance to a termination and the dancer to a table amongst his companions, where he took a hearty swig of ale, and with a fearful oath declared that he could 'dance all night and floor the _____ fiddler any time.' We learned that it was a common thing for youths frequenting this and other concert rooms to appear as amateurs in dancing and singing. If they display any ability, they are encouraged to appear frequently. The vanity which operates with all amateurs induces them to bring their friends and acquaintances to see how well they can 'do it'. The keeper of the house reaps the benefit, to the ruin of the youths, who, in too many instances, are led to adopt as a profession those amusements in which at first they indulged only for 'a lark'.

The dancing 'took' so well with the audience that the group of lads from which the other was selected put up another amateur to sing a song. He could not be more than sixteen or seventeen years of age. His clothes indicated that he was engaged at some foundry.

He was very dirty, with lanky hair, matted with filth, which could not conceal a large development of self-esteem and a low moral region. He held his cap before him, twisting it round with both hands, and was just beginning to sing, when one of the ladies called out, 'Drop that; it won't do tonight; there are people here who won't like it.'[12] Turning round, she whispered to us, 'He was going to sing that _____ song again.' The song was changed, much to the annoyance of his 'pals' as he called them, who made numberless suggestions as to the selection to be made for his vocal effort. At last, in a low, vulgar voice, he commenced a song disgusting in words, filthy in hints and allusions, and entirely obscene. The proprietor was in the room, but of course interfered not with an exhibition which appeared to give so much satisfaction to the amateurs and their companions, who formed the majority of the company. The professionals, too, had no reason to complain, for their labours were lightened, and the vain youth was never within 'two pennyworth' to be allowed to display his talents in public. The youths praised 'Tommy' to the skies for being 'plucky' enough to give 'mouth' to the words of the lewd song; they swore that he was a 'first-rate brick;' and as to his singing, why, 'leave it there'. The prices charged for drink are high, and the drink is of the worst description; yet the men and boys drink freely; another, and another still, and still another glass is called for, until 'the brain begins to swim', and then at midnight the motley crew are turned into the streets to find their way home or to worse places. What a preparation for the Sabbath!

4   The sparring match

In the last paper we saw how some of 'the Fancy' beguiled their leisure hours. In order to see the character of these 'manly British boxers more fully developed, it will be necessary 'to see these men at work;' and for this purpose we visited 'a sparring match.'[13] There are houses at which 'the science of boxing is taught at all hours', and 'profound and plucky professors' earn their bread, literally, 'by the sweat of their brow', in training the novice who is ambitious 'to flesh his maiden mauly', or in instructing 'fast young men' 'how to floor the peelers'. This class of sports (?) enjoys to some extent a literature of its own. 'Slang' of the most extra-ordinary character is in general use, even amongst the educated and aristocratic supporters of 'the ring'. These men would be horrified if it were stated in their hearing that one ruffian had struck another a violent blow in the mouth or nose, causing the blood to gush forth in a frightful manner; but they 'enjoy it rather' when it is said 'he got home beautifully on Bob's sucker, and drew an unmistake-able supply of the ruby;' or, 'he popped in his left very neatly on Sam's smeller, and opened up a fresh paint pot;' or, 'he cleverly reached his kisser, and turned on the tap from the darky's bunghole.' So general has this form of expression become, that the 'retreats of the Fancy', at least those of a respectable (?) character, always append to the advertisements this significant sentence – 'The whole literature of the ring kept at the bar?' The specimens given will show the necessity for this, and explain our motive for introducing such phraseology.

Sparring matches are got up nominally for the benefit of some pugilist, but really for the benefit of landlords, who in most cases have a youth in hand that they support and 'back' to fight; they therefore hold 'a sparring match' now and then, to raise funds to supply the fighter with food or get him into training, and so prepare him for a 'gallant, scientific, fair, manly, stand-up mill.' The appeals that are made to the public by these pugilistic professors, in advertisements and through the press, exhibit great ingenuity, and not infrequently display literary ability. It is lament-able to see undoubted talent thus prostituted. A sparring match was recently introduced thus: 'Now is the time or never for all

Englishmen to join heart and hand to prevent their truly national sport from being put down and utterly extinguished – the foreigner's *stiletto* substituted for the English *fist!*' In another announcement, speaking of the pugilist whose benefit was about to 'come off' – 'A_____, through unforeseen difficulties, has got into limbo; and as he has a wife and eight children, of course he is extremely anxious on the subject of the future. We do trust that none of his *brethren in arms* will neglect this call of charity. A gamer or better bit of stuff for his weight never peeled than the *beneficiaire*.' And as a further inducement to visitors, it is added, 'In this classical retreat there is everything in abundance to recruit the strength, cheer the spirits, and ease the heart. Lessons in boxing at all times. Gloves provided.'

The sparring match at which we were present was announced as a 'Grand scientific display of fistic talent,' for the benefit of a Liverpool celebrity who had just been involved in a fight which ended in 'a draw', that is, both men were so horribly beaten and bruised by each other that the umpire could not decide which of them was the victor. The admission to this 'sparring treat' was – 'Front seats, 1s.; back seats, 6d.; to commence at seven o'clock prompt.' The house where it was held is noted for all the sports of the fancy – fighting, running, ratting, dog racing, badger baiting, and their concomitant vicious practices. The squalor and filth to be met with in the street and neighbourhood are a commentary on our boasted sanitary progress and 'improved dwellings for the working classes.' Beershops and brothels, gin palaces and gin drinkers, wretched women, giddy girls, bloated bullies and blackguard boys, semi-nude outcasts, and mud-loving, mischief-making manikins, here abound. The houses are the oldest, and but one degree removed from the filthiest, in the town. We reached the place at seven o'clock 'prompt'. It was low and dirty-looking. We entered a small parlour, in which we found half a dozen young men, whose appearance at once pronounced them to be 'professionals', and whose conversation proved them to be so. On inquiring if the sparring match had commenced, we were told, 'It is time enough; the coves very seldom turn up till about eight o'clock.'[14] A man came forward from the kitchen, and enquired if we had tickets. He was prepared to sell, and we purchased for the front seats. One or two young men from a foundry sauntered in; they bought tickets, smoked short pipes, drank ginger beer or ale, chatted with 'the bruisers' about fighting in general, and the late fight near Birmingham in particular. The landlord was a stiff-set, sinewy, wiry man, civil and obliging in manner. He kept the conversation well up, and appeared to be 'well up' himself on all manners appertaining to his profession and practice. He told the company of a singular match which he expected would come off. Two men were matched to fight, walk, and run for £50 a side – to fight on Tuesday, walk on Thursday, and run one hundred yards on Friday. This was looked upon by the company as a remarkable feat, 'such a thing as never was before nor ever would be again.' There appeared to be several men present who had nothing to drink. They were fighting men, destitute of cash – some of them were almost destitute of clothes, and the landlord explained that 'the poor coves were out of feather' and 'nearly on the stones.'

A man came in who treated the company to half a gallon of ale, and, as the landlord put it on the table, he said, 'Come now, chaps, this will help you to moult,'[15] which we supposed to be another and probably more expressive form of saying it would cheer their spirits. When nearly an hour had elapsed, and the company had received several additions, we were asked to 'come up stairs to the sparring saloon; it's cooler and more comfortable.' Of this invitation we speedily availed ourselves. The sparring saloon was also used as the dog-fighting and rat-killing saloon – the 'rat pit', as it is called, having been taken asunder and placed in the corner of the room. The place was spacious, the room of the next house on the same floor having been taken in, as we were told, 'so as to give us proper room for our work.' The ceiling was very low, and the place had a close unhealthy odour. The windows were speedily opened, and we obtained better air and a view of the street. The gambols of some drunken sailors on the opposite side created amusement, and helped to while away the time. The walls of the room were literally covered with portraits of celebrated pugilists, pedestrians, rowers, dogs, rat-killing matches, and a large engraving of 'the great mill between Broom and Hannan for £1000 a side', with a key to it. If these portraits of British boxers could be relied on, a collection of more brutal-looking beings we never saw. The company spent their time in examining the engravings, and manifested nothing like dissatisfaction at the delay. Most of the young men were decent-looking mechanics, and walked about the room quite as seriously as if they had been waiting to hear a scientific or instructive lecture. About twenty persons had now assembled, and a little bustle in the corner of the room where the pugilists had assembled gave indication that business would speedily commence. A young man very smartly dressed entered the room, and was most cordially greeted by the boxers. His hair was cropped very close, and from his conversation and his frequent allusion to 'bagging the bobbies', it was evident to what class he belonged, and how his showy dress had been obtained. He amused the men very much by a recital of some of his hairbreadth escapes.

It was close on nine o'clock when the gloves were brought in, and the two men stripped to 'set to.' The poor creatures had little difficulty in stripping. One of them was the tall young man whom we had last seen at the 'Milling Crib',[16] 'shaky on his pins', and afterwards 'regularly doubled up.' The other was a stiff-set fellow, of determined aspect, and as an old man by us observed, 'snake-headed and flabby.' When the gloves (which were filthy looking articles) had been properly secured on the men's hands, they walked into the centre of the room, shook hands, threw themselves into a variety of fighting attitudes, and began to strike each other with such earnestness as to call forth requests from the spectators to 'Keep out', and 'Take it easy,' 'Don't be so savage', &c. The tall youth said his 'crabshells[17] were too slippy;' he therefore took off an indifferent pair of shoes and displayed stockings which were filthy in the extreme, but destitute of heels, and thus relieved, he again faced his opponent. They struck each other very savagely; even the men by us who appeared thoroughly to understand the science, complained of the ferocity, and considered it was not sparring but fighting. After beating each other about the head and breast until they were exhausted, they would walk about the room or sit down for a few minutes, until they regained sufficient breath to enable them to beat each other still further. As they warmed with their work, and administered what were considered effective blows, the audience, on the call of one or other of the professionals in waiting, applauded. After about twenty minutes, the order was given to the boxers to 'rally it off', and we then witnessed what the old man by us called 'nice rapping, and a very decent spirit for young 'uns.' A coarse-looking fellow, with high cheek bones, large mouth, flat nose, low forehead, a massive neck, now walked into the middle of the floor, and throwing down some coppers, said, 'Now, chaps, tip them up some coppers to get them a gill; they are both out of work.' Several of the spectators in response to this appeal threw coppers on the floor. As soon as the slim youth was dressed he picked up all the money and left the room. On inquiring for his opponent, whom we missed immediately on the conclusion of 'the rally', it was said, 'the poor cove was sick in the yard.'

It was a matter of surprise to us that the celebrated man for whose benefit this spectacle was got up never made himself known, if, indeed, he was present at all; and further, that there was no person to direct or control the extent or nature of the enjoyments provided. It did not surprise us much to find that we had been deceived in paying a shilling for a front seat, when there was no distinction between front and back; neither were we astonished at the meanness of the stout, able young men, who might obtain an honest livelihood by some industrial occupation, making beggars of themselves, or battering their bodies to gratify a vicious and depraved taste. These things were not to be wondered at, seeing that it was 'old English and manly sport!'

After a short cessation of hostilities two men 'peeled', and had the gloves fastened on their hands. One was called P_____, the other 'Johnny', 'a noted fist of the Liverpool ring.' P_____ was the man who had come forward to solicit alms for the former combatants; 'Johnny' was sottish, savage-looking, unshaved and filthy. The portion of shirt he had on appeared to be held together by dirt. After shaking hands, they looked earnestly at each other and began to *fight*. When two or three blows had been given, it appeared 'Johnny' was drunk and could not stand. P_____ waited nearly ten minutes for him to come round. In the meantime a tall, well-built, healthy-looking young fellow entered the room, and became 'the observed of all observers.' On enquiry we found this 'Topping Miller' had a short time before, in a pugilistic encounter, *killed* his opponent: hence the interest excited by his appearance. 'The Hero of the Redan', or of 'a hundred fights' could not have excited greater wonder and astonishment than did this man-killer amongst this gathering. Seeing the men idle, and 'Johnny' 'shaking himself together', this great hero called out 'Time', and, looking contemptuously at 'Johnny', he told him to 'go in.' There was now some terrible hitting before these brutes satisfied themselves or their 'brethren in arms.' They struck each other as hard as they could, wherever they could. They grinned fiendishly at each other. 'Johnny' sprang tiger-like on P_____, and sobered himself by such means. After a few rounds of this sort the men were ordered to 'rally it off', when another collection was made. The man-killer threw down fourpence, and called on the audience 'not to be ashamed to fetch out the coppers, for 'Johnny' was "hard up".' The money appeal was not warmly responded to, energetically as it was made.

The disgraceful exhibition on the part of 'Johnny' drew forth from the spectators many severe strictures on his conduct and character. A mild-spoken young man who sat beside us, and who appeared to know the whole of the men present, regretted very much 'to see Johnny cut up so badly,' adding, with a sigh, 'He was at one time a very pretty fighter, hard as steel, and a glutton at milling; but he's lazy, and has ruined himself with lushing.' Herein may be seen the whole life of the boxer epitomised. Yet even this would fail to warn many young men that surrounded us, and whom we noticed so deeply interested in the manner every 'hit' was given. The collection did not prove very successful, and the professionals, as is generally the case, had no desire to 'set to' for the fun of the thing. They had passed this stage, and would now only 'mill for money.' One of them walked into the middle of the floor, and holding up 'the gloves' in a tempting manner, said, in his most persuasive tone, addressing the company, 'Is none of you coves inclined to have a set-to? Your'e very shy to-night. Get up, some of you; there are chaps here that can give you a wrinkle, and put you up to a move or two, if your'e short.' But no one responded to this eloquent appeal. We learned that it is quite common for amateurs to 'show' on such occasions, and by this means 'get their hand in.' They spar here for fun, and are afterwards found fighting in earnest, or for a livelihood. The professionals in this class, as amongst others, are ever ready to puff up, spur on, or or flatter the vanity of young men already vain enough of their ability. Thus are weak-minded, lazily inclined youths led to adopt as a profession what they began as a pastime. Look at 'Johnny' a short time ago – *he was an amateur*. He put on the gloves at a sparring match to save the bones of a professional, and to gratify his own depraved taste, and he is now what many amateurs around us will become – a drunken, dissolute, degraded scoundrel.[18]

The audience had been gradually on the increase, and had now become large by the influx of a crew of sailors, out for a spree. They were carefully waited on by the professionals, and 'stood something stiff' for 'Johnny.' We were surprised to see several respectable-looking young men turn into this dirty saloon, devoting their hours to such degrading pastimes. The landlord and a very loquacious waiter carried round large jugs and cans of ale, and filled up the glasses as required, charging twopence per glass, of which there might be five to the quart. The ale was said to be 'worse nor anything.' Twenty minutes elapsed before hands could be obtained for another 'set to.' After a deal of pulling out, punching, and persuading, a nice-made young man, rather respectable-looking, was induced to get up and strip, in order to face the tall youth who 'had good stuff in him but could not feed.' The coppers which had been begged after the first mill had obtained for him a gill or two, which was clearly indicated by his flushed cheek and glassy eye. Here he was, ready again to pummel any one, or let any one pummel him, in the hope that when it was over there would be a good collection. These fellows 'took their licking with a relish,' and the applause of the audience was very general. We had seen enough of such an exhibition, and whilst these men were engaged we left the room, passing on our walk through the crowd of half-drunken, filthy, blasphemous wretches, who had assembled inside and outside to witness the grand, scientific and manly display of fistic talent.

5 The dog fight

During the visits to the 'Canine Tavern', described in the last chapter, we learned 'that a dog fight for £10 a side' was to come off on the Tuesday following, and as this demoralising pastime presents attractions for and employs the leisure hours of great numbers of the working population in this as well as other towns – nay, is indeed looked upon by hundreds as an amusement – we deem it proper, notwithstanding the revolting nature of the details, to lay a few facts on dog-fighting before the public.[19] Not a week elapses in Liverpool in which several dog fights do not take place, some more or less openly, many, particularly those involving large sums of money, strictly private. All persons present at the prize fights are supposed to be confederates, or to some extent have a pecuniary interest in the result. We saw, with much surprise, in the public prints, within the last few weeks, that one 'respectable aleseller' of the town challenged the dog of another 'nobby tavern-keeper' to fight for a certain sum. The weight of the dogs was fixed, and the money was said to be 'ready any time.' This fight, as we have already announced, was stopped by the police last Monday, and the gathering assembled to witness it fully corroborated all we advanced, yet the promoters of this savage and brutal sport (?) enjoy the privilege of being licensed by her Majesty's board of inland revenue to supply her Majesty's liege subjects with 'beer and tobacco'.[20] It would appear from this public challenge that dog-fighting is about to be more openly prac-tised, and we may look forward to the time when the columns of the sporting journals will be devoted to the details of the dog fight, with the number of rounds fought, the appearance of the combatants before and after the fight, 'the points' made by each brute, and the 'glorious future which awaits such gallant achievements', just as we now see space devoted to men fighting, &c. And why should not this be so in the age of progress?

When a fight between two dogs is arranged, the money or a deposit down, and the weight at which the dogs are to 'come to the scratch' fixed, the dogs are said to 'go into training', and their owners set very industriously to work to bring out the full powers of the animals, in order to secure the money to be contended for and protect their backers. It must be borne in mind that the money staked is frequently the result of subscription, and many a poor fellow who earns his wages by wielding the sledge-hammer at the forge risks a portion of them on a dog fight. He has 'a fancy', and, after the manner of the horse-race betting man, he looks well to the pedigree, finds that 'the dog is of a good stock, and ought to fight, and nothing else;' and therefore will starve his wife and children 'to support his fancy.' As the day for the fight draws near the excitement at the Canine Tavern becomes intense. The state of the odds is regularly quoted, and men with serious faces talk of 'getting a little on at three to five,' or 'doing the homoeopathic trick at evens,' with all that air of legitimate business which you may see in Brunswick-street when corn is up, or on the flags when cotton is rising.[21] To look at the men in the tavern, no one could conceive the horrid means they adopt to make or lose their money. They talk in the coolest manner of fighting their dogs, or of dogs being killed in the pit; but there is one thing you never hear them name publicly, 'the trysting place.' You never hear them state the hour or house at which the fight will take place. This is learned in a quiet way. The tavern at which the fight is fixed to come off may be known the night before the fight at most of the sporting houses. You go to the host, and 'he tips the whereabouts.' In Liverpool the risk that landlords run in holding dog fights in their houses is said to be very great; therefore the landlords of sporting houses good-naturedly undertake the risk in turns. Besides this, there is a charge made for admission to witness the fight. This is done (so the dog-fighters told us) to cover the risk, or 'help the poor cove to pay the fine, if he should be nailed.' The time chosen is generally early in the morning, when the police are going off duty; and we were told that '*Sunday was a very good time.*' It would appear from what we saw and heard that dog fights in the town are as common on Sunday as man fights 'up the shore', or dog races at the 'Old Swan.' Ministers address the working classes at Windsor fields or in the Concert Hall and Park Theatre on Sunday afternoons; the dog-fighters set them an example of industry, and begin their work 'ere it is yet day,' always mustering, to use their own phrase, 'in great force, and no mistake.'

The 'dog fight' about to be described took place in this town, not long ago, on a Tuesday morning. There is something very revolting in the idea of rising early on a beautiful summer's morning, and walking to the foulest and filthiest portion of the town, to look on two dogs tearing each other to pieces, to gratify the vicious propensities of their owners and a crowd of interested spectators. But to see Liverpool life it must be done.

It has just gone five o'clock. Working men are on the move to their daily toil. We notice that several on their way 'drop in' to the grog shops, which are standing open like so many man traps, 'to have a drain,' as they term it. There are several coffee stalls as we pass, and at these we notice that workmen stop and get a bun and a cup of coffee for a penny. We see spring carts laden with carpenters, who, in these miserable days of free trade and ill-paid labour, have to be carried to their work.[22] They look very hearty, notwithstanding the injustice inflicted upon them by free trade, of which they were and are such bitter opponents. As we get into the centre of the town, the stream of working men widens, and we are regaled with the fragrance from the short pipes under way. We cannot help contrasting our object with the object of the passers. Indulging in a gloomy view of humanity, we reach the street where the fight is to take place. The riot, of which this street was the scene last night, has left some tokens in the broken windows of several houses, and portions of plates and dishes are laying about. There is one of the houses open. An old man is sitting at the door, trying to obtain what in this street he can never get – fresh air. He tells us 'there was only four taken to quod.' As yet we see no dog-fighters about. Presently two men come up the street. They look stealthily around 'to see if the Bobbies are about.' Finding 'the coast clear,' they go to the tavern door, and by giving a peculiar knock, which is understood by the landlord, they are admitted. Having got in, all is said now to be 'comfortable;' but before going upstairs the money is collected. Sixpence each is generally paid, but several men pay one shilling, and 'think that cheap enough.' The close smell of the room, after the debauch of the previous night, is very offensive, but we hear no complaint, all the visitors are so intent on the dogs. Both dogs have arrived, and are being rubbed down and prepared for the fight. The preliminaries require some time to arrange. There must be an umpire appointed and a referee chosen. The dogs must be weighed, and the owners of the dogs 'toss for scratch.' About thirty men are now present; some of them appear nervously excited. There is talk of 'beaks about,' or all not being 'safe.'[23] We hear the growling of the brutes as they get a glimpse of each other below, and immediately there is a rush up stairs, the men carrying up the dogs.

The room is a filthy place, filled with men in good keeping. The 'pit' in which the dogs fight is formed with boards, the lower portion of which is lined with tin, or in some cases zinc. It is about two and a half or three yards square, is thirty inches high, and is so arranged that it can be taken to pieces at a moment's notice and put aside, or more frequently into a closet which is at hand. At two of the corners small seats are placed, for the men who are in the pit attending to the dogs. 'The scratch' is formed by a piece of

string being placed across the centre of the pit, or in some cases it
is formed by a chalk mark on the floor. The chalk mark, however,
is liable to be rubbed out by the struggles of the creatures, and
more frequently by their blood. The men hold up their dogs until
the order is given, when one of the men, according to the result of
the toss, takes his dog to the scratch; that is, holding it by the neck,
he drags it to the cord in the middle of the pit. When he looses his
hold the brute runs at its opponent, which up to this time is being
held in one of the opposite corners, and the worrying then begins.
On this occasion the dogs were similar in weight – twenty-eight
pounds; one was brindled, and the other fawn-coloured. We have
their names, and know the names of their owners. The fawn-
coloured dog had the advantage in age, being much younger, and
was immediately backed by the company for sums which we
wondered how men in their positions could ever get together. The
dogs 'did not get hold well' at first, but 'did better' as they 'got on
a bit' – that is, the men were not satisfied because the creatures did
not tear each other sufficiently. When a dog is thrown, or at some
other particular crisis during the engagement, which we could not
well discover in consequence of the crowding round the pit, the
signal is given to take the dogs off, and they are loosed. Their
mouths are then washed and sponged out, their bodies are rubbed
over with some sort of liquid that has turpentine in it, their ears
are rubbed and pulled, their muscles attended to in the same
manner, and thus is the time spent until the signal is again given
for them 'to go to the scratch.' The growling of the brutes at each
other – the cursing of the men at each other and at the dogs – the
shouts of delight when the dog which an enthusiastic looker-on is
backing obtains an advantage – the crushing to the edge of the pit
– the heat of the close room – the sound of money changing hands
– the demoniacal expression of the men in the pit, and the terrible
excitement of all around, carry the mind far away from happy
England in the nineteenth century, and we look in vain for any
scene amongst the degrading exhibitions or pastimes of savage
nations, at all to compare with what surrounds us, and which takes
place in Liverpool almost every day.

But a few moments elapse when 'time' is called, and again the
dogs run at each other, and growling, gnawing, twisting, tearing,
biting, writhing, and wrestling, they go through another round. To
dwell on such a scene would be simply loathsome, and we forbear.
Enough has been said to show the horrors of this inhuman sport,
and it therefore remains only to state the result. The young dog,
after fighting three-quarters of an hour, was declared the victor; the
other, it seems, had no chance, and the curious notions of justice
which these dog-fighters have, led the owner of the old dog to 'give

in.' Had both dogs been of the same age, in all probability they would have had to fight until one or other had been killed in the pit, or until one had turned tail and 'would not scratch.' There was great interest manifested by all around to see the dogs when they were taken out of the pit, and the general remark was – that 'they were not cut much, and that it was a pretty fight – stiffish for the time.'

The principal director of this horrible sport was a celebrated pugilist, whose name we see has been mentioned in connection with the great £50 match which was fixed to come off last Monday. This man entered heartily and earnestly into the work, and tossed his money about from hand to hand in the most indifferent manner. When the fight was over, rattling his gold chain and jingling the sovereigns in his pocket, he called out, 'All hands to the beer barrel,' and there was a general rush downstairs for ale. We presumed the stakes were given up, for there was abundance of cash to spend. The revel now began in earnest, and during the smoking and drinking many instances were related of dogs being killed in the pit. Indeed, only a few days before this, there had been a fight, which ended in one dog dying in the pit, and the other dying very shortly afterwards; but, strange to say, the dead dog, it was said, won the fight. Won after it was killed? We could not understand this, but it was explained thus. 'Tip' fights 'Jerry.' In the last round 'Tip' is killed, and 'dies in his corner.' It is, we will suppose, 'Jerry's' turn to go to the scratch. If, when he is taken to the scratch, he does not run at the dead dog, he loses the stakes, and the dead dog is declared the victor. Such is one of the laws of 'the fancy.' The supply of drink that was forthcoming on this occasion appeared to be inexhaustible. Men who came out to see the fight, and then go to their work, remained, on the invitation of the director of this orgie, drinking the whole of the morning. At noon we again passed the place; drunken men were lolling about the door – one was being led home by his son, a youth of ten or twelve years of age; the house was completely upset by the carnival of the morning; wives would no doubt be abused, children ill treated and starved; men would be still further depraved and hardened in their viciousness; homes would be rendered miserable, hearts rendered callous, society degraded, and the town disgraced. But still the monsters of iniquity revelled on, glorying in the fact of the dog fight.

It appears to many incredible that scenes such as we have described can take place in a town like Liverpool, watched over as it is by an active body of police, and a large and active bench of magistrates. Thoughtful men say, 'Surely the magistrates do not know.' 'Why not write to them privately; many of them are earnest philanthropists, and take an active part in anything that promotes the moral and social welfare of the people.' Yes, we know this; but yet the fact remains. *The police do know* of the existence of these houses – they know that canine taverns are receptacles for stolen goods, that convicted thieves and daring burglars are there to be met with, that they are hotbeds of vice, hiding-places for villainous characters – yet the landlords have the licenses renewed, and thus iniquity thrives.[24] We boast of our superiority as a nation – of our progress in good of all sorts – yet neither local nor national legislators appear to take one effective step for the suppression of vicious and degrading sports. See what Brother Jonathan has done in the state of New York. It has recently been enacted that in the future every person 'who shall set on foot, or instigate, or move to, to carry on, or promote, or engage in, as a witness, umpire, or judge, or do anything in furtherance of any premeditated fight or contention between persons with their fists, or any fight between game birds, or game cocks, or dogs, or bulls, or between dogs and rats, or dogs and badgers, or any other animals shall be liable to imprisonment and fine to the extent of one thousand dollars.'

6   The Aintree carnival

Having described the preparations made for the Aintree carnival, attention is now earnestly requested to the carnival itself. The term 'races' is seldom or never used now. 'The Aintree Meeting,' 'The Autumn Meeting,' 'The Spring Meeting,' &c., may frequently be heard of; but it is not respectable to speak of 'The Aintree *Races*.' This may to some extent be accounted for by the fact that the majority of persons who assemble at such class of sports go not so much for the races alone as for other associations which may there be formed. Hence it becomes a meeting-place for all sorts of characters. A 'meeting,' therefore, let it be called; but the public should know of what this meeting consists.

Amongst all classes of society in Liverpool the great gatherings at Aintree are looked forward to with a degree of interest which is at once remarkable and instructive. The errand boy or young apprentice will at this time obtain a holiday, and having, perhaps, 'saved up' his pence for the purpose, will for a few hours in the year have an opportunity of enjoying the fresh air and tumbling on the green sward of the pleasant meadows about Aintree. Mechanics, young and old, think and talk about the races as an event in their life, and it is no uncommon thing in workshops to find money clubs formed, or saving boxes established, in order that when the day arrives the long looked-for and dearly loved spree may be entered upon with ample means to secure its usual termination. There are no other sports of a public, open-air character held anywhere else within an easy distance of Liverpool: hence the great popularity of the Aintree carnival. In Manchester, and many other manufacturing and large towns, days – yea, weeks – are periodically set apart for the recreation and enjoyment of the people.[25] In Liverpool it is not so.[26] Here bankers, merchants, brokers, clerks, shopmen, businessmen of all grades, and handicraftsmen of all trades and every position in life, have to work away from year to year in a dreary round of never-ending toil, the only recreation provided for them being those of that vicious and soul-destroying character which have been laid before the public in the former series of these papers. The desire for recreation, amusement, or excitement implanted within the human mind is, when properly used, directed, and controlled, calculated to exercise a most beneficial effect, socially and morally. It is only when the desire for amusement becomes a *passion* that it proves dangerous to individuals or society. There is no necessity why even a horse race might not be a healthful, invigorating pastime and rural sport. If it were properly conducted it might prove so. It is now surrounded by vicious practices, and mixed up with questionable pursuits, which have totally destroyed its original and simple character.

The mode of transit to Aintree has of late years undergone a complete change. Time was when the large 'float,' the spring cart,[27] the gaily decorated coach, were all brought into requisition to convey the visitors to the race ground. A trip to Aintree in a water-side cart, covered with an awning, a fiddler sitting on the front, and a couple of damsels dancing in the centre, was something to remember and talk about. But the road has had, in this case, as in many others, to give way to the rail. Instead of the crack of the driver's whip, you hear the railway guard's whistle, and the iron road now monopolises the principal traffic. There are, however, many persons who, in this respect as in others, cling with tenacity to the remnants of antiquity, and would as soon think of going to church, voting for a radical, or leaving off the orange neckerchief, as they would of going to the races by rail. To such persons the spring cart is a chief delight. The cushions round the sides, the red ribbons in the horses' 'blinkers', the sturdy, independent, and not unfrequently indecorous behaviour of the driver, and the rattling pace at which the horse is made to go, constitute a great portion of the enjoyment. Then again, by rail there is no stopping 'to get a gill.' You are crammed into a box, and whirled over streets and through a tunnel, and are at the course without any fun. By the road, with a spring cart, you pull up at Walton and perhaps again at the Throstle-nest, again at the Black Bull, and whatever be obtained to drink is never allowed to settle – the jogging of the cart prevents that; hence you reach the course in a tolerably excited state, and are in such manner prepared to enjoy the sports that await you. Contrast this with going by rail.

It is between twelve and one o'clock. The crush at the railway station is great, but the temper of the crowd is all that can be desired. A continued stream of passengers is pouring into the station, anticipated pleasure depicted on every countenance. The tickets obtained at the booking office are taken by a porter at the entrance of the platform. By this arrangement time is saved, but the company *save* nothing else. As fast as the carriages can be brought up they are filled, and trains are being dispatched every five minutes. 'Here's room for one.' 'Take your seats, gentlemen.' The train is in motion; still people press into the carriages. 'There is no room in here, sir.' 'Is n't there, though?' and in goes another, until, 'Now they are off,' and away they go. The carriage is calculated to hold thirty-two persons; here are in it *forty-five*, many of them not *thin*, huddled together, some sitting on others' knees, and several standing in a stooping position. Everybody says 'it's terribly close;' and 'if there should be a smash, won't the company be in for it,' is a sentiment strongly expressed by a half-drunken tailor, who sings, 'Down among the dead men,' and other equally cheering allusions, as the train passes through the Walton tunnel. This state of Calcutta black-holeism does not continue long, for in a few minutes the course is reached, and the change from the close carriage to the purer air of Aintree is very agreeable. The day is beautifully fine; the visitors were never so numerous. Carts, cars, whitechapels, and omnibuses are passing the 'Sefton Arms,' laden with passengers from town. Troops of pedestrians trudge on, their jackets being carried under their arms, their shoes white with dust, their faces black and glossy with a mixture of dust and perspiration. A large calico placard attracts everybody's attention. It is supported by two poles, and is watched over by two men, who, besides the discharge of this duty, distribute tracts to the passers-by. The placard displays, in very large characters, 'Remember Poor Palmer,'[28] which excites criticism and condemnation. Go down the road, and pass in at the entrance leading immediately to the back of the grand stand. Here is a man with a basket of books, which he calls 'The prize of your high calling, fourpence each.' They are Testaments. Close by him is a stout, active, loud-spoken man, asking every one if he has obtained permission from his minister to visit such a place. He distributes tracts to all who will take them. The ground for several yards around is strewed with tracts. On the gatepost is a small bill warning itinerant preachers and their followers off the course, and threatening prosecution for disobedience. Just here the cars, carts, &c., are packed closely together, the horses taken out, and the grooms attending to them. Here is a very primitive tent – a float covered with a waterproof wrapper, seats along the sides and across the bottom, and two barrels of ale are being tapped, which will be sold and 'consumed on the premises.' But pass on towards the grand stand; and now you are at once in the region where tents and turfites most do congregate. The bustle of business has commenced; crowds of people from every class in life move about over the fields, amongst the meat stalls, into the booths, and round by the hobby-horses.

Here are upwards of forty tents or booths fitted up for the sale of liquors. The bars of many are garnished by boiled hams and rounds of beef, large cones of sandwiches and baskets of crackers being added in some cases. The proprietor and his lady are in most

cases behind the bar dispensing the meat and drink. Waiters –
males with white bibbed aprons, females with lustrously bedecked
caps – glide about with trays and glasses. The proprietors of these
booths lay claim to the friendship of the visitors by announcing on
their signs where they hail from, and it is amusing to observe that
even in these matters clanship and class distinction prevail. Walk
into a tent the host of which hails from an inland town, say Bolton.
Notice the men sitting here on flimsily constructed seats, holding
small cups of ale or porter in their hands, and many of them
munching bread and cheese. What a contrast they exhibit to the
visitors in the adjoining tent, over which is a representation of the
'green immortal shamrock', and in large letters the motto 'Faugh-a-
ballagh.' There is no sitting down here. The old fiddler is perched
on a barrel in the corner. Near him is laid a board, about three feet
wide and eight feet long: this is the 'footboard', on which are two
girls, smartly dressed, and a man without a jacket, footing it in a
three-handed reel. The visitors crowd around to criticise the 'step-
ping.' The heat of the day, combined with the nature of the sport,
causes the girls to throw off their shawls. They are determined to
dance the man down, and he is equally determined to knock either
them or the fiddler up, and there will be no cessation until one or
other of these feats be accomplished. There is here no eating, but
a good deal of smoking and drinking, and further on in the day
fighting will be in favour. As a still more striking contrast, look in
at this tent, devoted to the members of the 'canine fancy;' the
keeper of it has a good dog, and is himself said to be 'no pup.' The
dog is chained to the side of the bar, and the scars with which the
creature's head is covered are looked on with admiration by the
men around, or rather the race of incorrigible scoundrels here
assembled, standing with their hands in their coat pockets and
biting their lips, wishing someone would 'stand a quart.' How
suspiciously they look on any stranger that enters! Or look at the
tents devoted to pugilism or pedestrianism, for there are on this
occasion several. At one of these the champion displays his belt
very ostentatiously on the front of the bar, and young men go in
to obtain drink in order that they may have an opportunity of
inspecting the trophy. Pugilists come in here to refresh themselves,
for there is a sparring booth close by, and 'Con Quin' persuades a
'novice', whom he has been battering about the head for the last
five minutes, that 'porter is the best stuff for making you plucky.'
Thereupon the 'novice', a young fellow, said to be an American,
but who looked and spoke like a 'genuine native,' paid for two
pints of porter, and thus rewarded the pugilist for cutting his cheek
slightly and tearing the collar off his shirt! What were the character
and object of those beings who threw sops to Cerberus? Thus it is

the tents are laid out that almost every class or profession may meet with congenial spirits or old familiar faces, whilst indulging in the 'draughts of liquid friendship and solid comforts' that are said here largely to abound. As a rosy-cheeked carter said, 'It's just like a Saturday night at home, a fellow meets with so many as he knows.'

Between the row of tents and the back of the brick stands, a sort of street is formed, in the centre of which are bread and meat stalls. One of these, the attendants at which are more dirty and slovenly than their neighbours, is called a 'soup house.' Many young lads seem to relish the hot liquid. The soup manufacture is carried on close by the edge of the pit, where the horses are led to drink. A knowledge of this fact might affect the sale of the article. A tall, fierce-looking man is engaged cutting up bread and ham at one of the stalls, and his cry of 'three pence a slice; carry it off, my hearties,' meets with a ready response. Near this is a camera obscura, to attract visitors to which a conjuror is engaged to go through a few tricks of sleight-of-hand. An invitation is given to two county policemen 'just to have a peep,' and they accept of the polite offer, and come out recommending the camera to the notice of the crowd. But the great attraction on this part of the ground is the sparring booths. There are two – one supported purely by native talent; the other is much more pretentious in appearance, and the names of celebrated men are mentioned as 'just going to set to,' beyond which the celebrated pugilists are brought on to the platform in professional costume and exhibited to the multitude. The Liverpool men have not so much to say as their professional brother from Manchester, and they find it to their advantage to drown his talk by plying a large watchman's rattle, the din caused by which destroys the effect of Johnny Magrath's eloquence. The admission to these booths is twopence each, and it is much to be regretted that on every occasion they seemed to fill.

Here is a tent for the accommodation of another class – more respectable people – at the corner of the road opposite the entrance to the grand stand. Look in here, and it will be seen more clearly what are the enjoyments provided for the people in every grade of life. This tent is very gay-looking in the interior. The bar is tastefully decorated. A very aristocratic title is suspended over the entrance. At the back part of the tent is a sort of select chamber or private room. Young girls and women are here – their faces daubed with paint, their persons profusely adorned with highly coloured dresses. They pass the time in drinking, laughing, and giggling with men – with merchants who on the Exchange and at home pass for gentlemen. The company at this booth is so very aristocratic and fashionable, the conduct so indecorous and unbecoming, that a crowd of persons in the humbler walks of life are attracted by the exhibition, and gaze on, as well they may, with astonishment. A spring-cart driver in the crowd says – '*Well, s'help me! if we was to pull our molls about so, the bobby would jug us.*' The response of a butcher is, 'That's about the size of it.' This tent is stated to be established by the notorious brothel-keeper and procuress, Madame _____. Her name does not appear, but her person does behind the bar; and a young gentleman in a very loose coat, and whose conversation is more loose still, sips wine with this bloated and brazen-faced hussey. And active as this young man may be on the Exchange in the morning, when cotton is on the carpet, leering and simpering as he is now, he will in all probability meet his mother and sisters in the evening without a blush. They are all male waiters at this tent, and outside are a couple of suspicious-looking attendants. There they are, walking backwards and forwards as if on the look-out for somebody, and not in any way appearing to be connected with this rendezvous. These are bruisers, or bullies, ready to adjust – of course in an amicable way – whatever little differences may arise, or to remove, by their gentle mode of entreaty, any gentleman who makes himself obnoxious to the visitors. They have been refreshed with sundry draughts of ale or porter, and are now smoking short pipes. One of the waiters, seeing the crowd increase – the observations from which are not agreeable – is winking to the bruisers to get the people away. So move off!

Just step across to the entrance of the grand stand, and notice the vendors of race cards. 'A card, gentlemen, a card; names, weights, and colours of the riders. Take a correct card, gentlemen sportsmen.' These persons differ widely from the vendors to be met with in town. Here they are all females, with sunburnt faces,[29] gaudily trimmed bonnets, bright-coloured plaid shawls, white aprons, and shoes with buckles. They are not gentle in their manners, nor do they appear virtuous or sober in their habits, yet they seem to be on good and intimate terms with many aristocratic members of the ring, who are passing in and out of the stand. Notice the peculiar telegraphic communications which are carried on between them and some stylishly dressed touts who are in the background. These characters do not depend on race cards alone for their living, but use the sale of cards as a cloak to hide their iniquitous practices. They have large pockets about them filled with filthy and obscene prints, which they sell at high prices, and by such means pander to the taste of many to be found at such gatherings – men whose soul aim and object in life appear to be indulgence in gross sensuality and animal pleasure.

Pass down the row of drinking, sparring, and dancing booths, and here is the field devoted to shows, merry-go-rounds, swinging boats, three-sticks-a-penny, &c. There are no theatrical booths. The tinselled Thespians confine themselves to town. There are no travelling menageries, and very few swinging boats; but what there are seem to be doing a great business. The space in former years devoted to shows is now devoted to donkey racing, and this sport affords much amusement to young and old. The races are very short ones, the riders not very active, and the donkeys are not abused. Good humour and innocent mirth are the rule. Lower down, nearer the plantation, are groups on the grass, enjoying a pic-nic. Gaily dressed country cousins ramble about with the bottom of their trousers and the cuffs of their coats turned up, carrying the everlasting blue umbrella, such a hot day as this, and eating away at the real Ormskirk gingerbread. Pass the bottom stand, and ramble up between the stalls and the course: what a busy and exciting scene! Here are gingerbread stalls, with healthy-looking women presiding over them – there are nut barrows, and perambulating shooting galleries, with sickly, drunken-looking fellows as proprietors; here are men and women with three-sticks-a-penny – there are young, suspicious-looking men selling 'cigars and a light;' here are Chinese jugglers forming a ring for the exercise of their profession – there are a shoal of young pickpockets fully prepared to exercise theirs, whether the ring be formed or not; here are men and women standing on stools singing ballads shamefully indecent, and the crowd of well dressed men around patronise the ribaldry by purchasing the songs; here are soldiers, smart and dashing-looking fellows, their caps bedecked with ribbons, and bearing on their breasts the emblems of their bravery – there are men destitute of legs, soliciting alms; here are a blind man selling lucifer matches, and a man with one arm selling religious tracts. Crowds are passing into the booths; hundreds are passing out and on to the stands. The bustle is becoming greater – the bell rings for saddling; and now prepare for the race.

7 The Aintree meeting

The bell is ringing, and preparations are now being made for the race. On quickly to the grand stand; elbow your way through the crowd of pleasure seekers as you best can; pass round the ginger-bread stalls, the American ice cream manufactory, the vendors of walking sticks, and notice, as you approach the enclosure, the groups of disreputable-looking men that are settling down to their business. These are betting men from all parts of the country, comprising all shades of character. The enclosure before the grand stand is called the betting ring. The railings are white on the inside, but black and slabby without. They have just received a fresh coat of tar, which must prove extremely pleasant to the olfactory nerves of the ragged touts and kicked-out stable scamps who pass their time peering through the palings, and receive a whisper now and then which they are not long in turning to account. Here, at the outside of the betting ring, but as near it as they are permitted to come, are assembled the lowest class of turfites: they are now very numerous and noisy, closely packed, shouting, and offering odds. They extend from the corner of the stands to the course; and it is lamentable to find among this degraded crowd so many men to whom the public give credit for purer practices and better sense. Here is a group that have subscribed a sum sufficient to obtain admission for 'one of the lot' within the sacred precincts of the ring: hence their reason for keeping so very close to the palings. How the young man with the loose drab coat curses the *tar* – how heartily he says he could kick Topham.[30] That man inside, with the dark tweed suit and cap to match, with a face strongly indicative of those practices which are said to produce 'cheeks which shame the rose's hue,' is the person on whom this group rely for obtaining the 'right office.' See – he comes from the centre of the enclosure towards where 'his lot' are standing, and whispers what he has learned in the ear of the stout man with a wall eye, who 'gives the office' to the others, and this group is dispersed; the members of it now walk, or rather crush, their way into the crowd of duffers, loafers, and men who live at the outskirts of honesty, loudly proclaiming what they are prepared to back or lay against. But pass on – never mind the generous offers of the slender youth who shakes a bag of half-crowns in the face of passers-by: he never earned the money, nor is it his own. Never mind the flaunting of feathers or the rustling of silks hereabouts. Never mind the procession of painted prostitutes that are just now passing from their carriage to the tents: press on, the ring is fast filling. Show your tickets. 'That will do, sir.' The ring is before you.

The crowd of well dressed men in the ring is very great, but it will be greater presently. Look! here the turfites come from the refreshment room; all the strongly marked peculiarities of the racing and betting fraternity may now be seen. The bustle is beginning, the books are in hand. The Manchester men and the Liverpool gentlemen are easily distinguished. The stand is fast filling. Many handsome-looking, elegantly dressed ladies, accompanied by tall, hirsute, fashionably attired men, take up positions for viewing the race. The gentlemen have opera glasses, in cases, slung across their shoulders. The glasses are handed to the ladies, and the gentlemen look patronisingly around. The horses destined to contend for the stakes are now being led round the enclosure – their numbers are already on the telegraph. The favourites are closely scanned and scrutinised by the practised eye of many competent judges, and their appearance and form are spoken of by these gentlemen in the usual slang of the turf. The excitement is beginning in the ring – listen to the murmur, then the roll, then the burst from the betting man. How thronged the place is – the meeting is 'well and fashionably attended.' Here are earls, viscounts, noble lords, honourable captains, gallant admirals, members of Parliament, magistrates, aldermen, town councillors, merchants, brokers, publicans, business men of every grade, and many men of questionable character; the comfortable easy-going country gentleman; and several representatives of the fourth estate. Many of the men here have, as magistrates, presided at county sessions lately; others have spoken at public meetings on the duty of making earnest efforts to purify and regenerate society. Several have been found on platforms, supporting, either by their presence, purse, or advocacy, missions to the benighted heathen, the Additional Curates', the Pastoral Aid, or Home Church Building Societies; and some of them will, no doubt, if they succeed to-day, stand an extra dozen of champagne in the evening, or make a very handsome donation to some religious or benevolent association. There are men here who have the noble ambition to become statesmen, guided, no doubt, by the principle that if they have the ability to direct the national sports, they ought to be entrusted with the power to control or guide the national councils. The jockeys mount; the horses pass from the enclosure on to the course and walk down, then gallop up and past the stand, preparatory to starting for the

prize. Now the excitement among the bookmakers and backers is
at its height. Innocent recreation, rational enjoyment, rural sport
are unknown amidst this infatuated gathering. Look at the anxious
faces and the highly nervous excitement manifest on all sides.
Groups are formed; these speedily become enlarged, or dwindle
away and become lost in greater groups, where the odds offered
secure more attention. The cry is raised – 'They are off;' the groups
are broken suddenly up, and all eyes are directed to the horses,
which are seen running down towards the canal turn, passing this,
the pace quickens, and the positions undergo some change. The
horses are now close together, pass into the straight run home, and
the excitement becomes more general. All the stands appear well
filled; the course, half-way down, is lined with spectators two or
three deep; gentlemen on smart cobs are rattling along the ploughed
gallop. Enlivened by the beauty of the day, the whole scene is
brilliant, gay, and picturesque. Now the vast sea of faces is turned
towards the distance chair, near which the beautiful creatures are
struggling for the mastery. On, on they come – you hear the rattle
of their hoofs; the pace is good, the goal is near, and the feelings
of the spectators find vent in such phrases as 'Blue has it,' 'No, he
has n't, yellow has it,' 'Not he,' 'Go it, yellow, the stake's your
own,' and the horses, whipped, and spurred, and bleeding, pass the
winning post with the fleetness of an arrow. In a few moments the
numbers of the first, second, and third are suspended on the
telegraph, and immense sums of money have been lost and won.

The race over, the vast body of spectators break in upon the
course, and there is a general rush to look at the winner. As the
horse is walked down to the enclosure the people press upon it, and
the aid of a couple of police is required to form a passage. The
stable boys, with bottles and clothes, are in attendance, ready to
wrap the animal up when the saddle is taken off. The horse which
the 'talent'[31] have been operating about has won, therefore within
the ring his appearance does not excite so much attention. The
turfites clear off; the ring is speedily cleared, so is the stand; the
refreshment room is visited, and men look cautiously over their
books whilst indulging in brandy, soda water and cigars. The 'great
event' forms the subject of general conversation. Whilst preparations are being made for the next race, stroll around amongst the
tents and stalls, and notice how the visitors pass their time and
amuse themselves.

Do not stay now to try your strength, or test your weight, or
discover what you well know. Go round by the upper part of the
enclosure, cross the course, jump over the railings, and get across
the ploughed gallop and into the centre of the oval. There are here
two tents apart from all the rest, and, as might be supposed from

their situation, not likely to do much business. This is a mistake. They are thronged with 'respectable' (?) men. Go to the bar of the first tent and ask for a glass of anything. There is no getting near the bar; the calls for drink of all sorts are more numerous than can be responded to, notwithstanding there are three male and two female waiters, and the host behind the bar. Go into the next tent. The crowd here is the same; the supply of drink is not equal to the demand. Go forward, or rather to the back part of the tent. There is a small apartment – a canvas screen protects the visitors from the gaze of the vulgar crowd; lift the screen; are you surprised? 'Come in, come in,' cry half a dozen damsels, 'what are you going to stand?' The waiter is opening a bottle of champagne, and a young man, who displays a republican and wears spectacles, hands a sovereign in payment. Do the obscene remarks of the women offend the visitors here? not at all; this is what they seek. The Aintree 'meeting' affords them extensive gratification in this way. Here publicly, in face of day, men can display their utter want of common decency, and by their conduct induce the poor unfortunate outcasts to display their utter want of modesty and shame. Turn away, turn away, the sight is shocking! Look again at the bar. It is hard to conceive that there are about fifty other refreshment booths, all perhaps thronged, although few of them possess attractions of the character to be seen here.

Close by this is the archery ground; a dark-eyed woman is engaged practising, and, as she says, 'teaching the young idea and the sporting gents how to shoot'. 'Only fourpence a dozen; have four penn'orth, gentlemen sportsmen, and learn in time, whilst you have opportunity, how to hit the bull's eye.' Near her is a young man engaged in a similar pursuit, but he has not so much to say as the lady. Young and old men try their hand, and evidently draw the bow at a venture. The only thing surprising about their shooting is how they manage to keep so far from the target. The old sailor with the two stout girls in company is loudly laughed at by the spectators; still he declares the fault is not in his aim – it is now the bow, then the arrow, next it slipped, or the sun is in his eyes, or he is afraid of hitting a dog that is near; it couldn't be his fault, 'for when I was in Africa last voyage but one I shot so many ostriches that the king of the tribe gave me fourteen elephants' teeth to drop it and go home!' Hallo, they are clearing the course; rush on, and get across to the stand, or you will miss the great event – the race for the cup. The people are taking up their positions at each side of the course; little boys, hundreds of them, lie down on the grass and put their heads between the legs of the men who stand over them. 'Mount up, gentlemen, mount up; two-pence each; you can see all round the course for two-pence.'

This is the cry from men and women who have erected crazy-looking stands down the side of the railings, a few yards from the edge of the course; and these are being covered with all classes, anxious to witness the event which has attracted such multitudes from afar. No persons but simple-hearted Irishmen, entirely innocent of any idea of the strength of material or the principles of construction, could venture to solicit persons to 'crowd up.' Look at the supports of that stand; the legs have been broken in two places, but the good-natured proprietor says, 'Sure, the rope 'll hould, and are n't I houlding on myself?' And there he is at one end and his wife at the other, helping to support the 'royal stand', on which are many persons, some of whom might have been expected to set more value on their lives or limbs, seeing the families they have left at home. Get on, get on. How they are crowding on to the stands – there never was such a sight. 'Admission to the stand, two shillings.' 'Go up' – 'It's all very fine to say go up,' says a worthy doctor; 'can I go through people?' 'Don't lose your temper, if you neglect your patients,' says a hearty fellow, who winks knowingly at his companion. The doctor feels this, and is silent. Up you go; there you are, on the top of the stand.

The scene from here is surprising. The course is clear, with the exception of *that* dog which is sure to run up, and be driven back, and hallooed down, and kicked across, until, driven to desperation, it rushes amongst the crowd that is gathering at the turn just above the judge's chair, and is seen no more until the next race. But notice the people around. The stand is crowded, and medical men are numerous. Surely they have not come to bleed people; they do enough of that in town. Do they expect accidents, and are looking out for work? Not at all. They know the value of excitement, and it is now getting up in earnest, and the doctors look pleased. Look over the back of the stands. There you look down on the whole of the tents. See the crowds moving in and out, up and down, to and fro, notwithstanding that the great race is now coming off. But what care these thousands for the races? Nothing; they never come to Aintree for the races. It is a 'Meeting.' And look at the back of the tent below. Two men, drunk and cursing each other's eyes, are pulling off their clothes to fight, whilst the friends of each support their man, and back him to 'lick the other blind.' They get out of sight. And now look at that man playing the bagpipes, and his two children, dressed in Highland costume, dancing. Look at those women regaling themselves in the uncovered portion of the tent just beneath. Listen to their remarks when they find out that they are observed. Notice the woman who beats her child so unmercifully because the poor little fellow will cry by reason of the pain caused by the filthy liquor she has given him to drink. Medical men –

there are seven of you here, eminent in your respective walks – why not some of you go down and tell that infatuated mother why her child cries? tell her also what her child may become by such a training. Never mind the race, you are not interested in the turf, and your noble profession ought to interest you in saving human life. But you have come to see the race: very well, look at it; next week will bring you plenty of patients – you know that right well.

The horses are now leaving the enclosure; only seven will start –'Wild Huntsman was scratched at 1.30.' They will start from the bottom of the course, consequently will pass the stands twice. 'I'll lay against Typee,' 'I'll lay against Brother to Gray Tommy,' 'I'll lay against Marchioness,' 'I'll lay against Vandal,' 'I'll lay against Pretty Boy,' is the cry on all sides. Men that do not appear to be worth a shilling – sunburnt fellows[29] with well-worn clothes – pass half-crowns and sovereigns about, and jingle many more. One of our medical friends joins in a half-crown sweep – seven members; he has by this an interest in the race to the amount of fifteen shillings. The horses seem long in starting but at last down drops the flag, and 'they are off.' It's a good start, and here they come. They pass the stand 'all of a ruck,' turn the stable corner, and then pace improves; and as the positions undergo some change, the glasses are brought into requisition on the grand stand. How eagerly they are watched now by hundreds whose very existence, in a pecuniary sense, depends upon the result of the race. They are getting near the canal turn, when crash goes the Irishman's grand stand, amidst screams of fright and curses of indignation. Just now a fellow crushes past the doctors, and hurriedly leaves the stand. Are some of his friends injured by the fall of 'the twopenny?' or can it be that he is a thief making off with his booty? Why does he sacrifice the view of this 'beautiful race,' if it be not to succour the suffering or to flee from justice? But no one thinks of anything but the race now, for the horses are coming up. 'Tom Thumb is beaten off,' 'Brother to Gray Tommy looks well in,' 'Typee is beaten – Typee is beaten,' roar hundreds of excited men; 'Lady Tatton has it – Lady Tatton has it,' 'No, no,' 'Now, Fordham, go it,' 'Call your horse – lift him in,' 'He has it,' 'It's Pretty Boy – it's Pretty Boy,' 'It's Tatton,' 'It's not – it's Pretty Boy,' 'Hurrah, hurrah.' Caps are twirled, hats are waved by winners, and there is a wholesale rush from the stand. The numbers are soon up – Pretty Boy first, Lady Tatton second. Pigeons, with ribbons round their necks, and some with ribbons streaming from their tails, are tossed up from the betting ring, and after performing a few circles over the stands they fly off, bearing with them weal or woe to thousands.

A good-looking farmer's daughter, who is accompanied by her father, now discovers that her purse has been stolen, containing two sovereigns and some silver. The farmer is very wroth, saying he knew something would happen, and he told her before she left home not to come to races with money in her pocket, for 'such spots are always snewing with thieves.' The daughter now recollects that when the twopenny stand fell a man who had been speaking of Pretty Boy pushed against her; but he was a decent-looking fellow – it couldn't be him! Get off the stand, and look about you. There are two county police with a man in custody. What has he been doing? What all his fraternity practise at such gatherings – picking pockets. Look at the girls running after the fellow, wishing to God it may be a 'summary' and not a sessions. The Irishman's stand is being repaired again. He says there was no one hurt, they were only 'shuk;' and what could they expect for the price? Cross the course again. There is a man dressed in Chinese costume, who has a number of ragged boys around him, beginning to form a ring. But see how the people are running this way. 'What's to do?' 'Oh, only some one going to quod.' No, not this time. Go closer – look! On a nutbarrow, borrowed for this purpose is laid a strong, muscular man; his face is ghastly, his hands clenched, his head cut and bleeding. This man, Thomas M'Donald, a sawyer, had attempted to cross the course, thinking all the horses had passed; but Tom Thumb, who was far behind the lot, knocked the man down, and caught him on the head with its hind feet. He is in a state of insensibility, and two police officers are taking him away to the hospital to die. His family will remember the Aintree meeting.

It is time to think about leaving the ground. What pleasure can there be, what healthy exercise or recreation, in a place like this? What are those carriages filled with ladies, surrounded by gentlemen who laugh, and drink, and puff away all care? These are the usual concomitants of a 'Meeting.' Here are several coaches filled with harlots. The drivers are in most cases trimmed out in some sort of lace. The horses' heads have large blue or pink rosettes, and the harness is bright and glossy. Here is a young fellow at one of the coaches, engaged in emptying a hamper of edibles, and the rosy-cheeked man with crape on his hat is looking after the champagne. '_____ the corkscrew,' says he, and breaks the neck of the bottle on the coach wheel, pours the sparkling liquor into a gill glass, and hands it to a girl in lavender-coloured satin, from whose head a plume of yellow feathers is waving, and who sits perched on the box exhibiting herself to the crowd. Pass on; at every coach you see well dressed men dancing attendance on these women, and at that where the very stout woman is eating oranges and throwing the peel at the turfites around, there are several men in earnest conversation. Cards have been distributed amongst the fashionable and sporting gentlemen during the morning, and in imitation of the cards of the horses these ladies' cards have written on them the colours in which their owners will appear, and are in this style – 'Matilda, primrose and pale blue,' 'Fanny, pink and French white,' 'Sarah, white and green,' 'Jemima, pink and blue,' &c., &c., the colours corresponding with the bonnets and dresses. The great event being over, lazy-looking and fashionably attired men cross the course and enter the ploughed gallop, drawing from their pockets the cards they have received, in order that they may the more easily distinguish their favourites. The girls, flushed with wine, waited on by bullies and pimps, watched keenly by their keepers, who are hovering about, are thus decorated to captivate the turfites. Some of them are very young, and notwithstanding their gay attire, look ill at ease. Anxiety and remorse have already stamped in indelible characters their youthful visages; and although the Melton pies are good, the fowls particularly fine, and the wine has flowed very freely, still they are not hearty. There is no joy here, nor can there be where innocence has fled and the consciousness of guilt is not altogether stifled. But leave them; enough has been seen to convince right-minded persons of the disgraceful exhibitions and practices which characterise 'an excellent Meeting.'

Before you leave the course, stroll down once more between and around the tents. The company has received large additions since the races began, and even now that they are nearly over people are still flocking on to the ground. Carts have brought loads of the lowest grade of prostitutes, and females of the humbler classes are very numerous. In the booths dancing is very general, and men half and wholly drunk stagger about in all directions. Women, with children in their arms or at the breast, in company with their husbands or friends, are eating and drinking, and seem to enjoy themselves in such fashion. The pugilists are now all far gone in drink, and their addresses to the crowd become more vulgar and disgusting than ever. The conjuror engaged by the proprietor of the camera is drunk, and persists in telling the people that he is a 'practical mechanic,' and has not sold his soul to the devil, as many suppose. A young man is being led out of the Irish tent with his face dreadfully cut, and a bandage round his head, whilst several women accompany him, swearing vengeance on somebody 'before the week's out.' Two carpenter apprentices have quarrelled over their drink, and are now crossing the field determined to 'fight it out.' Policemen are not about here; they find quite enough to do in keeping the respectable people within bounds, for drink is now telling heavily on all. Omnibuses and cars are beginning to move off. Away, then, to the railway station, and leave the revellers to enjoy as they usually do the Aintree Carnival.

In the railway carriage is a young man who says to a companion,
'My governor will expect I am at Wigan collecting accounts, and
I must work hard to-morrow to pull up for lost time.' Here, as in
too many cases, the allurements of the turf had withdrawn a young
man from his business for the day; and if nothing worse were done,
the vilest deception had been practised towards his employer.
Whilst speaking of collectors, the last few days have brought to
light circumstances which should be deeply pondered by employers
as well as by the employed. A short time ago, a young man, respec-
tably connected, came to Liverpool, and obtained a situation as
collector in a large establishment. One of the places of public
'amusement' which he first visited was the 'Salle de Danse;' it
presented attractions which he could not resist, and his visits were
frequent. One day he neglected to hand over to his cashier the
amount which he had collected, and in the evening he met with 'a
friend.' They entered a public house in a back street, and partook
of brandy. He recollected nothing further until the middle of the
night, when he found himself lying on a sofa in a dark room. He
arose and got into the street, but in such a confused state that he
could not find afterwards the house he had left; and thus he reeled
home. In the morning he found all his money had been taken – £11
of his own, and about £14 belonging to his employers. Whilst in
great distress of mind consequent upon his loss, he met another
'friend,' one who could 'put him in for a good thing.' The 'turf' was
shown to be the best and only means of restoring his shattered
fortune, for not only could the amount lost be won, but endless
sums in addition, by the purchase of a 'tip,' which would only cost
£2. Unfortunately, the advice of this 'friend' was acted on, and the
young man took his employer's money to pay for 'the tip', by which
he expected, and was assured, to win £240. The event came off
'crabs,'[32] and instead of winning anything, he lost £40. Again he
had recourse to his employer's money to enable him to maintain his
position and 'get round;' but he had gone too far. He is now an
inmate of the Borough Gaol. He has read Liverpool Life, and in
extreme anguish of mind many times exclaimed that to his cost he
knows the facts stated therein to be too true.

Many similar instances could be cited, for judges from the bench
have been induced to notice the frequency of embezzlement brought
about by turf practices. In Liverpool, the professional betting men
have recently received 'hard hits,' and several of them, who rode
and walked with their 'heads high,' have become defaulters, and are
now missing. One gentleman, in addition to other losses, is
reported to have 'dropped' £300 on the Lime Street ward election.
To such a length are men led by the gambling spirit engendered and
fostered by great and successful 'Meetings.'[33]

8 Sunday Night on the Landing Stage

There are few sights in Liverpool which are more surprising and gratifying to a stranger than the magnificent Landing Stages, at the George's and Prince's Piers. Indeed, to many 'natives,' these structures are a source of healthy and invigorating enjoyment; and thousands daily use them as such. In the nature of things this was to be expected. Hundreds of people whose business or means compel them to live in the more densely populated parts of the town, make a daily practice of taking a walk to enjoy the sea breeze and fresh air on our Landing Stages. What the Parks are to some towns, the Landing Stages are to Liverpool.

It is not to be wondered at, seeing the vast and teeming population which surround us, that the enjoyment of such a privilege as a walk on the Landing Stages afford, should be greatly abused. The fact of the public being allowed to use it without let or hindrance has caused this abuse; and the scenes witnessed here, on Sunday evenings more particularly, have long been a reproach to the local authorities. Still, on this as on all other matters which exhibit moral or social degradation, there exists a difference of opinion. This difference is caused in the main by a misapprehension of the facts. People who have not seen the Landing Stages on a Sunday evening, will not believe that the evil has reached that magnitude as to warrant its being publicly noticed in the Council.

The crowded state of the small Landing Stage on Sunday evenings cannot have escaped the most casual observer. It is a busy day with the Ferries. The pent-up artizan rejoices, and often indulges, in the Sunday trip to Cheshire; and an increase of several thousand passengers to and fro will, as a matter of course, affect the gathering on the Stage. But those who cross the river, for purposes of recreation, are not those who crowd the Stage, and call forth public indignation. No. Young lads and girls who began by going there for a walk, soon made it a meeting-place. Older heads, with more vicious intentions, then began to frequent the stage, and it has gone on from bad to worse, until now it is almost impossible for a female to pass to or from the Ferries without being subjected to the rudeness, vulgarity, obscenity, or profanity of the shameless hordes, of both sexes, who congregate on, and pollute the stage by their presence.

The girls who frequent the stage, and by their gaudy dress, rude speeches, and unseemly conduct, excite the disgust of all well disposed people, are not such as have given themselves up wholly to a dissolute life. They are not 'social evils' proper. The majority of them are engaged in some industrial occupation during the week, and this is their mode of enjoyment on the Sabbath. They here meet with young men, and the promenading of these groups, mingled with the jeers, laughter, and filthy conversation, is what constitutes the great public nuisance so justly complained of.

'Fast young men' were not long in scenting out what they term 'the game of the Landing Stage.' It is with no simple or virtuous intention that you see the 'pork-pie' and the 'turn-down'[34] bearing away to the Landing Stage, on Sunday evening. After meeting a girl here for two or three evenings in succession, and perhaps meeting her at a dancing class during the week, it is found easy to persuade her to accompany them to Eastham or Bidston, and in *five* cases which have been painfully brought under notice, the girls' ruin had been effected by these young scoundrels and by such means. Parents are now mourning the loss of daughters, and girls are now outcasts on the streets; and these fearful results can be traced to the permitted indecency and immorality on the Landing Stage.

But it is not the 'lower orders,' as some people term it, that are solely to blame for the disgraceful scenes. It is not the 'fast young men' either. The evil would never have reached such a magnitude had it not received more substantial support. On a Sunday evening recently, we noticed men of good position, (one of whom had filled public offices in this town, and had a wife and family at home,) leering and chatting with girls, whom they would in daylight, or in the public streets, be ashamed to acknowledge. There was noticed also one of our great public men who lives at this side of the water, landing from the Rock Ferry boat. He appeared to have been wooing the rosy god, or in plainer terms, he was partially intoxicated. He stood a little time by the south refreshment room, gnawing the head of his cane and reeling about now and then, noticing the while the girls that passed, and occasionally tapping some of them on the shoulder or hat. Having completed his resolve, he joined a group, and in a few minutes after was seen talking to a very young girl – a child, or little more – and by the eight o'clock boat this couple crossed to Seacombe.[35]

There were several of the young girls there under the influence of drink, and the gross indecency of their language was inexpressibly vile. The young men in their company seemed to be quite their equals, so far as foulness of speech and riotous behaviour were concerned; but the number of *aged men, of decent exterior*, who promenaded and seemed to enjoy the scene, was the most suggestive sight. To think of men who will walk to Church with their daughters in the morning, spend the afternoon with their amiable families, and yet devote the evening of the sacred day to the encouragement of such abominable profanity.

It sounds well at public meetings to hear men talking of taking 'a deep interest in all that concerns the people's happiness.' It is easy to condemn the conduct of the lower classes; but there is nothing that encourages immorality so much, or corrupts the manners of the lower classes more, than the looseness, the vicious indulgence, and the filthy hypocrisy of 'well-to-do people.' By their conduct they foster, feed and perpetuate all manner of evils, and were it not for them, brothels would not be so numerous, neither would the Landing Stage be such a great public scandal.

9 Scientific experiments and rational mirth

The establishment for the manufacture of galvanic apparatus and the enjoyment of rational mirth was a low dirty-looking building.[36] Over the door were a transparency and a bill on which appeared a clown's head with 'a broad grin' on the features, and the words, 'lots of fun every evening.' At the door there were some galvanic batteries and other apparatus, with the view of exciting the curiosity of the on-lookers. A young man addressed the crowd, inviting them to come in and witness the interesting and scientific experiments 'for the low charge of one penny.' Crowds of persons, chiefly young men, were pouring in, and we resolved to enter. We paid the penny to a red-faced broad-set, slovenly-dressed woman, who looked 'juicy,' and smelled strongly of the extract of juniper. It must have cost a considerable sum to paint this lady's face, so brilliant was it in colour; and there was little doubt that, whatever the colouring material used, the application had been made internally. She was evidently not without the milk of human kindness in her composition, for, although she prayed to the Almighty that she might get hold of the hair of her '_____ husband's head,' she in the intervals of money-taking lavished her delicate attentions on a dirty poodle dog which sat in her lap. On pushing aside a curtain we found ourselves in a square barn-like building, lighted by a gas pendant from the roof, for there was no ceiling. There was a form about four feet long at one side of the apartment, and this was the only seat-room provided. From a beam there were suspended two galvanic wires, and under them was placed a box for persons to stand upon who wished to receive a shock. In a corner of the room was a table supporting oranges, Eccles cakes, and a wheel of fortune, which were watched over by a very young girl. In a prominent position, in large characters, was placed the notice, 'Take care of your pockets,' – a caution which, judging from the appearance of the company, was not necessary. There were about fifty persons present when we entered, and the number was being steadily increased by new comers.

Strange as it may seem, up to this hour we had not the least idea that science or the love of it had taken such deep root and was bearing such fruit amongst the masses. We had read that in the United States of America there is an astronomical society that numbers amongst its members thirty-nine grocers, sixteen hog dealers, twenty-five joiners and carpenters, and but five ministers; and we knew also that in our own town there existed several societies for scientific purposes; but we were not prepared for the fact that three or four hundred persons of the lowest grade of society could be brought together on a Saturday evening to witness scientific experiments. The persons, however, were actually before us, and were anxiously waiting for the display.

In the absence of any person to direct the studies or conduct the scientific experiments, girls, boys, and men experimented on themselves. The contortion of their features and limbs was very painful to look upon. Their conduct was disgustingly vulgar; their language shamefully indecent and obscene. The batteries being very strongly charged, at times the experimenters were twisted about, and on several occasions they were knocked with such violence against the gas as to endanger the pipe. The rosy-faced money-taker noticed this, and remonstrated with the company in such gentle and elegant phrases as these: – '_____ your eyes, do you see what you're doing? You'll break the gas directly.' 'Now, do you hear! I'll turn it off directly, blast me if I don't.' 'If you don't mind what you're after, _____ the bit more shall you have to-night.' To one boy, who was inclined for more mirth than the place could afford, the lady said, 'Now, I *will* turn if off; _____ if I don't, you _____ set of fools.' She was true to her word, and disconnected the wires accordingly. With such an introduction to the lecture, what could be expected from the lecture itself?

We were not long in discovering that the interesting and instructive part of the exhibition was carried on in a room or shed adjoining that in which the crowd assembled. This shed, which was capable of holding about one hundred persons, was filled. Boisterous laughter and shouts of applause were heard from time to time, and these served to increase the anxiety of those who were impatiently waiting for an introduction to the *sanctum sanctorum*. One gentleman, a member of the musical profession, carried in his arms a child about six years old. He said, apologetically, 'I wish my daughter to know everything,' and for this purpose he placed her on an old stove in the corner near the door. From her elevated position the child could see the coarse behaviour of the men and boys who beguiled their waiting moments by experimenting with the galvanic wires; she could hear the fiendish and frightful oaths of these devotees of science; and she could witness her father laughing at the obscene jest or the filthy retort of youths and men deeply sunk in depravity. Poor child! in years to come she will, doubtless, think of what she saw and heard, and remember also the expression of her father, that he wished her to see everything. On the form was seated a mother sucking her infant; next to her sat a voluptuous-looking woman of easy virtue. They had both been indulging at the shrine of Bacchus, and were in that yawning, sottish state well known by tipplers as 'moreish.' After every yawn, the young woman exclaimed, 'I wish to God it was over.'

As we were contemplating the scene before us, the proprietor of the establishment came from the inner apartment. He carried with him a filthy-looking bladder, to which a tube and mouthpiece were attached. Upon inquiring how long we should have to wait before we were introduced to the 'rational mirth', he replied, 'In a few minutes; I'm going to give it to the last one now.' He returned into the room with a well filled bladder of gas,[37] and we soon heard more laughing, singing, shouting and swearing. After the lapse of a few minutes the door of the *sanctum* was opened; there was a great crush towards it, and at last we found ourselves in the next room. The apartment was a mere wooden shed, the filth of the ground being heaped up at the ends to form a sort of gallery. The atmosphere was very foul, and in this abominable, dirty hole, at least one hundred persons were crammed. The notice, 'Take care of your pockets' was here, too – suspended from the roof! There were crowded together boys of all ages, and in all stages of depravity and filth; young men from seventeen to twenty-five years of age, in various stages of intoxication; old men, who seemed to like the fun; and girls, young women, and mothers. The young men appeared to consist principally of carters, porters, sail-makers, and ship carpenters, and their language and behaviour were filthy in the extreme. Regardless of the presence of women and children, one fellow conducted himself in a manner which led us to regret that Newland's patent sentry boxes[38] had not been introduced into such dens.

The bulk of the audience took their stand on the raised positions. A strong rope ran along the outer side wall, and by means of a belt round the body, and a ring, the patients were tethered to the rope. We asked the proprietor the reason for such an arrangement. His reply was suggestive. 'The people that come here, whenever they take the gas, begin to fight, and we do this to secure them and ourselves, from injury.' The proprietor being completely 'done up' with his previous exertions, his assistant came forward to conduct 'the instructive and scientific' experiments. The assistant proved to be an abominably filthy fellow. The crowd had rendered themselves almost hoarse with cursing each other's eyes and sanguinary faces; polluting the already poison-laden atmosphere with their horrid imprecations; and he, instead of lecturing upon science, cursed the various features of the human face divine into a frightful manner, threatening to turn some of the scientific disciples out of the place, and to throw others into a region never mentioned in ears polite. He concluded by declaring that unless, 'Yees stand back, and keep order,' no distribution of gas should be made. A young fellow having at last been properly secured, he took off his coat and cap, and the experiments began. The operator held the nostrils of the patient whilst he was inhaling the oxide. For a moment or two the youth appeared to be stupified, and shut his eyes. In a second or two after he stared wildly around him, and then with set teeth and clenched fists he struck out, and kicked with maniacal fury. His intellectual development was extremely low; his moral region equally so; his temperament bilious; and during the excitement his face became thoroughly animalised, so to speak. 'If I had you at the Tranmere wakes,' shouted he, 'I would kick the _____ soul out of you.' He tugged at the rope, and tried to free himself; he swore at the audience, and yelled fiendishly. There was neither mirth nor method in this madness. It was a terrible spectacle for men to witness; and what must it have been to the poor children by whom this wretch was surrounded? Having become somewhat exhausted by his efforts, he sung a song disgustingly obscene. No attempt was made by the assistant to stop the singing; the song was listened to with very little interruption, and there was no disapprobation shown. A few of the audience were too young to understand the filthy allusions; but there was a wicked silence, a sly smile, and a secret satisfaction manifested by a majority of the scoundrels present that quite startled us. Some of the women even appeared to have an affection for the indelicacies which were introduced. The stimulating effects of the gas having died out, the young 'rough' was let loose.

Just at this moment there was presented a scene which no pen can describe. A nest of young devils appeared to have been unhived, and were savagely fighting for the nectar essential to infernal life. '_____ your eyes, did you not promise it to me?' shouted one. 'Hold your _____ tongue,' cried another. The divine name was associated with almost every volley of oaths – each horrid imprecation. Desperate were the struggles of the incarnate fiends to get possession of the dirty bladder which contained the intoxicating gas. 'Do you take me for a _____ fool, or a _____ idiot?' shouted out the assistant; and with a terrible oath he threatened to 'knock their _____ heads off'. One stronger than the rest succeeded in getting hold of the pipe attached to the bladder, and to him the privilege of being fastened to the stake was granted. He inhaled the gas, and before the assistant had withdrawn the bladder, he struck out with desperate force. Foiled in his aims, stamping, swearing, and slaking his tongue, he would have been no bad model of a chained demon. Although it was apparent that he was fighting earnestly to free himself, yet, as an innocent-looking boy remarked, he was 'swearing for fun.'

> And he, repulsed, fell into a sadness; thence into a weakness;
> Thence to a lightness; and by this declension
> Into the madness wherein now he raves.

During this dreadful exhibition of depravity, some of the spectators, not yet sufficiently familiarised with this form of vice, became terrified with the devilish incarnation, and expressed uneasiness and anxiety to escape from the den. One boy was so much overcome that he had to be taken away from the front, and the money-taker kindly and considerately allowed him an opportunity of witnessing the concluding scenes of this performance at a distance from the stake. To the great majority of those present this spectacle was evidently nothing new. We learned from their conversations that 'Tom', 'Bill', 'Jack', and 'Harry', all acquaintances of theirs, had on many occasions partaken of this life-giving oxide, and while under its influence had played such fantastic tricks before high heaven as would make the angels weep. The intimacy between many of the young fiends and the proprietor and his worthy assistant was remarkable; but, of course, it must be borne in mind that this was a display of 'scientific and instructive' experiments, and it was only to be expected that the lecturer and his pupils should be on the best of terms. It might be that some persons present had been misled by the announcement on the bills and the address at the door, but we regret to think that such were the exceptions – regular frequenters the rule. Most of the persons present knew, or had been informed by their companions, of the scenes which awaited them. The anxiety of so many to inhale the gas, even after they had witnessed the vicious display made by some of their associates, was strongly indicative of their love of approbation, and moral depravity. From inquiries since made, we learn that the influence of the gas does not remain on the patient for more than five or ten minutes, at longest; therefore we are led to believe that the inhaling of it was partially used as a cloak, under which these young 'roughs' could exhibit their vilest passions. The similarity of the performance of each patient serves to confirm us in this view. The first tethered wretch throws himself into a fighting attitude, spars, kicks, swears, fumes, and concludes by singing – once or twice interrupting the progress of the song to kick and swear more still. Just so does the second. The companions around know the performance so well that they can tell you what song will be sung.

What does this indicate? What instruction do these interesting experiments furnish, to those who have the elevation of the people at heart?

When the first effects of the gas began to subside, the youth before us began to sing 'The Battle of the Alma;' to the sentiment there could be no objection, to the style of the singing much. We had seen enough, and retired. In such way had several hundreds of young and old been prepared for the coming Sabbath. Next day we listened to one of our most eloquent divines describing the deep degradation of the poor African, but not a word of the deeper degradation at home. With the previous night's experience we repeated with heart and soul the words used during the service of the day –

Throughout creation's bounds *let there be light*!

10   Secular and religious gambling

It was deemed prudent to suspend the consideration of that deeply important subject, the sources of juvenile delinquency, during the festive season of Christmas and the inauguration of the new year. The one having passed, the other being now entered upon, it may reasonably be supposed that the public mind will become somewhat settled, to pursue with renewed vigour the serious business of life. Without further preface, therefore, attention is earnestly invited to those matters in which we are all more or less interested, affecting, as they do, the social and moral condition of a large class of this great community.

The destruction of the Gambling Tables, and the dispersion of the gamblers who were accustomed day and night to assemble in the yard at the corner of Lime-street, are matters for hearty congratulation by all who are striving to purify the moral atmosphere that surrounds the haunts and homes of 'the dangerous classes.' By whatever agency this has been brought about, the result cannot but prove highly beneficial to the town, and reflects the highest credit on the police who effected the capture. As early as June last, the attention of those in authority was directed to the existence of such a fruitful source of depravity, such a fearful school of vice, as might there be seen in active operation, in the very heart of the town. Seeing that the authorities have at last begun to discharge their duties – and that, too, it may be inferred from the judicious remarks of Mr Mansfield, in real earnest – it is much to be desired they will continue in this righteous course. Let them not rest satisfied with the destruction of tables in the streets, but go into the shops and houses where such things are known to exist. If a lottery or a raffle for a Christmas dinner can be stopped, why should wheels of fortune, mock auctions, and more questionable modes of gambling be suffered to exercise such a pernicious influence on the people? What is the difference between working men raffling at a beershop and religious professors raffling at a bazaar? Has modern civilisation reached that point where, in reference to the respectable (?) raffle, it will be said the end justifies the means? Justice in England is, or ought to be, even-handed: the poor can never be punished for their poverty; neither ought the more affluent to escape by reason of their superior intelligence. If either are vicious, or indulge in vicious pursuits, let the penalty be in each case duly inflicted. The necessity of one law for the rich and another for the poor will, after all, be no fiction, if the raffle at the beer shop be wrong and the raffle at the bazaar be right. Let us notice gambling of both sorts, secular and religious.

We visited a gambling stall or shop near the Sailors' Home. A wheel of fortune or lottery occupied one side of the den, a gambling table the other. The place was thronged with youths of both sexes. Of sailor boys there were a great number, of young prostitutes not a few. For the risk of a penny the chance of a valuable prize was offered, and the proprietor urged all to come forward, and many did. Although many pence were paid, no prize was drawn of the value of one penny whilst we remained. Here was the first step in the gambler's career, and the stall was doing a thriving business. A good-looking sailor boy was at the entrance, denouncing the place and proprietor in most emphatic terms: he declared that at the stall on one evening he was induced to play until he had lost 19s. He knew it now to be a decided swindle, and had the good sense never to try and win his money back; but how few are like him! These traps for simple-hearted seamen abound in this locality, why should they not share the same fate as the gambling stalls in Lime-street?

We visited a bazaar held for the benefit of a church.[39] The room was tastefully decorated, festooned with flowers, and scriptural mottoes were curiously worked in with evergreens. Stalls were presided over by elegantly dressed ladies, whose anxiety to secure purchasers and effect sales none could doubt. The room was thronged with visitors of a highly intelligent and respectable class. Mothers brought their sons, fathers brought their daughters – all had money to spend: this was the proper mode of spending it. Young ladies of pleasing manners and winning address perambulated the room with *lottery bags*. Most of them addressed every gentleman they passed, although they had never seen the individuals before, have not since, may never do so again. The object of this was to secure customers for their raffle or lottery. As a particular request, or a personal favour, you were asked to invest sixpence or a shilling, for which trifling sum the chances were that 'a set of dinner mats' or 'a beautifully dressed doll' would be secured. It was in vain that gentlemen urged their destitute state of bachelorhood, and that neither dinner mats nor dolls would be of any service to them. Every objection was met by these ladies, and the gentlemen were quickly informed that if they were not married they ought to be. All the arts for which the gentler sex are so remarkable were put into requisition, in order that a shilling, sixpence or even a penny might be obtained, and one more name added to the list of gamblers. These ladies gave no change. If the amount you sought to invest was one shilling, and you were simple enough to entrust half a crown to the fair fingers, you were done – decidedly done! In one case it was said the list was just filled up, and the raffle would take place immediately; but when the fair holder of the lottery bag was interrogated more closely, the admission was reluctantly made that she had obtained only *three* names, and her list required twenty, at three shillings each! Young girls – children – were here engaged in this very questionable employment, and they induced other children 'to put into the lottery for such a sweet little workbasket.' Here we see the sanctity of religion taken to cloak or cover up the most dangerous practices – and by such means are many well intentioned persons misled. Here are ladies making gambling-stall keepers of themselves, and the daughters of most respectable men spending their time in touting or canvassing for customers. And all this is done for what? To benefit a church! Where are the ministers? Do they approve of such conduct and practices, and call it 'a labour of love?' Has religion come to this, and must the temple be again cleansed of the 'money changers' and those that sell doves? Let the authorities look at it, and inquire why should these lotteries and stalls not share the same fate as the gambling stalls in Lime-street.

The holding of a bazaar, where 'useful, fancy, and ornamental articles' are sold for the benefit of a church or schools, may be admissible; but the holding of lotteries or gambling stalls at such bazaars is highly objectionable. They are, looked at in a moral point of view, utterly indefensible; and although ministers of the gospel are found availing themselves of such 'helps,' none have yet had the hardihood to defend the practice; and, looking at the precepts of that gospel these men profess to teach, their conduct in this matter is reprehensible. Well may the scoffer smile, and the cynic sneer, when they see principles, profession, and practice so antagonistic. The Egyptians are not the only race that love the 'flesh-pots!'

Religious professors, by their modern practices, create another source of juvenile delinquency – that is, sending children from door to door with cards and boxes to beg for missionary purposes.[40] Several cases can be given, showing the vicious tendency of such beggarly means to support what is believed to be truth; but we need only give one which came not long ago under our own observation. A little girl connected with a Sunday School was entrusted with a card, and instructed by her teachers how to go about collecting. She set about her work, obtained coppers here and there; but her moral training had not been sufficiently attended to, and the temptation of the sweet shop overcame her love for the spread of truth. She appropriated some of the money collected in the purchase of 'paradise,' and, little by little, she became a confirmed thief, and is now in the criminal class. Up to the time of her entering on the missionary enterprise, nothing was ever seen or known of her thieving propensities; and the probability is, that had she not been exposed to the temptation, she might now have been respectable and respected. Why should children be exposed to temptation in this way, for such a purpose? and how terrible the responsibility of those teachers who train children to habits of mendicity! Every Sabbath day sober minded people are shocked, and Christians ought to be ashamed, to see the hawking of missionary boxes from door to door by children, whose parents, if they could but see the evil seed that is by this means sown, ought at once to remove their offspring from such temptation. Many eminent ministers regret the necessity for Sunday Schools at all, because they consider them as so many testimonies to the unchristian state of parents. And what parent who is desirous of supporting a manly, independent spirit, and who wishes his children to display the same, would permit them to be made beggars, and endanger their moral character, in order that their name might stand high on the list at the children's missionary collection? Older heads and hands entrusted with money are overcome, lose their balance, and fall; and children, whose moral powers are not yet developed, but whose propensities are excessively active, can hardly be expected to stand a test which men of standing and character sometimes find it difficult to undergo. Ministers who object to the working classes taking a walk in the fields on the Sunday, and who shudder at the idea of any inroad on the day of rest, ought not to be silent on the Sabbath missionary begging box.

Now as to licensed houses where gambling is practised. These are well known to be numerous. The police can point them out by scores. We know one house – a beer-house – where card-playing is regularly carried on, and men are induced, week after week, to lose much time, and all their wages, and bring destitution upon their families in consequence. Their children, in search of food, are driven upon the streets, meet with temptations which they cannot resist, are led into crime, and go to swell the number of juvenile delinquents. Cases have come under our observation, have been inquired into, and the source of the depravity is the *card-playing beer-house*. Magistrates may enlarge gaols, and continue to build reformatories; all these and more will be required if these infamous houses are allowed thus to deal around social and moral destruction. Under the plea of playing for a Christmas goose, we know of one man who lost seven pounds *in a beer-house on a Sunday morning*; and there is not a Sunday passes that pounds are not lost and spent in this filthy resort. It is said that men who are fond of such unhealthy excitement, and are so far depraved, would be sure to indulge in it whether these houses were in existence or not. But how do they become fond of excitement – what has had most to do with confirming and gratifying a vicious and depraved taste? The licensed houses. Listen to a voice from the gaol: – 'I began going with some lads to a drinking shop. These lads began playing at dominoes and cards, and I learned, and the man who kept the house put us in a little place by ourselves, so that we could fasten the door if the police came.'[41] We have witnessed during the past few months similar scenes to those described by this convict – rooms set apart for boys and young men to play cards; and *this is knowingly permitted*!

Well known card-playing houses are situated in densely populated districts. There is one which has rendered itself notorious for the riotous conduct of which it is frequently the scene. We visited the place on a Saturday evening. The rooms are small, ill furnished, and filthy. The proprietor was 'drunk at the back,' but his wife was attending to the customers, who appeared to be working men, not of the lowest grade. The 'missus,' as they called her, had a drunken look, and wore a very gaudy cap. She addressed many of the men as they came in, and referred to a slate to see what they owed. 'Seven and sixpence,' 'six and tenpence,' and in one case fourteen shillings were paid, and when the man felt inclined to dispute the amount the slatekeeper replied, 'You got most of it on that night you played for the clock, for you would have me to get you some whisky.' The 'shots' being settled, the men settled down to drink and smoke, and after a short time went into the cellar. This was the carding room until it got later on; then all rooms were alike. There was a man here whom we had noticed from boyhood. He had a few hours before received twenty-eight shillings for his wages, had been home to clean himself, and from his wife, who was crying at the door, we learned that he had given her *twelve shillings*, to keep himself, wife, and two children for the week.

> He entered a licensed beerhouse next –
> A reeking and filth-filled room,
> Where, 'mid oaths and lust and lies, he must
> Have felt himself quite at home;

and when he had paid his shot and spent the evening here the whole of his wages would be gone. This fellow must have a good beefsteak on a Sunday morning to his breakfast, and would beat his wife if she was unable to procure him a substantial dinner daily. His children lived in terror of the father, and the eldest boy was frequently driven to the streets. Were it possible to investigate the circumstances of each of the twenty-eight men we saw enter this house, there is no doubt the result would be similar. Homes neglected, wives abused, children driven to crime, through the accursed vice promoted and encouraged by these licensed houses. Do we require an increase of magistrates, or do we not rather require that those we have should do their duty?

If the magistrates be anxious to do what in their power lies to check the growth of juvenile delinquency, and at the same time purify the pastimes provided for the people, let them turn their attention to other licensed establishments. At one of these, which occupies a prominent position in the town, may nightly be witnessed a scene that for grossness, immorality or obscenity stands almost unparalleled. Even what are called the decorations of the room pander to the worst passions of humanity, and vulgarity and lasciviousness are unblushingly proclaimed. Here are youths – many from the upper classes of society, mixed up with others in more humble positions. Smoking cigars, sipping ale, wine, or brandy, chatting with degraded girls, and examining 'the points' of the living tableaux constitute some of the features of the evening's entertainment, and those which would appear to excite most attention. There is singing, and much of that class which cannot be described. Between forty and fifty boys (they could be called nothing else) were the other evening in this place, and seemed delighted to hear a filthy song called 'the lively flea.' Now, the obscenity in this consisted more in the action and grimace of the vocalist than in the expressions used, although the latter were bad enough; but a more abominable song, as this was here given, one containing viler suggestions, could not be conceived. The girls laughed, the lads roared with delight, and one of them said '*he would do anything rather than miss such a treat.*' Are fathers surprised at their sons falling into a vicious course of life? Are merchants or tradesmen astonished that their confidence should be abused by such 'nice young men?' How can it be otherwise, when those who have the power to check the evil would appear to lack the will? The proprietors of such resorts look at them in a business point of view, and supply what they think will pay. But the great moral responsibility rests upon the heads of those who year after year license the iniquity.

And to go further and deeper into these dark and morally death-dealing practices, where, in any town making pretensions to progress, and professions of respect for morals, or manners, could be met with such a licensed promenade for prostitutes as we have seen to exist here? 'Minor theatres,' 'twopenny hops,' casinos, and singing saloons are all spoken of as having a tendency to promote the growth and foster the evils attendant on juvenile delinquency and public immorality. Without doubt such is the influence of these places; but all combined sink into absolute nothingness when compared with this licensed promenade for prostitutes. Here are children from twelve to sixteen years of age who are being trained, and have already learned much of the sin and trickery of the abandoned harlot. It is in vain you look in any of our provincial towns for a festering source of moral corruption as we see here. In London there is nothing so vile. In Paris the scene would not be permitted an hour, *if it were known*.[42] And we are assured, by persons who have been in most of the continental cities and towns, that the iniquity here is without a parallel. Liverpool, the modern Tyre – Liverpool, that boasts of her sound Protestant feeling, of the sterling character of her evangelical clergy, of the noble resistance made against an inroad on the Sacred Day, of her benevolent and charitable institutions, of her public baths, washhouses, free public libraries, and reformatories – has, to feed an insatiable cupidity, obtained an unenviable notoriety for permitting the social life of her inhabitants to be polluted by the corrupt and filthy stream which flows from this vile spot. Not only this, the scene is watched over by the representatives of magisterial authority; and are we not, therefore, justified in saying that these practices are knowingly permitted? To whom are the rightly disposed members of the community to look for the purification of manners and morals which are thus being corrupted? Not to the proprietors, clearly: their interest lies in keeping such places open and having them filled. We have heard over and over again, that the heavy current expenses of one notorious establishment are entirely defrayed by the money paid for admission by the troops of unfortunates who nightly throng the place. It is to be hoped that the proprietors have neither wives nor daughters to maintain out of such ill-gotten gains. It is the magistrates, who grant the privileges to individuals, who are in a great measure to blame, and it is to the magistrates the public should look. The public scandal, social degradation and misery inflicted on individuals by the existence of this promenade for prostitutes ought to make magistrates shudder for the consequences.

Again, look at the abominable and disgusting practices at the Salle de Danse, or the degrading pastimes at the Supper Rooms. We have heard a magistrate from the bench describe the scenes nightly enacted in the street as a scandal and disgrace to the town; but what would he have said were he to behold the 'chamber of horrors' within, and breathe for a few hours – for a night – the pestilential atmosphere of the place? And yet, well as these places and practices are now known, we scarcely find one minister of religion in the town who has the moral courage to stand forth and declare his open hostility to such soul-destroying vanities. We hear now and then the theatre abused and spoken of very improperly; but such abuse betrays a want of knowledge. The theatre may be the medium of conveying sound instruction in that form which to the national mind is popular; but the theatre and the promenade, the theatre and the dancing saloon, the theatre and the supper rooms, need not of necessity be connected. A visit to one for purposes of recreation ought not to involve the loss of moral character and self-respect; yet in many instances which could be given such has proved the result.

There is no more pitiful spectacle than to behold a minister of religion rising at a public meeting and telling, in serious tones, how he 'mourns over the iniquity of the age.' It is this crying, and doing nothing else – this mourning and not working, on the part of the ministers, which allows the evil to spread. He who 'went about doing good' mourned over Jerusalem, but the latter was the result of the former. The scenes we have witnessed and described during the last six months should have been visited, described, and denounced by ministers. It is clearly their work. Their sacred calling invests them with peculiar power. Their education and training ought to nerve them for the duty; and their zeal for moral purity, if nothing more, should render apathy abhorrent. But no; controversial lectures, speeches at public meetings, and 'mourning' at tea parties, occupy the portion of the time which ought to be directed to the pleasures, practices, and pastimes of the people, unless 'the pastor of the people' and 'the shepherd of the flock' are to become the poetic fictions of a by-gone age.

Part two
Low life: home, family and neighbourhood

11 The social condition of the people

The Sketches of Liverpool Life would be very imperfect if we omitted to notice 'The Homes of the People'.[43] There is much written and spoken just now concerning the labouring classes. Their habits, their homes, and the improvement required or sought for in these matters are being placed before the public in a variety of ways. Each man who speaks or writes professes to have discovered the true and only remedy for all the evils – moral, social, domestic or political – under which the working population is said to groan. It is idle to talk of anything in the way of improvement, says one, unless you first of all impress the mind with the importance of religion. Another is convinced, and declares with equal confidence, that the one thing needful is total abstinence from all intoxicating drinks. A third erects the standard of education, and is of opinion that were the education of the people properly attended to, all other good would follow. A fourth says, Give the people comfortable homes; let them have houses to live in, and not 'abominable filthy styes,' where all decency must of necessity be set at nought: then, and only then, you may expect to wean men from their degrading habits, and lessen the attraction of the card-playing beer-house or the glaringly lighted gin palace. The men are not so much to blame, says a fifth; it is to the women, the wives of working men, that you should look if you ever expect to influence their social position. Let a man have a good wife; to this end educate girls in such a manner as will enable them to become frugal and thrifty, patient, painstaking, and clean in their habits, and so form proper partners for working men. This done, you need not fear the result. In all these proposed remedies there may be – nay, undoubtedly is – a portion of truth, but of no one proposal can it be said this is all you require in order to place the moral and social progress of the people on a sound and satisfactory basis.

How few there are of the reading or thinking portion of the public who really know what it is that constitutes the life of the working man. To what books, to what reports, to what statistics can you refer and be enabled to see what are the hopes, fears, joys,

sorrows, temptations, and triumphs which go to make up the social
life of the labourer? Then as to his dwelling, his home, where do
you find that depicted? The character of the street or court may be
described; the peculiar construction of his house may be pointed
out; the condition in which it appears on a given day may be
accurately noticed – yet what false views these all may give of a
working man's home. That improvement in the construction of
dwellings for the humbler classes is much needed admits of no
doubt. That this improvement has begun, and is being carried out
amongst us, is a gratifying fact, which it will be our duty to allude
to hereafter. But that improvement in construction or ventilation of
a house will effect the wonderful change in the character of the
inmates that some well intentioned persons expect and look for we
do not believe. An intimate acquaintance with the various classes
amongst our working population, and some observation of their
manners and customs, induce scepticism in this particular.

The suggestions that are thrown out and the plans that are being
adopted for bettering the condition of the people prove one thing
– the anxiety and manifest earnestness of the so-called upper or
middle class to alleviate the sorrows or mitigate the sufferings of
their brethren in humbler life. All that seems necessary, therefore,
now, is *direction*. The earnest and determined *will* is apparent, yet
the *way* is not made clear. In the matter of the amusements and
pastimes of the people we have shown what they are, leaving it for
others to point out what they should be. So in the social life of the
people, as shown in their homes, we purpose to point out what it
was and is, leaving it for those who are anxious on the subject to
say what it should be. For obvious reasons names and localities
must be withheld; but the facts will lose nothing of their interest to
the social reformer on that account.

A very large majority of the working classes of this town reside
in 'courts.'[44] Those constructed before the Health of Towns Bill
passed are ill-contrived, badly ventilated, miserable-looking dwellings. In some districts there are whole streets composed almost
entirely of such; for instance, look at Duckingfield-street in the east
of the town; Albert-street and others adjoining in the south; and
Hornby or Paul-street in the north. These court houses are
frequently four stories high, 'straight up and down,' and contain
four apartments – a cellar, a living room, and two bedrooms; and
often in these houses two and sometimes three families reside. At
the top of the court stand the open cesspool and privy. The houses
adjoining these are sometimes let at a lower rent: thus poor
creatures have a premium offered them for the loss of their health
and the possibility of cutting short their days.[45] The rents vary
from 2*s*. 9*d*. to 4*s*. 6*d*., according to locality. The class of houses

built since the operation of our health committee it has been felt are a great improvement on the older courts, the law compelling builders to have such blocks of dwellings 'open at the ends,' and otherwise ensuring modes of ventilation and cleanliness. In order to show the social life of the people, we request the reader's company to one of the courts in our town. It is not one of the worst class, but may be looked on as second-class, the houses and people in which will represent a great number of those that surround us. There are in it four houses, the rents of which are 3s. 3d. per week. This court is approached by a narrow passage, and in the passage are two houses, or rather the entrances to them. The court is about four yards wide, is flagged, and there are two houses on each side. The character of the inmates is clearly indicated to some extent by the exterior, yet in these matters it is not always safe to judge by appearances; therefore enter house Number One.

This house, a few years ago, was the residence of a shipwright who held a responsible situation, and whose relations were in a respectable sphere of life. He received two guineas per week as wages; had his wife and two children (girls) to support; the other children were earning their own living, and two daughters were married. The house contained good furniture, which presented the appearance of ill use and neglect; and everything about the place was disorderly and careless. It was not positively a dirty house, but was in all respects slovenly. If you wished to sit down you would have to move a towel, a basket of potatoes, or a knife off the chair before doing so. The ashes would be heaped up under the grate, and the breakfast things would not be 'sided up' at eleven or twelve o'clock. The proprietor came home drunk three or four nights in each week. He abused his wife, broke the furniture, took a great delight in breaking crockery ware, on one occasion pulled down the mantelshelf – yet, notwithstanding this course of conduct, *he was regular in attendance at a place of worship on the Sabbath*, where he was seen by his father, who was an office-bearer in the church. His wife was of a very respectable family, but had – through the conduct of her husband, to a great extent – become an habitual drunkard. She drank ale, rarely ever touched spirits. She generally received a portion of the wages on Friday night, and was sometimes helplessly drunk before noon on Saturday. There was a talking parrot in the house that used to imitate the children crying and the wife's screams when the husband was abusing her. The drunken woman's noise, the screaming of the bird, and the lamentation of the children from day to day, rendered them anything but pleasant neighbours. The children were ill clothed, irregularly fed, and, as might be expected, used language to their parents which was lamentable to hear. Both husband and wife are since dead, and one of the daughters has become an outcast on the streets. She declares her father's conduct drove her to this wretched mode of life.

The second house was the residence of a man engaged in the building trade. He had a wife and three children; his wages were 24s. per week; but he frequently worked overtime, and thereby earned considerably more. This man's father is a tradesman in the town, has brought up a large family, and is now a respectable man. The son who resided here was a sottish, stupid-looking fellow, who formed low companionships, married young, and seemed totally indifferent to all domestic comfort. His wife, when *clean* – though it was a rare occasion to see her so – was a decent-looking person, but her habits were idle and dissolute. The house contained very little furniture, and that of the meanest description. The children were in the main indebted to their grand-parents for clothing, and their education was almost entirely neglected. The man left home in the morning soon after five o'clock, and did not return until evening, unless he was working near enough to come to his meals. He took his coffee and bread and butter with him for breakfast, and many times the same for dinner, and rarely ever obtained a proper or comfortable meal. In this matter he represents the great majority of working men. His wife, left to herself all day, found companions in the neighbourhood, and at No. 1 she was a frequent visitor and guest. When No. 2 had cash she spent it with No. 1, and these kind offices – so they were spoken of by these people – were returned, and thus were the earnings of the men worse than wasted. The husband in this case did not abuse the wife; he did not beat her, yet he took no interest in either her or his home, and Sunday seemed a miserable day to him, for he had no clothes to appear decent, therefore rarely went out. His brothers, who were unmarried, came sometimes on Sunday to see him; then the large jug of beer would be sent for and obtained, a regular carouse would take place, every one in the house, children excepted, would be drunk at night, and on Monday morning there would be a quarter lost, or sometimes the whole day. The wife had pledged the husband's credit wherever she could, and all the little shops in the neighbourhood, down to the cellar where potherbs were sold, had occasion to bear her in remembrance. She is since dead, the husband has the eldest daughter keeping house for him, and the daughter has given birth, not long since, to a child, *said to be by her own father*! And further, in the same house where this degraded wretch now lives, may be found a brother who is said to cohabit with his own sister.[46]

At No. 3 resided a mechanic. He was a good workman, very expert at his business, worked 'piece-work,' and could earn a large sum of money in a short time. He was dirty and slovenly in his attire; his wife was the same; and the house presented a destitute appearance. The man scarcely ever went to work before Tuesday or Wednesday, at which time the earnings of the previous week would be squandered, and he was compelled to work in order that he might eat and drink; indeed, this latter seemed to be his principal support, and, as we have frequently heard him say, he 'lived on suction.' There was very little furniture in the house, and there appeared to be scarcely the necessaries of civilised life; pots and pans had to be borrowed to cook victuals for the family; yet this man earned more than many a hard-working shopkeeper who has to pay large rates and a double income tax! He could, if he liked, earn from £4 to £5 per week. This house was noted for women meeting to have a smoke. The place at times was reeking with the fumes of tobacco, and one of the neighbours – a tall, clean-looking woman, who lived in the next court, and who had a beautifully clean dwelling, and *cohabited with a man who had left his lawful wife* – might be seen frequently walking about smoking a long pipe.[47] The other smokers had a larger development of secretiveness, and enjoyed the 'weed' by the fireside, where, with the assistance of the 'half-gallons of fourpenny,' they traduced the character of all the neighbours who would not join them, and looked upon themselves 'as good as any of um, although we take our glass now and them.' The proprietor of this house left the neighbourhood for Sheffield, and we lost sight of him.

These people appeared to be totally indifferent respecting the education of their children. It cost them twopence per week to send a child to school, and this sum could not at all times be raised for such purpose. They could, however, muster funds every Monday to have a tea party at one or other of the three houses, to which friends from a distance would sometimes come to join them.[48] On these occasions there appeared no lack of meat or drink, and immediately after the arrival of each visitor *a little girl would be sent off to the grog shop for spirits.* She would return with the bottle carefully concealed by her apron, and was thus being early trained in habits of deceit, and accustomed to the use of ardent spirits. There was generally a great bustle to get all indications of the tea party cleared off before the time at which the husbands might be expected home – that is, supposing them to be at work – and the women separated with very loud protestations of friend-ship for each other. When 'my man' returned from labour there was a very poor meal for him, and even for this he would have to wait until the kettle boiled – the wife telling him the while 'as how Dick has been so cross there was no doing any good with him; and she was not able to get a thing done this afternoon.' In some instances we have known 'a little sup' to be saved for the husband, and this atoned for all the neglect; but more frequently the man saw his wife's condition, did not feel disposed to quarrel with or abuse her, and, therefore, lighting his short pipe, he left the house, and found solace in the well lighted room and comfortable fire at the jerry shop, where he could get 'tick.'

The fourth house was inhabited by a young man and his wife, who had the appearance of being recently married, and this was their first house. It presented to the most casual observer a striking contrast to the other three. The window, with a neat muslin blind attached, was clean; the steps were daily scoured; the centre of the floor was covered with a carpet, and the stair in like manner. There was not much furniture, but what there was had undergone a good cleaning and polishing. The grate was well blackleaded; the fire was clear; and the hearthstone was scrupulously white. A spirit of order, comfort, and cleanliness was in everything apparent. A few books on a small shelf, under which was an arm-chair, indicated how the young man spent his leisure hours; and the ball of blue yarn and knitting needles on the table showed how the young wife passed hers. This man earned 25s. per week, and no Saturday elapsed without some small addition being made to his household goods. His wife and himself went regularly to some place of worship on the Sabbath, and they seemed in no way to mix up with the neighbours. This man is now a master tradesman in the town. Sobriety, frugality, and earnest labour, on the part of himself and his wife, have constituted the main elements of their success.

To this court, thus inhabited, no scripture reader, town missionary, or minister ever came during many months that it was under notice. The parish doctor had to find his way there some-times, and minister to the wants and bodily woes of sick children and parents; but the spiritual necessities of the people were totally neglected. Yet the town mission was then, as now, in what is called active operation, but none of its agents ever came here. Not far from this place there was a house where a missionary held a weekly meeting. Being anxious to see what was the character of persons who attended these meetings, and the nature of the address they were called together to hear, we visited the house on several occa-sions, and have therefore been duly returned in the number of hearers. The missionary was a middle-aged man, of moderate ability. The number in attendance varied from fourteen to nineteen, and were chiefly women and children. They were in most cases of the humblest class, and many of them presented pictures of poverty and wretchedness. A few working men sometimes turned in, but these were rare exceptions. This missionary commenced the meeting by singing and prayer; he then read a portion of Scripture, and addressed the people in the way of explaining some particular passage. He appeared to have read 'Jenkyn on the Atonement' carefully, and his address evinced the correctness of his memory. We heard nothing of the blessing and dignity of labour, nothing of self-reliance and manly independence, nothing which would excite or stimulate any person present to adopt habits of domestic economy, but much that the poor people could not understand. The abstractions with which he attempted to grapple were, to our mind, very much out of place, and the earnest simplicity of the gospel narrative was completely lost sight of. 'Whether faith be a gift of God or a work of the Spirit' seemed to us a secondary, or, indeed, altogether an indifferent matter to these poor people. They had probably to struggle with poverty and pain, and needed consolation and encouragement to enable them to fight the 'battle of life.' They were exposed to trial and temptation, and needed succour and support. What would they gain in this direction from the 'straw-splitting' of theological dogmas? Let the ministers who take a deep interest in the moral, social, and religious well-being of the masses see well to this; and if it be found that some poor creatures are asking for the bread of life, care should be taken in every case that they are not presented with a stone.

We found at the conclusion of these meetings that tickets for food were being eagerly sought after. It is quite possible that persons may be induced to attend meetings of this character with a single eye to the loaves and fishes, and no doubt great caution and discrimination are exercised. We hope this is so now, because, as we shall have to show, cases have come under our immediate observation where the greatest imposition, deception, and hypocrisy had been practised.

It must be borne in mind that the inhabitants of this court all breathed a similar atmosphere, their houses were all similar in construction. They all drank the water from the red sandstone, only some of them adulterated it with other fluids. They had all ample means for maintaining themselves and their families in comparative comfort. Yet look at the contrast in their habits and home. What influences would have altered the dispositions or practices of these people?

12   An Oriel prospect

The Christmas Festivities appear to be in no way neglected or slighted in the region upon which we now enter, and the effect of them is seen after many days. No sooner had we turned out of Cherry-lane and entered Oriel-street, than the vegetable refuse, broken mugs, and filth of all sorts bore evidence that the people here, in the expressive language of Mr. J. L. Toole,[49] had been 'a-going it.' In all probability the sweepers had been in the street on this morning, yet here at noon the place bore no evidence of having been swept for a month, and on seeking for an explanation it was given, as the result of considerable experience and close observation, that 'about and after Christmas it was always the same.' In courts where the sun never penetrates, in alleys where pure air is unknown, in cellars where even daylight is carefully excluded, in garrets where the bare boards form table and bed – the spirit of Christmas, so far as feasting and jollity of a sort expresses it, never fails to reach. In many cases the people themselves bore testimony to this. People whom you could hardly suppose had ever been able to obtain a decent meal's meat, and who had barely sufficient clothing to cover their frames, pleaded the Christmas sprees as an excuse for their filthy condition. It would be all right in a little time, they would get into working order again soon, and then the courts and street would be kept in such condition as to merit commendation rather than reproof.

There are thirty courts in Oriel-street, and all built upon a very similar model, yet they vary very much in character and appearance. There could hardly be a more striking proof of the influence which one or two tidy women exert upon a whole colony than you find in this street. Indeed, each court may be said to have a distinctive peculiarity, caused by the attention which, more or less, is paid to the outward appearance of the houses, and class distinctions are as strongly marked, indeed, perhaps more strongly marked, than they will be found in any other class of society. The courts, particularly at the lower end of the street, on the left leading to Vauxhall-road, have the appearance of being built about the same time. The houses are small and very inconvenient, but the courts have mostly wide entrances, and are tolerably well flagged, the difference which they present in appearance now being clearly dependant upon the character of the people that reside in them. There are ten, and in some cases, eight houses in each court – five or four on each side, – and for the use of each court there is an open ashpit at the top, and a very small privy on each side of this. One may perhaps form some idea of the foulness of these places, before means were adopted for having them regularly inspected, when it is seen the nuisance that they still create notwithstanding the improvement that has been effected.

Sheer idleness in some cases, helplessness in other, and indifference in many, lead people to neglect the most obvious requirements for their own cleanliness and comfort. In more than one instance we came upon women who were making an attempt to clean up. The privies are cleaned in turns (or ought to be) by the residents in each court. But to see the way in which women set about it was to see how wretchedly ignorant many poor people are of the simplest work of a domestic character. In one case, where a court was horribly dirty, (not in Oriel-street,) and the person whose turn it was to clean the place was desired to turn out, what did she do? A boy was told to take the coffee kettle, without a spout, – the only domestic utensil that the house appeared to contain, – and this he began to fill with water from the tap in the court, and then souse it over the filthy court. In another case, where *the Sunday spree* and a drenching rain had caused an accumulation of slop and filth at the entrance to a privy, we found a woman hard at work cleaning this away, and this she was attempting to do by means of a little birch rod! It was not a besom, – never had been one. It was simply a halfpenny birch rod, well worn; and although she plied this vigorously, and had ample strength, she could make little way against the heaps of refuse and puddle. The stench the while, as she said, was 'nearly blinding her;' but at it she went with her little rod. One could not help but think, on looking around the place, that some one would surely turn out and lend this woman a good besom, a spade, a shovel, or a brush; but while we remained no one did so, and we left her hard at work. As she said, 'anyone as wanted to know what cleaning was should have that to do of a Monday'!

The first court that we entered in Oriel-street was No. 30. It is in a very dilapidated condition, and there are eight houses unlet. The public house at the corner of the street had the use of one of the houses in this court at one time, and there was a communication through; but we cannot say whether that is so now. This we can say, we don't remember to have seen houses anywhere in a more dilapidated condition, or houses that have been worse used. The roofs are all now leaking; and well they may be, for what with the pigeon fanciers breaking through the roofs to make traps, and using these traps on other occasions as means of escape for larger birds than pigeons,[50] there is no keeping roofs in repair. There is not a whole pane of glass in any of the windows, – hardly a whole frame. Every door shows marks of violence, and steps and flags have 'come in for a share of the ill usage. In some cases the skirting boards have been torn off for firewood, the handrails have been found extremely useful in case of 'a row,' and the boards have been known to be ripped from the floor when the exigencies of the housekeeper required that a pot should boil speedily and coals were not at hand. It is not at all likely that anyone would now think of putting these houses in repair: it would almost be cheaper to rebuild them. We were not surprised to find so many of these houses untenanted; but we were surprised to find what tenants there were *without water*. They had been in this position for three months. We have spoken with the agent on the subject, and he has an explanation to offer; but in meantime the people have to steal the water they want.

When the people here and in the next court, which is similar in character, were pouring out their complaints, – the evils they had to endure, the dreadful state of the houses, – it occurred to us to ask some of them why they remained in such wretched places, as, for a few pence more each week, which might be saved from the grog shop, they could get much better residences, and in a more healthy situation. One old woman stepped forward to reply. She had lived there a long time – we forget how many years; she had found friends and neighbours there; a neighbour was not to be met with in any place or every day, and it was not easy to leave a spot which she had known so long, and where, in sorrow or in joy, she had met with sympathetic hearts. She put the case in very homely language, in a most telling way, and her old eyes glistened as she gave utterance to words which were the natural language of the human heart. 'True for you, Biddy,' was the response; 'God's truth, you've spoken this day, if you never speak again,' and then, warmed by the old woman's burst of genuine feeling, others began to gush forth in expressions which showed what a dear, very dear thing *home* is, be it ever so humble.

Of course it was only fancy, or, at all events, imagination; but, when these women were giving utterance to the heartfelt love of home, and describing in a simple way the ties, yes, sacred ties, which bound them to this miserable plot of earth, the court looked better, their houses had a better light thrown upon them, and they and their children seemed to have manifested a stronger claim upon the consideration of any who can give them help. We may be told that these people are not by any means sober people. We may be told that their mode of life would not bear a strong daylight to be cast upon it. We may be assured that all hope of raising such by any or every sort of leverage is at an end, and they must just be left to their fate and allowed to bring up children to become worse than themselves – but we refuse to believe it. There is always hope whilst the love of home exists; and this little spark may be fanned into a flame that would light up a pathway by which, perchance, they could escape from the social and moral quagmire into which ignorance and idleness have cast them.

The fifteen courts on the left of Oriel-street contain 129 houses, and, averaging eight persons to each house, look what a colony this is. Then there are the front houses – two between each court, the little shops, and the cellars. A walk down one side of the street alone is instructive as to how people live. The courts at the lower end, near Cherry-lane, contain the most wretched people, and their household arrangements are of the most miserable description; and in several other courts evidence is given to the most casual visitor of the riotous character of the inhabitants. In some cases the landlords have placed wooden shutters inside the window frames, finding it useless to replace the glass panes. In other courts you find houses neatly kept, the conveniences clean, and the people altogether of a better class. The goods kept in the little shops convey a good idea of the class of people who frequent them. The courts on the other side of the street are more confined, and the people have here to contend with the smell of petroleum, which in Courts No. 7 and 9 is quite unbearable. There are some well known characters who seem to reside on this side of Oriel-street, and the female portion of the inhabitants are quite indifferent to a sense of shame, young girls vieing with married women as to who can be smartest in obscenity. There were men lounging about here who evidently didn't like to be looked at.

13 Marybone and further on

What are the Police Instructions respecting Stalls in the Street? People hear something about fruit stalls, from time to time, but what has Major Greig[51] or the Watch Committee to say about the 'fish stalls' in Marybone? 'None of 'em says nothing,' was the answer given last week near the corner of Maguire-street. But what has the Health Committee to say in its defence for allowing the people who reside at or near these street corner 'fish stalls' to inhale all day long the effluvia which they send forth? The stall-keepers are certainly cheerful and lively people, not particularly shy as to their opinions on passers-by or lookers-on, and their conversation is not checked in its rapid and sometimes turbulent flow by any of those obstructions which decency or propriety is apt, in other classes of life, to interpose. Perhaps the residents in the vicinity find their compensation in this, for it must vary the monotony of many a cheerless life, and furnish hints moral and educational to listen to the warmly sustained discussions which frequently arise on physiological subjects, but chiefly confined to the eyes and limbs of those who take part in the debates. But even this is a point on which there exists considerable difference of opinion, for whilst one resident of Marybone stoutly maintained that the 'Rows was nothing to the stink,' another declared that 'The stink licked the rows into *fits*.' We should like to hear from some active member of the Health Committee, – some man who does not confine himself to simply attending all the committee and sub-committees, but, in addition, goes round amongst the dens and rookeries of the town, quietly to see for himself, (such, for instance, as Mr. J. J. Stitt,)[52] – what he thinks about the 'fish stalls' in Marybone.

What is called 'fresh fish' may be met with chiefly about Midghall-street and Maguire-street. How fresh it is, the odour tells you. Sawney Pope-street seems to be devoted to salt and dried fish and greens. About eleven o'clock in the morning there is quite a market held here, and no more suggestive sight, as to the wretchedness which abides in this locality, could be met with than to see the poor people making their markets. Half-naked and shoeless women purchasing for a few pence the chief meal of the day, and yet withal there is a flow of wit amongst them, and little rills of humour come babbling by you, by which eyes are brightened up, and you see lithe forms trip away with apparent glee to miserable homes. The dried fish seems to create no nuisance, and very likely to have it so cheap and so near their homes is a convenience for the poor people; but as for the *fresh fish*, or, at least, what we saw of it, the further it was off anybody the better.

This much is passing. We were on a visit to the courts in St. Martin's-street, Blenheim-street, and Wright-street, and took the 'fish stalls' in our way. The courts in these streets are not so large, neither do they appear so confined and crowded as we find in other parts of the town; but there are to be found in them features which readily indicate the evils which are here nourished and brought up. The houses have all cellars, which at one time were inhabited. In many instances these are altogether closed now; in others they are used for storing and chopping chips, and have an entrance only from the outside. Where the cellars are closed the outside entrances should be filled up. A capital illustration of the beneficial effect of this may be seen in 'Duggan's-buildings.' The landlord has here filled up the cellars and the entrances, flagged the court, and done it well, and the place now forms a really clean and pleasant (so far as a court in such a street can be pleasant) playground for the children. But, in the majority of instances, the cellar entrances are open, and in many they are not even protected by railings. They are simply traps for the poor little children to fall into, and several instances were given us by parents of their children 'tumbling in and getting their limbs *bent*.' Beyond this, so long as these entrances are kept open, they form receptacles for all sorts of filth, which is moistened by the rain, and sends forth into the court and dwellings poisonous vapours. No one can attach a right idea to what is meant by 'all sorts of filth' in these courts but those who go in to look upon it, and no language could possibly convey any sense whatever of the evils to which, what may appear to many, the neglect of a very simple precaution gives rise. We see that, in London, an eminent physician has traced the rise of smallpox, which is now ravaging a portion of the city, to this cause:– Neglecting to remove 'decayed vegetable matter and all sorts of filth from amidst the crowded residences of the poor.' If the fever cases which we now hear so much of in Liverpool were traced to their sources, it is more than probable that some such 'simple matter' would be found to give rise to them.

There are two good reasons for filling up all these cellar entrances. First, on the ground of cleanliness; second, to protect the little children from being maimed, and, at the same time, furnishing them with a decent place before their parents' doors on which they might play; and surely the Health Committee will find time to ask some of their officers to inquire into this matter.

We made rather an unexpected discovery in the first court we entered. There were four houses in it, and it was very close and not very clean. Two of the houses appeared to be unlet, and one of the residents at the other side of the court said that they were unoccupied, but a loquacious little butcher's boy, who had followed us into the court, here interposed and said that his master rented the two houses and occupied them by *sausage manufacture*. The machine, which the boy described as 'a regular good 'un for chopping anything up,' was said to be in the cellar, but it was not in operation at this time and we had no opportunity of seeing it at work, but could very well understand the advantages which must arise both to sausage-makers, sausage-eaters, and all around, from having food prepared in such a well-contrived and excellently ventilated spot as these court houses. Of course, manufactories of this sort are all under the inspection of health officers, and of course the people at Cornwallis-street[53] know all about this sausage court, and of course the medical officer has been there many times. So of course no one need put themselves out of the way about it on the score of health. Certainly not. We simply refer to it in passing, and ask isn't it a sausage-machine in the right place?

Several of the courts were found to be in a very filthy and neglected state, and exhibited on the part of the people the most supreme indifference, if not contempt, for any species of outward cleansing. The excuses given in some cases were very sorrowful and in others very amusing. At one house we found that two children were lying dead, and the court and its conveniences were as filthy as could be conceived. A lanky man, in a navvy's garb, came out of the house, and in the coolest way explained that it was no use cleaning up until after they had the children 'put away,' for there would be a bit of stir on at the funeral, and a 'few friends would be coming up;' but when the festivity had been got through the place would be cleaned, as the women could then settle down to their work. In another case, where the woman who had neglected to take her turn in cleaning was met with, she gave as her reason, 'I was waiting until I got my dinner over. You have a better stomach than I have if you could go to work and clean such a spot as that before you had your dinner.' This was thought by the neighbours to be 'not bad,' and it was added, 'Leave Kit alone for shutting any one's tater trap.'

Before going into further details respecting the courts in this locality, we desire to call the special attention of all concerned to the condition of No. 7 Court, Blenheim-street. There are here two privies, with ashpits, at the top of the court, and the wall of a large biscuit manufactory adjoins them. The smell from these places is most foul and sickening. We were at a loss to account for the great difference in the air of the court compared with others of similar construction in the same street. A woman, with greenish complexion and unhealthy aspect, who lived in one of the houses adjoining the privy, soon explained it. *The boiler of the biscuit factory is close to the ashpit and privy wall, and the heat from this must keep the filth in a state of constant fermentation.* Beyond this, the woman said that at times the steam from the engine came through the wall into her cellar, filling her house with foul vapour, so that she could not see, and driving her into the street to obtain air to breathe. She said that she had been to the biscuit factory to complain about it, but could get no satisfaction but that it was 'all good for trade.' She professes to have spoken to the police all to no effect, and she asks very properly, 'Am I and my children to be stifled and poisoned by inches, in a Christian land, without anyone lifting up a hand against it?'

We do not intend to add one word to this poor woman's question. It is startling in its simplicity and earnestness. We would like it to ring restlessly in the ears of every member of the Health Committee, demanding a reply.

14   Driven from home

Some people who have read much, and talked a great deal more, are inclined to doubt the statement, that thousands of working men are driven from their homes to the grog shop or beer-house, by reason of the inconsideration, ignorance, slovenly conduct, or slatternly habits of their wives. 'A man should be the master of his own house,' say they, 'and should order all aright! If this were done, houses would assume a different aspect, wives would be more like what they ought to be, and children would be better cared for.'

It is idle – a waste of time and means – to argue with such philosophers. They are wise in their own conceit, and never have spent an hour in a working man's house; least of all have they 'lived his life.' But there is another class, a more hopeful band of men, who, although they mix with the mighty ones, are not of them. These are 'the salt' of Social Science Associations. They will listen to facts, will weigh evidence, will exercise judgment, and seeing what intricate and paradoxical matters they are dealing with, will not rush to conclusions – for such men we submit *facts* in support of the statement that working men, in thousands of cases, are driven from home to drink, or worse, by the conduct of their wives.

Here is a street or court of modern houses. Externally or internally so far as their construction is concerned, there is nothing about them to prevent their being neat, clean, cheerful dwellings. If the construction of the house influenced the habits of the inmates anything approaching to the extent many suppose, the people hereabouts ought to be models of industry, frugality, and cleanliness. Take one house as a sample, and what is found?

A working man returns from his labour in the evening. He has walked a mile and a half to reach his home. He finds his children playing about the door, and his wife out. The alarm is sounded that 'father has come,' and the wife bustles up the steps to meet and return with compound interest her husband's frowns. The children have been playing indoors until they were tired – have thoroughly upset the house. There is no sort of preparation made for the husband's reception, and hardly a decent chair for him to sit down upon. He looks upon a cheerless fire, an unswept hearth; a few half-washed rags are dangling from a line, and unwashed crockery is on the table, or under it. The wife bustles about, knocks the child out of her way, and makes a show of work. The other children are just now turning in from the street, dirty and hungry. The cupboard door is open, displaying broken cups and plates, with gaudy floral patterns – the flowers all green, the leaves red and yellow. There, too, is seen half a loaf of what is termed 'bought bread' (as if all other were stolen); and as there is a chair near the cupboard, a little urchin mounts this, lays hands on the loaf, and helps himself, or may be said to 'dig into it like a two-year old.' The man waits patiently until his meal is prepared. He partakes of it, and is not pleasant or communicative during what is usually considered the most social repast. It is with great difficulty that he speaks civilly to the children, and in half an hour he is seen to go out of the house, smoking his pipe as he passes down the street to join other men in like affliction at the beer-house!

The man now spoken of is the type of a large and, it is much to be regretted, rapidly increasing class. And can it be wondered that such men leave home and seek elsewhere for that which is here denied them? Not at all. Here the wife has such a poor perception of her duty that she does not even know how to take care of her house. There is nothing joyous, nothing cheerful, nothing inviting about wife or house to keep the man in it, where he might enjoy himself by his own fireside, free from all temptation. The wife is given up to filth, and nurses her children in it, and forfeits all claim upon the favour or affection of the man. The powerful influence of a neatly kept and orderly conducted house upon a man's life and conduct this woman never could have seen or known. What is the consequence? The man is driven to drink – he and his wife quarrel – the children are neglected, morally and physically. Will our good brother on the Social Science platform say what he would do with such a wife as this?

But we have spoken of what this working man sees at home, and will now speak of what he does not see, but what many know he might see every day. He turns out to work at half-past five in the morning, and trudges through the streets with his coffee can in his hand, and his bread in a small, not very clean, check bag, under his arm. At the time when he is sitting down to his breakfast (his table being the stone he is engaged in hewing), his wife has not risen from bed. The children have been astir since father left home. Some of them are roaming about the house in their night clothes, not being able to find their day clothes, or not being able to dress themselves if they could. The half-past eight bell rings. Then the mother begins to stir herself. The children ought to have had their food prepared, and ought to have been on their way to school. Now there is no time for anything of the sort; there would have been no fire made, but the husband is one of those good-natured, considerate men, who always makes the fire before he goes out. There is no time to wash the boy; no time to make the girl's hair tidy; no, nor even to tie her frock. A slice of bread, with treacle daubed over it, is placed in the child's hand, and it is sent off to school, and has there to endure the chidings of the teacher for what it must know and feel to be the mother's neglect.

Well, having got her children off to school in such a fashion, mother sits down to get her own breakfast; and then she has the whole forenoon at her disposal, in which she does her house work. Does she do it? Does she set to work in earnest to try and improve the appearance of her house? Does she try to put a different face on her door step? Does she displace that dirty and ragged window blind? Does she even wash up her breakfast things, sweep her floor, put her chairs square, or give them a touch of her furniture brush? Does she clean her grate, whiten her hearthstone and give brightness to her fireplace? Does she sit down and mend her children's clothes? or, having done any of these, does she get her knitting out and try to get a little stocking off the needles, to surprise her husband on his return to meals? She does nothing of the sort; she is altogether indifferent to the discharge of household duties – has never been trained to them, has no love for them, takes no pride in them, and wishes the 'bothering house' was far enough.

With a *housewife* of this class the children are a difficulty; they interfere with what she considers her enjoyment. Accordingly, those of them who do not attend school are told in very expressive terms, and not in a mild or endearing manner – 'Now, you childer, be off out and play,' which simply means this – go and dabble in the gutter; go and make mud pies in the street; go and take your chance of being run over by a cart; go and try and pick up seeds of consumption; go and profit by what you see around the gin-shop door; go and learn to curse and swear, to lie and steal, as other children turned on the street by the disgraceful habits of their parents have to do. Having got rid of the children who are able to run about, and having almost shaken the life out of her infant, at the same time telling it to '*hould yer noise*,' she will wander off into a neighbour's house to jangle, or a neighbour will come into hers, and one or two more will soon turn up, until quite a little congregation is formed.

There are no remarks made on any neighbours who don't join in this sort of thing. Oh dear, no! If one woman in a court or street is bent on keeping herself to herself, – to use the common expression, – or is bent on keeping her house clean, and her children out of the streets, she is not called 'proud' or 'stuck-up' or a 'touch-me-not.' Oh dear, no! There are no remarks made as to how her clothes are obtained, or what she was 'afor she came here.' Oh dear, no! These comfortable morning meetings never entertain subjects of this nature. There is something else to do at them; and they are held very regularly, until a brawl takes place in consequence of Mrs. Topping telling Mrs. Nipper that Mrs. Quick's last shawl was obtained from the Scotchman! 'And there are some people, she will not mention names, as think Mrs. Quick is no better nor she ought to be.' This, being retailed, and having, by every hand it passes through, the retailer's profit added, becomes a very serious affair; and the disgraceful brawls which we meet in streets and courts are the result of such a state of household management and habits of life as have been described.

But how is it with wives of this sort whose husbands come home to dinner? If the wife gets through her scandal-mongering visits before eleven o'clock, she is considered to have been pretty smart – may be congratulated on having done a very fair morning's work; and has therefore ample time to look after the preparation of her husband's dinner. It will be interesting to see how she sets about this.

Look at that woman – a modern housewife – crossing the street. She has an old dingy shawl thrown over her head; this is held together by her teeth, and is made to answer the double purpose of a bonnet and to cover her ragged dress. Her gown is open at the back, having only one pair of hooks and eyes to hold it; and, as Paddy would say, 'that pair is odd ones.' With her old shoes down at the heels, and her stockings exhibiting such an excellent mode of ventilation that wicked boys cry out, 'Missus! how are you off for potatoes?' – with a few coppers in one hand, and a little blue-edged plate in the other, slip-slop, slip-slop, there she goes. What a spectacle is this of an English housewife going to market in this age of progress! Notice her conduct at the butcher's shop. That large dish, on which are displayed all the little offcuts, outside bits, jagged ends, or withered chops of meat, is what she sets her eyes upon. How she pinches the pieces with her not over-scrupulously clean fingers, as if she was such a good judge of flesh meat. How she turns over piece after piece; and then, having made a selection, how she will higgle with the butcher as to price. The butcher, however, in most cases, is very independent. He seems well acquainted with his customers; and the stinging remarks which he not unfrequently makes to wives of this class, one would think, ought to force them to form different habits of life, if only they might escape his scalding sarcasms. But this modern housewife is not easily disturbed; and she can, as she expresses it, 'mostly in a general way speak for herself.' She can give the butcher full change for anything he sends; and employs herself in doing so, whilst fumbling in her pocket for the few coppers to pay for her 'plate of bits.' Then she has potatoes to look for, and there is another higgle and delay with the woman in the cellar; then there is the cooking to be entered upon; – all of which creates confusion of an indescribable character. Her cooking utensils are of the most meagre description; and if she have, by jangling, tale-bearing, gin-drinking at tea, or quarrelling about her children, closed the doors against her where she used to borrow a saucepan or a frying pan, she will have nothing left but the tin kettle and the penny gridiron to fall back upon. Not once or twice, but four out of six days, during several weeks, the writer has seen working men at noon sitting down to burnt bits of meat and badly cooked potatoes – the table without covering – the plates all sorts and sizes – only one knife and fork for the family; and such a want of common decency, such an absence of tidiness about wife, children, and house, that it is surprising how men can endure or women can allow their houses to fall into such a miserable condition.

The way in which these wives spend their afternoons is still more instructive, because it shews, – what those who will not or do not mingle with the people can never rightly see, – how the money goes, and why thousands of hard-working men in constant employment are continually upon the verge of pauperism. Look at it as one will, afternoons spent in a court of houses exhibits a very appalling picture of an English home. The wife will not have time to wash up what few dinner dishes have been used, for no sooner has the husband left the house than the wife is at the next door, or swaying about at the court end. If she have a daughter grown up, the child will be left to 'clean up' as it best can, the mother being engaged in making arrangements to spend the afternoon. There will be quite a commotion in the court as tea-time approaches. A party has been arranged, relishes have been sent for, and, if needs be, clothes have been pawned to obtain them. It is not unusual for the visitors at these court parties to furnish their own tea-cups, the house where the entertainment is given not being able to boast of any superfluous stock of tea things. In one case that we enquired into there was a very unpleasant interruption to a tea party. The husband came in sooner than was expected; and finding a good display of earthenware, and several women in a state of excitement, he set to work and made what he called a 'gravel walk with the mugs,' and in his rage converted his wife and some of her friends into the garden rollers. We often hear of such cases; but the cause is not given. Not long since, the public were told of a working man going home one afternoon and throwing what was termed 'a washing mug' against the window of his house, smashing it to atoms. This was a stupid act; but look at the cause. Why did he do this? It was Friday afternoon. He had gone home early, expecting something to be ready for him, but found his wife was out. One of his children was there, crying. It wanted food, it wanted washing, it wanted clothing. He wanted some of these too; and worked hard, hoping, week after week, as he said, 'that Nan would come round,' and help to get them. He saw by the side of the door, and under the window of his house, the large 'washing mug,' containing clothes. He had seen this for two days before just in the same place. Driven to desperation by the negligence of his wife; feeling that, whatever he did, his home could not be more miserable; reckless of consequences, and blinded with the intensity of his mental anguish – he smashed his window, thus adding fuel to the fire of his embarrassment.

Let us now shew what effect such domestic infelicity, such slovenly houses, such reckless lives of parents have upon children. This cannot be estimated; least of all should it be overlooked. Strange as it may seem, however, this is practically lost sight of by men who are working earnestly to improve the education, and, as a necessary consequence, the social condition, of the people. The sectional divisions of Philanthropy have something to do with this. Each section erects a standard; men rally round this, fight under it, and believe that their cause in not only above or in advance of any other, but that it is the particular cause destined to triumph, and all others might as well be left unheeded.

Take one section as an instance – that of Education, or School-training. No one can deny the benefits which this confers; no one can deny the zealous labour bestowed upon it. But if men begin to think that the school can do everything that is necessary for the poor man's child, as too many do, and are led to overlook the influence of home and its associations upon the growing mind, they set facts at nought.

Whilst feeling grateful for all that is being done for the scholastic training of the labouring man's child, we would urge on the attention of those in authority the necessity of looking to *home*. There it is where the character is formed. The lessons given there are never lost. And it is vain to expect children to be orderly or virtuous when the lesson of the school is practically denied by the conduct of the parents at home. Here is a case from every-day life – one which any reader, without much trouble, may verify for himself:-

A well-educated, intelligent mechanic, in whom his employer felt an interest, and whose welfare he was anxious to promote, had neglected to attend his employment. This had occurred several times, and generally on Monday or Tuesday. The employer was not willing to attribute this to the intemperate habits of the man. He had no reason for suspecting anything of the sort; therefore thought the best way would be to visit the workman's home, and learn what prevented him attending to his duties. It was noon on Monday when this visit was paid. The house was one of a long row, such as are inhabited by the better class of artizans – such houses as have, so far as construction and surrounding circumstances are concerned, nothing to prevent them being made comfortable dwellings. The door was opened by a little girl, a weak-eyed, ill-clad, neglected little creature, but intelligent for her years. Mother was not in. Father, the child supposed, had gone to work, but she had not seen him that day. The house was indifferently furnished, and what good articles of use or ornament were in it were in a dirty state. The floor bore evidence of a recent conflict; dishes or plates having been objects of special vengeance, the remains were scattered about, and the younger children were amusing themselves with the fragments. It was desirable that the mother should be seen in order to learn something of the father. 'Could mother be brought soon?' 'Oh, yes; she had only just gone into the next house.'

The child was sent for her, and almost immediately 'mother' made her appearance. She was in slovenly attire, and slightly intoxicated. The account she gave, in answer to enquiries, was, that she had not seen her husband since morning; did not know when he might be found at home; and, unless he came home better-tempered, did not care. The question was put as to whether the man could be seen if a call were made in the evening. Now, mark the reply. 'It's of no use you calling here in the evening; there will be no one in, for I always go to theatre on Monday night!' 'But do you take your children to the theatre?' 'Well, as you must know every-thing, I always take the youngest with me, and put the others to bed.' Further enquiries respecting this case, and conversation with the father, whose youngest child spent Monday evenings in the gallery of a minor theatre, revealed the fact that his home was a fair sample of twenty homes in the same street. For years the man had struggled to try and bring about a better state of things at home, but his wife's habits, strengthened and confirmed by evil companionship, could not be conquered by anything he did. Although earning good wages, he was continually in debt, and had to wear such clothes as made him almost ashamed to mingle in the society he had been used to. His neglect of work was occasioned, in the first instance, by the domestic broils consequent upon his wife's conduct. As he said, what heart had he to continue earnest in labour when he saw the result of it – the wages squandered – his home comforts set at nought – his children allowed to pine in hunger and wretchedness – he himself to be involved in debt by the deceit and treachery of her who ought to have been his helpmate. On one occasion, after taking home thirty-five shillings on Saturday, he found, on Monday at noon, his house taken possession of by bailiffs, for rent. At the same time the rent book, which his wife laid before him, showed that the amounts had been regularly paid. Then it was that the discovery was made (no uncommon practice amongst women of this class) which proved the book to be a forgery, skilfully executed by some of his wife's designing neighbours and friends. The landlord's rent book showed that, for some time, week after week, his wife had been encroaching on the 'rent money,' and thus had allowed 'arrears' to accumulate, in order to enable her to gratify her depraved tastes. What could this state of things result in? Just what is usual, what is *well known*, to the sorrow of many working men. The man's spirit sank within him – he was driven eventually to drink – pursued a reckless course, and is now sinking rapidly – has lost his situation and character for industry, and he will ere long, in all probability, fill a pauper's grave, and his family, what of them remain, will have to be supported by the ratepayers.

This man did not latterly treat his wife with any kindness – he displayed no affection towards her – they quarrelled – he abused her – she would have the last word, and perhaps he gave her the first blow. But what was the cause of their quarrel? Untidiness, extravagance, utter disregard to his comfort. Where a woman has lost that on which she is so foolish to rely, beauty of person – when she has not art to soothe, or sense to console or encourage man – when she is found to be totally destitute of that practical wisdom, sometimes called tact, which can invent a thousand little arts to supply her deficiency in beauty or in style, and so maintain her balance of power – when the dashing young girl from the dancing class becomes the wife and mother, and has nothing to support her but the lessons she is likely to have learnt at these iniquitous places of resort – need we wonder at the homes many working men have? When any man reflects on the scenes of his early life, and accustoms himself to think of the many trivial acts constantly repeated, how they impressed themselves upon his mind, and led to the formation of ideas and opinions which have had something to do with his life ever since, what can he expect from children who daily witness the scenes which such a home presents? That which could reasonably be expected is found. Would that all working men, and all those interested in the welfare of working men, would ponder it.

A few years roll on – behold the change. Look at the Criminal Court, St. George's Hall. There, in the dock, stands a young girl, pale, blear-eyed, her whole frame tremulous with emotion, tears streaming down her cheeks, and loud sobs breaking forth as the peril of her position burst upon her. By her side is a broad-set man, with dark cropped hair, large coarse features, and of a forbidding aspect. His dark restless eyes, at length attracted from the witnesses, the jury, the bench, now fall upon the miserable girl. He takes hold of her ragged dress, and giving it a twitch, says audibly, 'Drop it; blubbering'll do you no good.'

Here is the daughter of the mechanic and his slatternly wife, charged with pocket picking! The girl (who has seen nothing at home to prepare for domestic service) has been 'sent to place.' She was soon discharged. She was then sent to clean up at a public house, and was turned away from that. Place after place (such as they were) her mother obtained for her, but she was not allowed, or did not feel disposed, to stay. The mother then began to treat her with greater indifference, almost with cruelty. She was driven from home, was glad to get anywhere to escape from the drudgery of labour which she had never been taught to love, soon found companionship, the result of which was that in three months she stands in the felon's dock, associated with a man deeply died in vice, on a charge of pocket-picking.

But look behind the dock – in the gallery. There, standing close up to the stout iron rail, is a woman without a bonnet, her bloated face plunged at intervals into the folds of a dirty and tattered shawl. How she groans and clutches her hands, as if in deep mental agony. That is the slatternly wife! – the mother of the trembling creature in the dock! She who had neglected the child, yes, driven the girl from home, and is now waiting to hear her wretched doom. Does she feel the full force of her responsibility – Does she even obtain a glimpse at the part she has played in her daughter's ruin? It is hard to say. This much is known – her daughter is acquitted, and mother and daughter are seen soon after in the crowded compartment of a gin palace!

Now let us look at the influence of ill-conducted homes from another point of view.

Most people who pass by or have occasion to visit the markets on Wednesday or Saturday mornings cannot fail to notice the number of boys, – wolfish, sharp-visaged little fellows, in tatters, – that hover about the vegetable carts and standings. Under carts – dodging around casks of apples – craftily sneaking by women who are bargaining – singing 'Dixie's Land' for a hunch of bread – or snatching a carrot from a heap, and running into a bye-street to gnaw it – now in the hands of a stall-keeper, and frequently in the hands of the police, chased, hunted, worried – these neglected children, disguise it as we may, are throughout all this pursuing a most effective educational course.

Comparatively few of these little fellows take to this mode of life from choice – they are driven to it. It will surprise many, but it is nevertheless true, that a large proportion of these boys are the sons of working men whose earnings are something considerable; at all events, are such as, if properly expended, would keep their children from prowling about the street in search of food, and exposed to all the evils of the criminal class, with which, under such circumstances, they are sure to be thrown in contact.

In many cases, indeed in most, the father knows nothing whatever about the mode of life of his son; least of all does he expect that the lad is being trained in thievery. An illustration will make this matter clear to the reader.

You see that little boy at the corner of Rathbone Street, in Nile Street. He is capless, shoeless; his legs look raw with the cold, and his eyes are sore from bad air and neglect. He is with three other boys about his own age, all in rags, all hungry, all looking for something to eat. It is now eight o'clock on Saturday morning. The boy has not tasted food since yesterday at noon. His father left home this morning, between five and six o'clock, to go to his work, and soon after this the boy, pressed on by the gnawings of hunger, crept down stairs and out of the house, and here he is, with companions in misery, looking out for breakfast. A carrot, or a turnip, is greedily devoured. Whether it be begged or stolen, there is little difference in the taste. He goes on to the steps of the spirit vaults to eat what one of his companions has laid hands upon; and whilst there – whilst crouching and drawing his limbs up off the flags for warmth – a stout 'market woman,' passing out of the vaults with a jug of smoking liquor in her hands, treads, not by any means lightly, upon the boy's foot; and when in agony he cries out, she 'scufts him' for being in the way. He goes up Back Parliament-street limping and crying; and is there met by a 'Home Missionary,' whose heart is touched, and whose sympathy is excited by the boy's woes.

This boy is the son of a man who is in current employment at a forge, and he has been there for years. His home is one of four small houses in a court in B_____ street, and a more wretched abode it would be difficult to conceive. The windows are broken, the floor has hardly ever been washed; there is no article of furniture to be seen except a small oblong table with thin legs – not even a stool or a chair. The fireplace is tumbling down, and the mantelpiece has been smashed. The walls are streaked and smeared with dirt; and yet hereon hang two portraits – two coloured prints – 'Tom Sayers' and 'J. C. Heenan,' in fighting costume and attitude.

The boy's mother, with an infant at her breast, is seated upon a broken box. She is repulsive in appearance; and has no garments to cover her but a bedgown, which was originally white, and a striped petticoat. She has on neither shoes nor stockings. She seems in no way humiliated – does not feel the degradation of her position. 'A working man's wages are not much,' she says, 'even if one got them all; and when one does not get half of them, what can you expect?'

This, then, is the state of things here. The husband spends his evenings from home, does not bring more than half his earnings to his wife. She cannot manage to make the money procure food for the family all the week, and on Friday and Saturday 'all hands have to go short.' Hence it is the son takes to the streets; and, so that he or the other children are not about her asking or crying for food, the mother seems to care very little where they are. Some weeks the boy gets school wages, and is sent to school. More frequently the small sum cannot be spared; so it comes about that the boy falls into the hands of other teachers than those certified by the Board of Education.

It is every way much to be regretted that this is by no means an exceptional case. Ask those whose business it is to mix with the working population, and they will tell you that such homes are very common; and then you will hear them launch out in railing against the improvidence of the people. But, before condemning the father, hear his case. Who would, if they could help it, stay in a home where there was not a chair to sit upon, and where, as the man says, 'you'd have to lie on the floor to take your smoke!' When the man did take more money home than he does now, his domestic comfort was no better cared for; and what simple articles of furniture he had brought about him at one time, were soon smashed by his wife's carelessness, or disposed of to supply her with drink. Remonstrance with her was of no avail, and generally led to quarrelling; and, as was ever likely, the man was thus *weaned* – nay, driven – from his home, quite as effectually as his son is driven to the streets.

Is there not every inducement held out to a man, thus circumstanced, to spend his evenings in the beer-house or the vaults? That the man is not a thorough drunkard, is proved by his keeping his situation so long. He wants warmth, light, and cheerful company when he leaves his work; and he can have none of these at home, as he says, 'no, not if I was to take home three pounds a week, I couldn't have um!' What is he to do? Who can help him?

There is every probability that some of this man's children will work their way into the felon's dock. The father may be called upon to support his son in a reformatory – may be compelled to do this whilst writhing under the stigma cast upon him by circumstances which he feels himself so powerless to prevent. It may be said, 'Surely the father might know how his children spend their time,' but acquaintance with the habits of working people proves that it is the mother who is in reality the chief guardian – has the full control – has the formation of habits and character left to her. It can hardly be otherwise. Perhaps in the main it is right it should be so. Why, then, do our social philosophers roll forth such terrible thunders upon the heads of the fathers? Whilst in no way attempting to palliate the offences which many workmen commit against their wives, families, and, consequently, themselves, let the women be dealt with. The sympathy that is expressed for many 'poor things' simply adds fuel to the fire of their self-indulgence, and is perverted into an apology for their misbehaviour and gross ignorance. The women who really deserve sympathy seldom get it. They battle with their drunken husbands, keep their houses in order, and their children out of the streets; and their labours are unknown, even to many of their neighbours; and the 'Missionaries' never see occasion to 'report' such cases. Whilst there are many *bad* husbands – brutal, stony-hearted ruffians – there are others who would be both *good* husbands and good fathers; but they are driven from home – driven to drink – driven to 'scoundrelism' – and their *children* driven to crime, by their slatternly wives.

15 Smothering children

Murder must foul, as in the best it is:
But this most foul, strange, and unnatural!

In Liverpool, for the year ending June 30th, 1862, inquests were held on eighty-one smothered children! A very large proportion of these were slain on Saturday evenings or Sunday mornings; and many people wonder how this could be done. We will lift the veil.

Look at that labourer's home. It is in a court; the top house on the left, adjoining the cesspool. It is Saturday evening. There has been an attempt made to 'clean up.' The centre of the floor has been brushed – the cinders have been partially removed from beneath the grate. There is a basket on the floor, near the fire-place – a clothes basket – and apparently a bundle of clothes in it. This has been moved from place to place by the housewife as the process of 'cleaning up' has been going on. Now that this business is over, the basket is placed in a nice 'warm corner.'

The door opens, and in bounces a rough-spoken, slovenly woman.

'Well, Mrs. Peters; you've cleaned up in time! I've brought you the shilling you lent me on Tuesday; and there's a little drop of the right sort, by way of interest' (pulling out from her bosom a small bottle containing spirits).

'Ah dear, you're very good,' is the reply. 'I'll just put my lips to it: but I expect my chap home directly, and we're going to have a bit of a round to-night.' (Takes a swig at the bottle and coughs.)

'It's well to be you, Mrs. Peters, as can get out with your man. He sticks to you, he does, and teks things as they come. He's not alus snarling or sulking, like the fellow at our house. I often says to him, "You'd have something to snarl at if you had a few children yowling at your heels. How would you be if you was like Peters?" But, bless you, he cares nothing for my talk now. You'll hardly believe it, I dare say, but, as true as you are here, that nagur of mine just comes home, pitches the brass on the table, and cuts away to his cronies; he has hardly time to get a bit to eat, if there chances to be a bit ready; and it seems a trouble to come near the house at all. There's no taking me a-walking on Saturday night, nor any other night. So I comforts myself as I best can.'

She finishes what Mrs. Peters had left in the bottle, and takes herself off.

Immediately the husband, Jack Peters, arrives, and brings with him a fish. This is ordered to be cooked whilst he goes to be *scraped*. (Working men never speak of going to be shaved, they get a 'penny scrape;' beyond being very expressive, the term may be most truthful.) The children turn in from the street, now that their father has come home, and they are banged about, here and there, during the bustle of getting the fish cooked and the tea ready. One boy is knocked over, and nearly tumbles on to the basket of clothes in the 'warm corner.'

A weak cry from the basket, and a loud coarse exclamation from the mother follows, 'The devil is in you! I'll murder you. Do you see what you've done? You've wakened the child, and nearly crushed its life out, poor soul!' And she fumbles amongst the bundle of rags in the basket, and draws therefrom an infant, very red in the face and very loose about the neck too. The poor boy who had knocked into the basket is now kicked on to the stairs, and remains there sobbing and crying until father comes in, when all this has to be stifled, or there may, from the representation of the mother, be another 'hammering' for him.

The tea is soon got over, Jack, eating, as he says, with a will, now ejaculates, 'It's a denged good fish,' then handing a piece to one of his children, and again urging his wife to 'mek haste, or all our chaps will have been eased of their blunt.' The man is in a hurry to be off. The tea things are all left scattered about the table unwashed, and the children are told to 'mind and behave yourselves while I'm away, or you'll catch it.' The old shawl taken from the corner of the cellar door, where it has been hanging for days, is thrown over the shoulders of the mother, the infant is rolled up in wrappering, and taken in her arms, then covered with the shawl, and away the man and wife go to spend their Saturday evening.

'Where are you going, Jack?' the man is asked by a neighbour when he gets near the bottom of Mill Street. 'Oh, I'm only going to show my ould woman the best way into Gore Street,' is the reply; and with a sly laugh Jack Peters steps into the large vaults which have a back entrance in the street named; his wife carrying the child follows him, and they are in a moment in the midst of a crowd of men unshaved, and women untidy, all talking and drinking – a very Babel of tongues – one phase of the working man's Saturday night.[54]

Wife and husband have a drop of something warm. The child under the shawl seems uneasy, but Jack tells his wife to 'stop that music,' and the woman adjusts the infant's head and says,

'Whatever do you want?' She then sits down on the form in order
to 'make all snug.' A friend turns up. Well, really, who would have
thought of meeting him? This occasions delay, and another glass.
'It's not every day we kill a pig,' says the friend, 'so let's have
something on the strength of it.' The time passes very pleasantly.
Wife and husband are apparently free from all care. What laughing
there is amongst them and the friends they meet. What fun about
Jack's wife 'alus carting a child about with her.' This is borne very
good temperedly for awhile; and when the place 'is getting hot,'
they break away from the company, and the market is reached;
here purchases are made, and in Rathbone Street more treats are
given and partaken of with right good will.

They have now been out from home three hours. (What have
those little children been doing at home the while?) They think of
turning their steps homewards. They feel rather tired – do not look
so pleasantly at each other – indeed are somewhat inclined to 'sulk.'
They do not walk very sprightly, and that last treat which they took
– that conversation with the carpenter 'as used to live beside them'
– seems to have mystified them. The husband gets near home, and
then says, 'I'll go no further – you may go on. I'll just have my
nightcap with old Bob; ler us have hould of the basket. I'll have just
one drain, take the basket with me, and then come home.'

There is no mild or tender epithet applied to the husband now.
No! lisping out curses and threats, the wife crosses the street to
reach her home. It is very dark. In her efforts to gain the side path
she stumbles against the railing of one of the cellars. The force of
the blow dashes her off the footwalk, and she would roll into the
gutter, but is stopped by a friendly hand. The child cries piteously.

'That kid has nearly got a squelcher!' says a young fellow, who
is passing, to his companion.

'Aye,' was the reply, 'luk how she staggers; she'll put the stunners
on it afore long,' and he leads her towards the court end.

The mother, after many heavy lunges and slips, which threaten
destruction, arrives at her own door. Bang she goes against it. The
little children understand this, and run to open the door. The
mother, hot, surly, almost speechless, drops down upon the first
chair she can reach. 'Undo my shawl, you childer,' she stammers
out; that is all she can utter; her head sinks on her breast; her
infant has been allowed to roll into her lap; and the children, who
have been for hours awaiting the return of father and mother, now
do what they can to get the child quiet. Oh, how piercing are the
cries of that infant! and there is the mother, stupidly drunk, totally
unconscious of what surrounds her.

'There's a pin running into it, Billy,' says the little girl, 'it
wouldn't cry so for nothing.'

Poor Billy looks for the pin; how rudely he handles the little infant, to be sure.

'Its feet's cowld, that's it. Ger'em to the fire,' says the girl; and thus these children – infants only themselves – seek to comfort the suffering babe, all to no purpose.

To increase their alarm, the mother, what with the drink, combined with the closeness of the house, is now totally overcome, and falls from the chair, amidst the screams of infant and children. This brings in a neighbour – an old woman – who takes the infant, and sends the boy off for her husband.

'Here's Mrs. Peters in for it again. Jack and her have been off as usual,' says the old body to a huge man whom the little boy has brought. 'Take her up stairs and lay her on the bed, will you?'

'Well s'help me,' is the first ejaculation. Then the huge fellow lifts up the drunken mother as if she had been a child, and, after several 'spells,' carries her up to bed.

'This is rum work,' he says, after he has laid the drunken mother on what is called the bed, and has come down stairs, and is looking about him at the children in the miserable room below. 'That room is enough to choke a fellow. The smell in the place is as bad as the canal bank.'

'Didn't you open the window?' asks the old woman.

'Not I; I was too glad to ger out. Them as has beer aboard may stand it, but I couldn't, and I'll not stop here neither,' and away he goes.

The father not turning up, the old neighbour desires the children to get off to bed; and whilst they are doing this, she opens the window, and bathes the mother's temples with cold cloths, which restores her to partial consciousness. The infant has, at the recommendation of the mother, a sup of gin, or 'some of that cordial out of the cupboard,'[55] given to it, and is soothed; so much so, that it is laid on the bed besides the mother, and is quiet. No washing, no change of clothes. As it has been all day, half stifled sometimes, nearly choked or crushed to death at others, soiled and weary, but now very nearly at rest, there it lies!

When the father came home last night, or morning, neither mother, children, nor neighbours can tell. How he got to bed or when he cannot tell himself. The light of a Sabbath morning beams through the dirty striped blind of that bedroom window, and there is seen the father breathing heavily, the mother tossing nervously about, and a dead babe lying between them.

Will a verdict of 'accidental death' or 'overlain by its mother' be sufficient to atone for the death of this babe? Coroners may continue to talk twaddle – sapient jurymen may 'ask questions' – social science philosophers may read papers – and 'learned gentlemen' may blow each other's trumpets afterwards, but this smothering of infants will continue to increase, unless the terrors and majesty of the law be brought to bear upon it. The sooner people in this, and in all other matters, begin to call things by their right names, the more speedily will morality and honesty be promoted. To speak of the death of a child which has been smothered by a drunken parent as 'accidental,' is a prostitution of language.

It may, however, be desirable that 'smothering children' should be looked at from working people's point of view; and with that object we will notice a case which is not, unfortunately, an uncommon one as to its results, and it did not, perhaps, call forth in the mind of the 'general reader' any special subject of remark. But, during the inquiry, it did appear as if flashes of light were unconsciously thrown upon a comparatively obscure phase of humble life; and yet only just sufficient was revealed as to render further inquiry necessary, in order that the knowledge gained might be made useful.

An infant has been SMOTHERED! But there was a remarkable peculiarity about this case. The child was slain upon *Monday night*, and not on Saturday or Sunday, as is the usual fashion; and beyond this, there was a coolness exhibited by some who ought to have been deeply interested, which was well calculated to excite surprise, if not suspicion. In consequence of this, it was determined to sift the matter a little further, and, if nothing more could be gained, there would be some facts brought to light which might help go towards a solution of the question – 'How are so many children smothered by working people?'

Accordingly, means were adopted which produced the following narrative, from the lips of a woman who said she could 'tell all about it':

'I was just putting the dinner things away that Monday, and the children had *got off somewhere*, either to play or to school, I forget which, when Mrs. K., as lives in the top house in the court, came in, with her baby in her arms. "Mrs. B.," says she, "two or three of us have made it up to go out for a bit this afternoon. We have some shopping to do, and as it is fine we thought you might join us." You know we often do go out a bit the beginning of the week, afore our money is all gone – it's no use going after. Well, I said I didn't mind; but I hoped they weren't going far, because I had my child to carry, and it's getting big now, and heavy. (Look what legs it has on it – bless it!) Mrs. K. takes her drop, you know – not as I says anything against that, so as it's done in reason, and no one's the worse for it; nor not as I would say anything against her as a neighbour; but she does take it rather sweetly sometimes, and her husband and her has rows ever so many. He turns her out in the street – swears he'll be hung for her yet – and it's no wonder, when you know what a tongue she has. Not as I care to say anything against anybody, you know, although Mrs. K. didn't do what I'd ha' done, neither. But on this Monday she looked to me to be on the steady tack. She told me she had got all her husband's clothes out of pawn – that her husband and her and the children had been at Cheshire[56] the day before, all was made up; and, as you may be sure, I was very glad to hear all this; so I agreed to go out with them a-shopping.

'In about half an hour after we all set off. There was four of us out of our court, and we called in F_____ Street, at a friend's, to see if she would join us. The poor thing was not very well, and a man had just been in reading to her, and he had left her a tract, which was lying in the window. We were all very sorry to see how ill she luked, and had a bit of talk, to try and comfort her; but she coughed a deal, and didn't seem to heed us much. After a bit, Mrs. K., who alus was silly good-natured, starts up, and says she, "Well, it's a poor heart as never rejoices," says she, "and it's no use supping sorrow out of a wooden spoon; so I'll be my sixpence to any of yours, to get a drop of something to cheer Mary up a bit." Well, I didn't think it would do Mary any good, or perhaps I didn't think much about it; leastwise I didn't like to be thought stingy amongst my neighbours. It's not likely. If you have to live in Wiggin, you must do as Wiggin does – high life or low life is all the same for that. So I gave sixpence, and one of the childer – a good-sized girl, as was attending to her mother – went out to fetch in some gin.

'The poor sick woman had no heart to take any drink, but after a bit we sent out for some port wine for her, and she took some, and we were all getting quite comfortable, when a young man came to the door. He was very nicely dressed, a very pleasant spoken man, and I knew him in a moment; so did Mrs. K. He was 'the Scotchman'[57] as we both dealt with, and was surprised to see us here. However, now as we had met, and as we none of us was bad customers of his, he couldn't be off giving us a treat when he was asked for it. So with that he sent out for a drop of something short, and as Mrs. K. only owed him thirty-five shillings, and was paying off regularly at a shilling a week, she, while the girl was out for the drink, and we was all chaffing the young chap a bit, got a dress off him, at least, you know, she chose the pattern, and would send for the parcel to his shop. My husband had swore if I ever ordered anything from a 'Scotchman' again what he would do, or else I was very much inclined to have something, especially as the young fellow had been so kind, and had with him the nicest patterns as any of us ever seed. Besides, he made such enquiries about the woman as was sick, that he quite made up with all of us for any imperence which he had given us when we couldn't pay up. So we drunk his health, and told him we was only joking when we said we could get in London Road for fourteen shillings the very same shawls as he was charging us thirty-eight for. We had a real good bit of fun with him.

'When the "Scotchman" went away we got away too, and in Scotland-road we went into a shop and got ourselves a nice pie each; and while we were eating this Mrs. K.'s child was very restless, and got agate of crying. With that, says she, "Let's go up to our Hannah's; it's not far off, and she'll make us a cup of tea, and I can lay this noisy nagur down." She used to call her little lad a noisy nagur regularly. Well, thinks I, it isn't often I go out, and it's a long time since I've seen Mrs. K.'s sister, – not, I think, since she helped to lay out my little Dickey, – so I'll go. We went into a street off Soho-street – a kind of terrace place; but before we went up the steps Mrs. K. says to me, "We are all going there for our tea," says she, "and it's as little as we can do to take a drop of cream with us." "To be sure, by all means," says some of the other women, and we turned into a vaults – there's lots of 'em about – and got a bottle of gin. Four of us could hardly go into a vaults for one little bottle of gin, so we each of us had a glass of ale, and then we went up to the terrace. Mrs. K.'s sister Hannah was at home; but her husband had been drunk all Sunday, and they had a row because he wouldn't go to work on Monday morning without she gave him a shilling. Well, she gave him the shilling, and he went right off and got drunk again, and she had at this time in the afternoon just got him to bed. She wasn't in a very good humour; but she made us as welcome as she could, poor thing, and we got the fire made up, and soon had a goodish cup of tea.

'We had a good deal of pleasant talk about all the rows as we had ever been in with our husbands, all the illnesses we had gone through, all the shops we had ever dealt with, all the houses we had ever lived in, all the neighbours we had ever had, and all the shifts we had been put to to get bread; indeed, I can say without a word of a lie that we were very comfortable indeed at Hannah's. I had thought of getting my man a check shirt and some stockings when I came out, but my money was going; still, as I felt in a sort of a comfortable way, says I to myself, What's the odds? I knew that my man wouldn't be home afore eight or half-past, becos he had to call and pay his club money,[58] and I knew that if the children wanted anything they could get into the house; so we stayed on, and after a bit Hannah's husband came down stairs. He was very sleepy-looking, and very sulky at first, seeing such a lot of women and children; but Hannah had a good cup of tea ready for him, and a drop of gin in it, and he soon began to talk away with us quite free like.

'But I should have told you before this, as we was going up the steps to the terrace, Mrs. K. slipped a little bit on one side, and went bang down with her child, falling a'most right on top of it; and as the steps was very nasty and sharp, she grazed her shin bone, and cursed a great deal about it. The child cried a good deal at first; but when she got it into the house it went off into a kind of dose, and seemed as if heavy with sleep. We thought at first that the child's head was hurt; but it cried too hard for that!

'We had been sitting nearly an hour after tea, when Hannah's husband jumps up, and says he, "What's the piece at the Adelphi?" says he. None of us could tell. He then called a little boy off the terrace steps – I think it was his own little lad; – "Go and get me a bill of the Adelphi," says he, "and look sharp." The lad soon brought him the bill. "Aye, just the thing," says he, "Hannah, I'll have three penn'orth to-night; it's *The Spectre* _____!" something he called it – "a first-rate piece, and it a'most licks *The Colleen Bawn*. I'm off." "You're not going alone," says Hannah; "what have I done as I can't go to have my pleasure as well as you?" "All right," says he – "all come, if you like; I'll be glad of your company, if you bring your brass and your bottles with you."

'Well, two of the women said as they wouldn't go – they daren't go. They must get home, to get their husbands something to eat; though, as Mrs. K. said, for the matter of that, it wasn't one Monday night out of fifty as any of their chaps came home without calling at the public house to have a game or two at cards. Besides, we all knowed as one of their chaps had a dog in training, as he was going to fight; and if he did happen to get home early, he would rather be trying his dog's wind in the top room than luking after his tea. But, come what would, these women would not stop, and they would not go to the Adelphi. So there was no keeping them.

'Well, after a bit, Hannah got ready, and Mrs. K. got her child up, and we set off to the Adelphi. There was such a crowd in Christian Street. Hannah's husband got the bottle as we all gave something towards, and he got the money to pay for us all to the gallery, and so we crushed in amongst the crowd. I was afraid of my child, and had hard work to keep it from being squeezed quite flat; and how Mrs. K. got on I can hardly tell, for she was talking so fast, and had got agate of quarrelling with some young man as crushed her, and for a little while we were separated. However, we all got in, but when I got up in the gallery – oh! how my head did reel. The place was so hot, and everybody was so rough; I says to

Mrs. K., "You'll have to excuse me; I must get out; I'll be suffocated," and I began fairly to gasp for breath.

'I could see she was not in a very good humour; and I could see, too, as the drink was making her eyes roul about and her tongue to go very fast (indeed, I felt quite sick with what little I had taken, and how must she be?) She turned round on me quite sharp. "Mrs. B." says she, "you never was the kindest of neighbours, and you never was worth anything in a spree," says she; "you're a canting, Methodee humbug, as takes tracts in; and I suppose you think the Adelphi not good enough for you. Go in the boxes at Hengler's," says she, "and tek yer ould limping husband with you," says she. And she clapped her hands, and clapped 'em again, and put her child in Hannah's lap and clapped 'em again.

'It was no use talking to her there, else I could have given her the rounds of the kitchen, and polished her fender off too. Talking to me a that road – me, as had got her trust; as had gone for a note to the charity when her husband had left her; me as never said an unkind thing to her! My blood was up, but I saw there was no one there to back me up; and as all the people were enjoying her a jeering of me, I began to move away; and for all Hannah's husband tried to keep me, and tould Mrs. K. he would put the stunners on her if she didn't shut her trap, I crushed my way on to the landing, where I rested awhile, and then I got out of the theatre, left her to it, and made my way home.

'It is not for me to say, you know, what was done to the child, or how Mrs. K. got on in the theatre, or how many rows she had with other people there, or what she had to drink when she got out. It's not for me to say, either, for I don't know, what time of night she got home; but I heard some row in their house about two or three o'clock in the morning, as if her husband was either trying to get her up stairs or kicking her down; and it didn't surprise me a bit to be told the first thing in the morning that *Mrs K.'s child was found dead in bed*. There wus an inquess, of course, and they said it was a haccident! Very likely, indeed!'

Thus far the narrative. It will be left for every reader to draw his own conclusions. The pregnant facts are worthy of earnest consideration, by working people themselves, as well as by all those who wish to be useful to them, but don't know how.

But there yet remains one other case of child-smothering to quote; and this gives a still further insight into the habits of working people, and the sad indifference some women display to the health or life of their children. In this, the father, a tradesman, with his wife and her sister, leave home at eleven o'clock in the forenoon, and proceed to a public house, to spend the day in drinking. It is one of the 'race days,' and as evening approaches, the party make their way to a house in Scotland-road, in order that they may 'see the people coming back from the races.' This mother leaves at home an infant six weeks old, described as 'a fine healthy child.' It is in charge of a grown-up sister, who seems to have been tolerably well acquainted with the habits of her mother; for she is said to have taken the infant several times during the day and evening from *the house to the spirit vaults, where her mother was carousing, in order that it might be suckled.* It is eleven o'clock at night before father, mother, and aunt reach home; and then they are all in such a drunken state that they cannot be prevailed upon, have not power, to undress themselves; but all three lie down on one bed, just as they have rolled in from the public house!

The daughter is worn out by nursing the infant and looking after the other children (for the family is large), and at midnight she takes her baby sister into the room, and lays her beside her drunken mother and father. In the morning, soon after daybreak, the child is found dead. Blood is oozing from its mouth and nostrils, and an alarm is raised. The policeman is sought out; and he soon sees how matters stand, and questions the father. The lie is ready on this father's lips. He says that the child has been sickly from its birth; that it has been subject to convulsions; and that it has doubtless died during one of the attacks. The mother, bad as she is, does appear not to have had her conscience entirely seared; for she bursts out, on hearing the statement of her husband, 'It's no use telling any lies about it; the child was smothered:' and on the evidence being laid before a coroner's jury, they commit the woman for trial on a charge of manslaughter.

We are not surprised to learn, much as it is to be regretted, that the practice of smothering children is not confined to that class of life from which our illustrations are drawn. A recent writer in the *Athenaeum* seems to think that it is rife amongst the middle and upper classes; and, in effect, he defends infanticide in the lower class, because it is so prevalent in the others. After speaking of the mode in which children in middle or upper class life are killed by suffocation, this writer says, 'In many cases the event never reaches the ear of the coroner, the respectability and position of the parents satisfying the neighbours that there can be no need for a painful investigation . . . But, whatever course the affair may take, the parents meet with nothing but commiseration. They are prosperous – and therefore to be pitied. But let the external condition of the dead child's parents be the reverse of comfortable, and hideous suspicion forthwith takes the place of Christian charity. The young mother who, after ten weary hours of toil in factory, or with needle, or out charring, sinks supperless on a wretched bed, and, utterly overcome with physical exhaustion, unwittingly gives death to her month-old child, is nothing better than – an improved murderess.'

Now we do not, on the one hand, 'regard all the infants that are killed by accidental suffocation, or by being unintentionally overlain, as victims of deliberate murder;' neither, on the other hand, do we regard the mothers of these slain babes as entitled to special sympathy. We have seen, in our vagrant sheds at the workhouse, a mother with a babe at her breast sitting down to a miserable supper, which she had earned by grinding a certain quantity of corn; and the state of exhaustion and fatigue which the poor creature exhibited was such, that no one need have been surprised had she – when sleep fell heavily on her – overlain her babe. But the cases we have given differ altogether from this, and the circumstances of the parents admit of no such defence. The facts, so far as Liverpool is concerned, are against all who would seek to defend the smothering of children on the ground of the parents' 'physical exhaustion.'

Even in the case of the homeless vagrants who take refuge in the 'sheds,' the smothering of a child is of very rare occurrence; whilst, amongst all the cases which have been reported at the Coroner's Court, there has not been one in which such a defence as physical exhaustion on the part of the mother could have been set up with any show of reason or probability. What the cause of infant suffocation may be in other classes of life, it is not our purpose to enquire, but, so far as regards working people in Liverpool, it can safely be set down to the frightful prevalence of the vice of DRUNKENNESS.

Seeing that the law does not accept of drunkenness in palliation of any criminal offence, it is well calculated to excite surprise how it is admitted in defence of smothering children; and that it is so, the reports of the Coroner's Court daily prove. In the cases which we have given (which form a fair sample of the majority), the children's deaths can be fairly traced to the intemperate, vicious, or degrading habits of the parents; and all these appear either to result in or flow from the use of strong drink. Saturday night, when marketing; Monday, out shopping, or at the theatre; Thursday night, 'going to see the people come from the races;' drink begins in every instance what ends in the smothering of a child.

We are not hopeful that legal interference can mitigate or cure the evil habits of people as regards drinking, and would never care to see it tried; but we hold that men, or women either, may be led when they cannot be driven. They might be persuaded to alter their habits (and many are) if appealed to in the right spirit. Anything that will draw the mothers away from seeking their sole enjoyment in the revelry or 'spree,' of which drink constitutes the main element, will give them higher aims, and will prove the most effec-tual check to the smothering of children. But it is worth while thinking what is to be done to stay the plague in the meantime.

16   A bad servant manufactory

It is an admitted fact amongst a large class of people that Domestic Servants are difficult to meet with, and not much worth when obtained.[59] That they are dressy, idle, ignorant of household duties, impertinent, and inconsiderate, thousands are ready to prove; and recently a writer has gone so far as to say, that 'sixty per cent. are of the criminal class.' It will be evident to any observer, that a great change *for the worse* has taken place during the last twenty years; and this, notwithstanding the progress which education has made. But as there are two sides to this question of the degeneracy of domestic servants, and the public seldom see or hear of but one, it may be useful to endeavour to draw attention to the other.

Domestic servants are, in the main, the children of working men. They spring up and are trained in the working man's home. Those who know what these homes in too many cases are, and what fearful havoc drink has made amongst them – how fathers and mothers squander their earnings and neglect their families – will be at no loss to account for the degeneracy of domestic servants. People engaged in education, seeing how girls are neglected in household training, have endeavoured, in some cases, to impart at school what children should be trained to at home. But failure meets them at every step. Mothers are known to set their faces against the training of their children in what they term the 'drudgery' of domestic duties. A large class of mothers – the majority of working men's wives – know nothing of the dignity or value of this most womanly labour; is it then at all likely that their children ever can? But suppose that a girl has been in some measure trained at home; she can scour, clean up, perhaps wash after a fashion, and is able to 'drag children about.' A place must then be got for her. She is only 'in the way' at home; and if she has not formed the companionship of neighbour's children, who visit minor theatres, dancing saloons, or even worse places, she is more fortunate than might be expected. Her training at home, age, and inexperience disqualify her from entering the service of what is conventionally termed 'a gentleman's family;' and she will therefore be placed in a humble situation, hoping, if she be well disposed, to work her way up.

Now here begins the manufacture of *bad* domestic servants. The home training is not all that could be wished, but these *first places* to which girls are put give them a bend in the wrong direction; for 'as the twig is bent the tree's inclined.' An illustration from real life will show best what is meant.

You see that long row of houses at the outskirts of the town, with fancy bay windows and small grass plots in front. The Venetian blinds are supplied by the landlord; so are the gas fittings; so is that 'glass case' in the corner of the small parlour, in which are displayed pieces of Derbyshire spar and 'our china tea service.' The houses are inhabited by clerks – a draughtsman in a foundry, and several of what are usually called respectable mechanics. Our friend Smith (a very uncommon name, everybody knows him) lives in the second house on the left, that one with a plaster horse before the fanlight and over the door. He has not been married long, and this is his first house. His wife is a tradesman's daughter; she can read, write, knit, do crochet-work, sing, and dance. She is supposed to have some knowledge of dress-making – is said to have been brought up to *that*, but she had never been used to house-work. Smith never saw her do anything of a domestic character before marriage, 'except serving out the shrimps at a pic-nic which they attended in Eastham wood,' but he liked her style, has now married her, and has to keep a girl to do the house-work. To such a place is a poor girl generally sent, to begin her education as a domestic servant. This 'mistress' is one of that class of women whom you will continually hear complaining about the difficulty of getting decent girls.

The house is small, and there need not be much to do if either mistress or servant knew rightly what ought to be done; but they are both in a comparative state of blissful ignorance on the subject; and yet this mistress expects, and broadly proclaims her expectations, that, – because she gives the girl *Ninepence* or *One Shilling* per week, – 'considering the wages I give, the girl ought to do everything without any bother;' and simply because the mistress expects so much, and gets so little, there is quarrel after quarrel, fault-finding without end; the girl is driven without mercy, abused without stint, and eventually got rid of in a hurry.

Now, if this mistress were a housewife, and could train a girl – would have patience to show the child how to work, and the best method of arranging and getting through it, and the girl were, in the face of this, idle, inattentive, and slovenly, no one need be surprised at her being sent about her business; but Smith's wife is ignorant, overbearing, and displays towards the girl not even the common consideration due to her age and sex; and she is thus duly qualified to spoil a good girl and make a bad one worse.

Smith's ignorance on domestic matters is not so surprising, when it is considered that he admired his wife for the manner in which she 'served out the shrimps.' Still it is very amusing to listen to his woes about girls. He seems to have no notion that when he is detailing to you, as you walk down together in the morning, how there were no chips in the house to make the fire – no bread, or butter – and how he had to come out without his breakfast – that these things tell altogether *against his wife*, and not against the servant.

If a poor ill-clad girl was sent out amongst the neighbours on a cold morning 'to borrow a loaf, some eggs, and a slice or two of ham,' it would not surprise us to find that she who went a-borrowing came back sorrowing, because the bread, ham, and eggs were not. Yet Smith will detail to you experiences of this sort by the yard, and wind up by saying that servants are the pest of his life, and that he has no comfort or cleanliness in house by reason of them.

If Smith's wife understood the duties of an English housewife, a young, strong woman like she is, with time and opportunities for the proper management of her house, she would not bring in a poor girl to worry and scold. She would not feel it any disgrace to scour her own floor, or make her own bed, or clean her windows, or her door step; although she is a tradesman's wife, she would not disgrace either his name or his calling by going down on her knees to clean her grate or polish her fender. She would by such means secure sound refreshing sleep for herself, health for her offspring, and domestic happiness for her husband; instead of which she dawdles her time away – does not know what the real comforts and happiness of home consist of – keeps a girl – changes her every fortnight or three weeks – wastes her husband's earnings – and all for what? To keep up her 'position,' as it is termed.

There is meanness and snobbery in the class, socially, far above that now under consideration, but there is nothing so wretchedly shabby, so disgracefully mean, as the treatment which poor girls receive at places like our friend Smith's. Talk of the rich snubbing the poor – of the upper ten cutting a tea dealer or ship chandler – of a South American merchant's wife declining to meet with a cotton broker's – these matters can be well understood, and heartily laughed at; but the treatment which Smith's wife gives to her servants is far beneath all this. No woman, nor man, has a right to take any one beneath her or his roof in the capacity of servant, unless they have well weighed the deep responsibility resting upon them by reason of such a step. Yet, in cases innumerable, girls are taken in to slush and slave – to do the bidding of vain, ignorant, empty-headed, inconsiderate wives, who have never been taught, and never try, to control their hasty tempers; wives who are too proud to stoop to learn anything – to ignorant to teach – and who are the first to cry out, when their poor drudge at ninepence a week has left them, that domestic servants are the pest of their lives.

If a girl has the misfortune to get into such 'a sham' of a place as Smith's at first, what a false impression is made upon her mind. And is it not well known that Smith's is the type of a large, increasing class? The worship of 'appearances' leads thousands of young married couples to keep servants – to 'keep girls' – who have not proper means nor cultured judgment to be entrusted with the keeping of anything so sacred.[60] It may be said girls must go somewhere; they must have a beginning. True; but if working men brought up their children in cleanliness, industry, and thrift, they would as soon think of cutting off their right hand as allowing their daughters to go where such shabbiness, hypocrisy, and outside show were practised. Reckless or indifferent parents care not where their children go, so that they get rid of them; and it is because there are such multitudes of reckless parents, and thousands of dressy, idle, shallow-brained women, married to Smiths and Browns – it is because the girls are so rude and untutored, and their first mistresses are so lazy and ignorant, that the race of female servants has degenerated, and they are branded as the pests of the household.

17 How Jem Burns bought a new hat

Jem Burns is a bricklayer, and lives in one of the streets leading from Great Homer-street up to Everton. He has a wife and four children, of whom he is often heard to speak in high terms of praise. His house is not very well furnished, the articles being in every instance more useful than ornamental. Any attempt at show would be out of keeping with the man and his house, yet withal there is an air of comfort about both, which cleanliness and orderly habits on the part of the housekeeper are always sure to impart. Jem says that he finds it very hard work to live comfortably and pay his way out of his earnings, especially if the state of trade and broken weather be taken into consideration. A stranger listening to Jem's talk would be led to suppose that all the care of the household devolved upon him, and that his wife had no share in the business. But Jem does not stand alone in this particular. How many men there are who have clean houses, comfortable homes, and properly prepared meals, and who attribute all these advantages entirely to their own conduct. In the majority of such cases, if the truth were fully and unreservedly spoken, men could tell very little about how the home was managed. They earn wages, not as large as they would like, not as large as some whom they know, but they earn money by their labour; they take this home, and, some way or other, their wives keep everything in order, and they have a pleasant fireside to sit down at; and that is all they really know about household management. Jem's knowledge amounted to little more than this.

Jem's wife, Liddy, often hears her husband talking very largely as to the efforts he has made from time to time to pull through a bad or slack season with his family. If a friend calls in, and the conversations turns upon the state of work, or the price of provisions, or family matters, all of which are almost sure to turn up in an hour, Jem is pretty certain to launch out as to how he manages to 'keep all square and the wolf of poverty from the door.' With true womanly tact and sound judgment, Liddy never breaks in to contradict Jem or claim for herself any merit which is due. She knows Jem's temper, and would rather lead Jem to convict himself of the injustice that he does her than tamper with their domestic happiness, or assert her rights in such a way as would be certain to ensure a domestic broil.

Jem has on two or three occasions been entrusted with little commissions of a domestic character, and in every instance he has failed, – nay, more than this, to conceal his failure he has tried to deceive his wife. If, therefore, Liddy can (when Jem is showing off how very successfully he manages the house) get him to tell one of the instances in which he failed, her joy is complete, and she is amply avenged.

The other evening an old friend was smoking a pipe with Jem. The children had been put to bed, and Liddy was, as she terms it, busy in siding up and preparing for next day. There had been a good deal of talk about managing a house and buying things in on the part of Jem, and, by some sudden turn in the conversation, Hugh Stowell Brown's name arose.[61] This was just what Liddy desired.

'Jem,' said she, 'do you recollect buying your new hat to go to Mr. Brown's lectures?' and she laughed very roguishly.

'I should think I did,' replied Jem. 'Well, tell Frank about it. I could never tire of hearing it.'

And so Jem was led off into the recital, which had better be given in his own language as near as possible.

'Soon after I came to live in this house a printer came to live next door to me. I thought at first it was from bad habits, but I found out afterwards that it was from brisk trade, that he kept late hours. We hardly ever saw each other except it was on Sunday, and then I used to see him reading a paper at the door, for he always brought home lots of papers, and was good-natured about lending them. He was the first man that mentioned Stowell Brown's name to me, and asked me to come and hear him at the Concert-hall on a Sunday afternoon. I went with him one Sunday, and told Liddy all about the meeting when I came home. Woman-like, she asked me how the men were dressed, and all that sort of thing. I told her as well as I could, and then she said, "Well, Jem, you know if you go there you must go decent. You mustn't go with that old cap on; you must have a hat; it will make you look more like other men." I never was very particular about my dress, but it just struck me then that she was right about the hat, and, thinks I, some day I'll get one. But nothing would do for Liddy but the next Saturday night I must go down Scotland-road and buy myself a hat. "Don't give more than eight shillings," says she, "but I'll give you nine, and mind now, you lay the money well out, for I've been a long time saving it, and I intended it for something else; but never mind, it shall go for Stowell Brown."

'Well, you must understand that I hadn't been used to buying anything for several years. Liddy mostly got me whatever I wanted, but as I had never cared to stir from home much on Sunday, I had never got a decent hat, so here I was off to buy one. When I got to the corner of Great Nelson-street, who should I meet but Tom Johnson, and he seemed in very poor feather. "How goes it Tom?" says I. "Very queer," says he; and then he told me how there had been a strike in their trade, how he was out, and what a trifle he had to live on. He was going then to "a house of call"[62] to look after some subscriptions, and he asked me to come along with him a bit. We hadn't seen each other for a long time, so I went with him. The "house of call" was somewhere close on Marybone, and when we got in, there was a lot of chaps singing and drinking. I wasn't a teetotaller, so we sat down and had a gill of ale each, and then a man came in with a petition for subscriptions to bury a child. None of us could well stand against that, especially as we had children of our own, and it was no use talking to the poor fellow then about putting the child in a burial club. So we gave some coppers each, and that was settled. I thought all the time about my hat, and yet I couldn't well run away from Johnson; but, having spent a shilling of my money, I found myself now down to Liddy's price. I was thinking about making a move, when a man came in to sell little dolls. They were little beauties. I never saw anything like them, and only sixpence a-piece. He didn't speak very good English, but made it out in some way that he had been wrecked coming from France, and these dolls were all that he had been enabled to save from the wreck. He imitated a coffee mill and a water pipe running, and seemed such a poor, simple fellow that I bought a doll from him, and very thankful he was.

'Johnson had got his business done when the doll was bought, so we set off together, down Milton-street into Scotland place, and there I found an auction going on. Thinking there might be hats for sale at the auction, I went in, but found the man selling scarcely anything but old bed-clothes and women's dresses. Johnson and I got crushed into the room, and after a while a fender – a parlour fender – was put up. Sixpence – a shilling – "Going!" says the man, and all that sort of thing. "It's very cheap," says a man beside me, and I thought it was. I had heard Liddy saying something about a fender that she wanted, so now was my time. I bid for it, and a fat old woman bid against me; but I would not be done, so bid up to three shillings and got it. When I went outside it did not look so good or strong but a bargain is a bargain, says I to myself, and I carried it off.

'Now the thought struck me – What about my hat? Well, Johnson and I looked into the windows in Byrom Street, and could see nothing likely to my figure, for I had only five shillings now. We went down into the Haymarket, but on enquiring at the hat shops, found that the "common class of goods could not be recommended," and all the hats at five shillings that they showed me were either too narrow in the rim or too small in the head. When we came out of the hat shop, "I'm very hungry," says I to Johnson. "So am I,' says he; and just then we saw a girl selling pies, and we got one a-piece. Of course I paid for them. I couldn't expect a man who was out of work on strike to "stand" for me. The pies were well peppered – "nicely seasoned," Johnson said – so we must each have a glass of ale to wash them down; and we went into a little beerhouse somewhere about the Old Haymarket, I think it was. There was a great crowd of people in, young lads mostly, some middle-aged men, and a few women without bonnets or caps. We had not been at the counter many minutes before a man with a swelled face, a broken nose, and the side of his head covered with sticking-plaster, came up.

"'Now, my sporting kids," says he, "what are you going to stand for 'the Pet?' Down with the browns and don't be stingy. It's us what makes England what it is and prevents it being anything else. Dibs! Dibs! – In with the dibs for 'the Pet,' that risked his life to show his pluck," shaking a low-crowned hat in our faces and rattling the coppers in it.[63]

"'It's the old game, Mickey," says a man behind me, addressing the bruiser: "you are carrying the milking can round, and you'll take good care to skim the cream off. The 'Pet' as you luk most after is yourself."

'A fierce oath was the response to this remark; and, seeing where I had got into, I looked for my way out, and found it. Both Johnson and I breathed freer when we got out, and at the corner of Shaw's-brow I pulled up to count what money I had. My money was all right, but my doll was gone! It had been taken from my pocket whilst I was in the crowd! Johnson had the fender; I felt glad that was all right.

'And now came the difficulty, – What was I to do about my hat? What account could I give to Liddy about her money? There was the fender – that was something; but I couldn't wear a fender upon my head when I went to hear Stowell Brown, although I have heard him tell about a minister's wife that went to chapel with a chest of drawers upon her head. So Johnson and I considered, and the best thing he could suggest was that I should go into Fontenoy-street. There, at what he called the translator's[64] I might meet with a very good hat for about three shillings or three and sixpence, box included, and to this suggestion I readily gave way. Immediately afterwards I found myself roaming about the old clothes and old hat shops, and was not long in fixing upon "a very nice hat, respectable wear." I got it, after a good deal of higgling, for two shillings and tenpence, and paid fourpence for a box. It looked, as Johnson and I thought, quite like new, and we both assured ourselves that Liddy would never see the difference. So, after we had another pie each, and something to it, I parted with my friend, and walked away home with my new hat.

'I had not gone far before I recollected that Johnson had my fender. I ran back and overtook him, but my fender was off after the doll. We had it when we were at the hat place in Fontenoy-street, and I recollected an old woman at the door (when Johnson laid the fender down whilst he examined my hat) saying it was a very nice one, and just like her Mary Jane's; but neither of us could recollect anything more of it. We went back to the shop, but the old man had never seen a fender. He dealt in hats, he did; what use were fenders to him? He was mortal saucy, we both thought.

'When I got home, Liddy was tired with waiting up for me, and she said something rather sharp, so the hat-box didn't get opened that night, but in the morning wasn't there a stir on! I heard her before I came down stairs. She knew all about it – at least she said so; and as I did not feel much in the humour of being talked to, I said very little, and let her have her own way. Every hour of that morning she kept finding out some blemish in the hat; and with her turning, twisting, and throwing it down, she made me wish I had never seen it. I never liked it very well, but it did look much worse when she had taken the gloss off it with handling. In the afternoon my friend the Printer called in for me to go and hear Stowell Brown; and off we went. It has always struck me as a very queer thing; I don't mean to say that Stowell Brown knew anything about my Saturday night's adventure, but that Sunday he had a good deal to say about "Speak the truth and shame the devil," and he did fit it on to me like old boots. He actually told of men "chiselling their wives" out of their wages, and all sorts of things like that. My head did feel very hot; and when the lecture was over, and I was going home, I told the printer all about my hat, and I afterwards confessed the truth to Liddy.'

Jem no doubt sees and feels, but takes a roundabout way of admitting it, that, either for good or evil, a working man is very much in the power of his wife. If he has a good one, and has good sense, he interferes very little – the less the better. If he has a bad one, he must grin and abide – there's little help for him. The foolish expenditure of money in which thousands may be seen to indulge any Saturday night – not speaking of intoxicating drinks – will show that 'how Jem Burns bought a new hat' is no fiction.

18 The mysteries of the courts: at Christmas time

The courts in Thomas Street are not yet all described. There still remain some very painful scenes to be shown. But although the threshold of the subject has been hardly crossed, some interest has been excited, and this has called forth a variety of hints, suggestions, and detailed accounts of actual experience. From amongst the latter, as the time seems favourable, we select a description of 'a court at Christmas time,' as seen by a working man. We are fully convinced of its fidelity, and have, for the sake of clearness, interfered little with the arrangement. We hope to hear of the simple story being read in many a working man's home:

'It's a good while ago, and was in a year that Christmas Day fell upon Saturday, when I was compelled to spend it in a Liverpool court. I was brought up and served my time in a small village in Cheshire. Eight years after I was out of my time I fell out with my master, and in hot blood threw up my place and came to Liverpool to look for work. I had a wife and four children. It was a hard job to leave the house where all these had been born, and the village so dear to me in many ways; but it had to be done, and there was no help for it. I recollect that I made very short work of the parting, and I tried to laugh whilst I shook my wife's hand, and at the same time the tears were pumping up and nearly blinding me.

'I soon got work in Liverpool, and I lodged with a shopmate, for it was some time before I could afford to send for my wife and family. But I managed to get them here before Christmas: I had worked hard for this. When they did come the job was to find a house for them. I had no time to look after it, and my wife was quite strange to the town, its ways and its people. As I was working at a yard at the south end, the house, to be useful to me, must be near to my work; so, after a deal of hunting, to try and get anything at about our price, and for want of anything better, we took a house in a long court, not such a way of St. James's Market. The place didn't look so dirty as many courts we had seen, for there was a good fall in it. The houses were single, straight up and down, and not badly built; but, for want of drainage, the cellars were very damp. For all this, people lived in these holes, – at least, on one side of the court, – though there was no entrance for them from the court, and they were lighted by very small windows. There were, besides, several things I did not like about the court and people; but my wife had been knocked about so to get any place to put our furniture into, that I felt it would go against her grain if I made any strong objections. Besides, on talking it over, I found she was not in love with the place, but she must have some sort of place at once, until she could look about her.

'We went into our first house in Liverpool on the Monday before Christmas Day. I thought, as I went down from work on the Monday night, and crushed by the crowd of all sorts that choked up the narrow entrance to _____ Court, "This is very different to your little cottage in the country, Billy, my boy," but it was no use crying over shed milk. Here I was, and here I'd have to stay, and when one's in for a thing, the best way is to stick to, and work one's self out. My wife had got the house very tidy, but I was sorry for my children. There was, it appeared, a dreadful rough set of children about, and on no account were mine allowed to go out and play with them, so they had been prisoners all day, and looked very different to what they used to do when they came clambering over the stiles to meet me as I left the yard. "This won't do for you, Billy," says I to myself, "and, what's more, it shan't."

'When the children were got off to bed, then it was that I heard what sort of a place we had got into. Why, before my wife had got her furniture put into any sort of order, she had been visited by half the women in the court – in a friendly way, of course. One and all wished her good luck; some wanted to borrow pans and mugs; some wished her to join them in a subscription to bury a child that was dead in the top house; others that had joined for a little sup of drink, wished her to taste with them; some wanted her to subscribe to a raffle for a fat pig, which had been fed in the cellar where it now was, and that was right opposite to the house in which I lived. We had not been talking long before there was a row in the court, and, on looking out, I saw two men, stripped to the waist, fighting in style. Every door was open, and here and there heads were pushed out of windows; and as the men slashed at each other the other women and children cried and screamed dreadfully. On inquiry, I found this to be the father and son. The father worked on board some steamer, and only came home once a week. Every time he came ashore he got something to drink, quarrelled with his wife, and turned her out of doors. The son stuck up for the mother, and father and son settled differences by a fair stand-up fight. Each has his partizans, and I saw that a good many fights would likely spring out of this, so I shut the door and sat down with my wife to think of the best way of getting out of the court. We were booked for a week, anyhow.

'My wife had a deal to put up with for the next few days from the people, because she would not go about with them nor drink with them, and she was in great trouble about her children. Out of the house the little things would go when they got the chance, and friendly with the other children in the court they were sure to be, in spite of all remonstrances. How could it be any way else? All day long the court, she told me, was very lively, for there were some men there who never seemed to work. They went out to get drunk and came home to fight, and hadn't time for much else. Some of them would come home drunk in the middle of the day, and others never turned out until it was getting near dark. The words which our little children were compelled to listen to, the tricks they would be sure to see played, the way in which the mothers behaved to their little ones, the sort of play they allowed them to indulge in, the sort of food that was given to them, the way in which they had to eat it, the dirty and ragged state in which they were always seen, and then, beyond all, the fierce brawling of men and women all day long, made my wife and myself miserable, and out of this nest of devilment we determined to get.

'But if the court was lively on the first night, what ought to be said of it on Christmas Eve? There were two raffles to come off. At one, that for the pig, there was a fiddler. He sat on the stairs, and men and women danced in a rattling way to his scraping. The woman who was raffling the pig came to my house to see if we would let our little girl fetch the ale for them. It was only from the beer-house at the top of the court, and she wouldn't have troubled us only her little lad had been shoved into the fire and had got his arm badly burnt! We both refused to allow the child to be put to such work, and with that the woman began to storm at us like a fury, and, before half an hour had passed, two panes in our room window were broken.

'As the night got on I was almost afraid to go to bed. The other raffle had got to work, and, although it was merely for a hand-kerchief, and was confined to young people and children, there was a complete riot over it. Men began to roll home now, mostly in a drunken state, and carrying something for the feast of to-morrow. Children were running about or were being kicked about, and far into the night we could hear rows, breaking of crockery, mingled with screams of children and curses of parents.

'I looked out just before twelve o'clock, as some singers had come into the court. They sang "While shepherds watched their flocks by night," and sang it well, too. I'll never forget the picture I saw there then. The court was in a manner of speaking still. The raffle people came to the door; out of many houses children ran and clustered round the singers. No one spoke above his breath, as the four young men and two women told the story of the Child that was born in Bethlehem. One thing jarred on my ear, and that was the hissing from the frying pans which were now under way in several houses. I had heard at my country home the singers at Christmas time, but I don't think the song ever touched me so much as it did on this night. I've often wondered whether the people in this court ever heard the glad tidings of great joy in any other way.

'Christmas morning opened with a child being scalded in one of the houses, and this accident roused the whole court. Then began the bustle of getting dinners ready and sending them to the bakehouse. Those who had got a goose took good care to tell everybody, for you could hear children going about begging or borrowing one thing or another in order that the goose might be cooked. Onions were in great request, and little children sat down on the steps to talk about what they were going to have for dinner. It amused me very much to hear women shouting at each other from door to door as to what sort of a fuddle there was at the raffle, and what they had got for their Christmas dinners.

'The house next door to that in which I was unfortunately fixed was unoccupied, and a heap of boys who lived in the court had taken possession of this, and were preparing to perform a Christmas piece. Those who could manage to get any fancy dress had done so, and dashed up and down the court to show themselves, and were the object of much curiosity to many grown-up people. The play was to come off in the afternoon, and all the fore part of the day was spent in "practising." Crashing of sticks, stamping of feet, firing pistols, and shouts of robbers, were what fell to my lot to hear of this practising. There seemed to be opposition companies, but those in the house part had the best of it. They charged a halfpenny each for admission, and when the boys, girls, women, or men got in, they might please themselves what lot they remained with. What interest people could have in seeing these little ruffians strut and bellow, one might well wonder at, but the people had had their dinners, and anything, as they said, in the way of fun was welcome to them.

'I did manage to get my wife and children out into Parliament Fields before it got dark, and I just got back in time to see the sweep that lived at the top of the court kick his wife into the street, and then throw a shovelful of soot over her, much to the amusement of the gangs of lads that were now coming away from the performance. The Saturday and Sunday which I spent in that court I always shudder at. I'm very sorry to think that, although we are told the world is getting wiser, the Liverpool courts are getting no better.'

19 Homes of the people

We will now transfer the reader to another district of the town, inhabited solely by the working classes. The street is comparatively modern, and contains no courts. The houses are what are termed double houses, containing front and back cellar, front and back parlour, four bedrooms, and compact yards. In almost every instance the front cellars are let off, and in these single apartments families reside. The houses let for £15 per annum, payable monthly, in some cases quarterly, according to agreement. The tenants let the cellars for 2s. per week.[65] The street runs narrow at one end, and here there are five houses smaller than the others, which let for 4s. per week. These were inhabited by men in the employ of the landlord, with one exception; and before proceeding to the larger houses in the street, we will notice these five, and their occupants.

At the first house resided a man who was in the employ of the landlord. He was a native of the north of England, and had been at one time in affluent circumstances; misfortunes had fallen on him, and he now had to turn to work. His wages were 27s. per week. He had a wife and two children. The wife had been well educated, so far as intellectual ability is concerned, and had learned several of what are called the modern accomplishments; but of household duties she was entirely ignorant – although she could work a beautiful collar, she could neither make nor wash her husband's shirt. She could sit down apparently comfortable and read the *London Journal*, whilst her children were rolling about in a filthy state, and her house was in the utmost disorder. In addition to this, she had become addicted to drink, which made fearful havoc of her health, and in a few months her personal appearance underwent a complete transformation: from a genteel, well behaved woman, she became a careless, bloated, hopeless drunkard. Her husband could not be called a drunkard – 'he took a sup on a Saturday night,' and on Sunday the bottle used sometimes to be in requisition, for the regular customers could get drink any day or hour from the vaults at the corner of the adjoining street. But he stuck to his work, and, being fond of his children, would have stuck to his home had it been made anything like a home for him.

He was also a kind husband, would make the fire before he left home in the morning, in order to save his wife trouble; and sometimes, when he came in to breakfast, he would have to prepare it himself. His house contained very good old-fashioned furniture, the use made of which we shall shew hereafter. The wife got her groceries from a small shop close by, where she had credit, and had run a large score entirely unknown to her husband. She sank deeper in debt week by week, because the gin bottle must be filled; and the wages were by such means mortgaged. When the supplies were stopped at the shop; when the coalman would give no more, and the potato dealer was pressing; when 'the Scotchman' threatened to tell her husband, and the collector hinted that the landlord, her husband's employer, would have to be informed – when, in short, she found herself completely run to earth, her husband would be informed of his position; a row would result, and a *loan* would be resorted to.

In order to obtain a loan, sureties were necessary. At the next door dwelt an Irishman, who was in the same employ: he had a wife and one child, a son. He was said to be 'a downright hard-working fellow when he was at it,' but he spent a considerable more time in drinking than he did in working, and would go on the spree for 'a fortnight at a spell,' would beat his wife, turn her and the boy out of doors, and pawn everything he could carry out of the house for drink – proving the truth of what was said of him, how hard he worked when he was at it. He was on excellent terms with the people at No. 1, and therefore was fixed on as surety for the loan. But his house was a miserable dwelling; there was hardly a chair to sit on; it did not contain altogether furniture that would amount to one pound; how, therefore, could he put on an appearance to become security for his friend? That was easily arranged. When the inspector of the loan society was expected to call, the principal articles of furniture would be moved out of No. 1 into No. 2. An eight-day clock, a good sofa, a few nice chairs, and a picture or two made the house look quite smart, and when the officer of the loan society, who was said to be a lay preacher, called, all appeared satisfactory. Another surety was got up in a similar way; the loan was obtained, and the money soon squandered. This furniture we have seen carried out to other houses in the same neighbourhood for similar purposes, a small commission being obtained for its use. The wants created and the woes inflicted amongst the working classes by the existence of loan societies, particularly those granting loans from £2 to £5, far surpass anything that can be imagined or described; yet it is found that the principal supporters and directors of what the late Mr. Rushton called 'abominable pests' are members of that section of

the Christian Church whose rules entirely condemn all usury, and
the venerable founder of which body considered it necessary to pass
such a rule as this – 'Not to pawn anything, not even to save life.'
What effect can follow the preaching of that man on the Sabbath,
who during six days is occupied by what are called 'the duties of
inspector'? *The society yields 10 per cent., and occasionally large
bonuses*! Such is one phase of modern Christianity. When a loan
was received, a good spree immediately followed, and then the
whole neighbourhood were informed how the loan was got, and
what was the character of all persons engaged in procuring it. The
drink did this; if nothing more, it made people very candid, and
they told each other in the plainest language the trickery that was
practised.[66]

At No. 3 a workman resided who had a large family. His wages
were 24s. per week. His wife was an industrious, tidy woman,
continually scouring her house, driving the children off her front
steps, and 'warming' her own children for going in the dirt. She had
a lodger, who paid 2s. 6d. per week for washing and lodging; this
helped her rent, and she bustled away and battled with the rise in
provisions and 'the bothering taxes' like a thorough English working man's wife. Her husband was a simple-hearted, hard-working
fellow; he knew little of anything save his work, and cared for little
else. He took a glass or two of ale when he went to 'the club' –
that was all; no one ever saw him the worse for liquor. On Sunday
he would take his children for a walk in the fields, and occasionally
take himself to church, where he slept very comfortably.

The other two houses were occupied by young mechanics and
their wives; they kept themselves very respectable, and their wives
vied with each other in keeping their houses smart-looking and
clean. They mixed little with the neighbours, rarely or never were
seen lolling at the doors, turned out to some place of worship on
the Sabbath, and lived in comparative comfort and happiness, their
wages being respectively 25s. and 24s. per week. One of them
joined a building society; the other put a small sum weekly or
monthly, as he could best spare it, into the Bold-street bank. Again
we ask, was it the construction of these dwellings, which were all
precisely alike – was it the ventilation, was it any atmospheric
effect, or was it the use of the water from the red sandstone, that
produced the remarkable difference in the inmates of these cottages?
Had any of these things at all to do with making 'the man a better
mechanic, or the mechanic a better man?'

When these houses had been occupied about nine months, the
whole of the tenants were summoned for poor rates. They all
objected to pay, on the ground that they understood the rates were
to be included in the 4s. weekly. This would not satisfy the

collector or assist to keep the poor, so to the parish office they must all go and appeal. The men who earned the largest wages sent their wives, who, covered as they were with filthy rags, presented an appearance of abject poverty; and having told a pitiful tale, in which there was no particle of truth, they escaped the tax. One of the young men appeared in person. He was asked why he refused to pay. He stated his objection, and gave further reason which ought to have weighed with the oracle that presided. The collector of rates, being in the room, was asked, 'What sort of house is _____'s?' 'A very clean, respectable house, sir, and he has a sitting at church,' was the reply. This settled the matter. The fact of the man being respectable, and having so much moral honesty and respect for religion as to occupy a sitting in church and pay for it, caused this justice to decide at once that the man must pay the rates in full. It was in vain he told what he had done or what he was doing for his family out of his limited income; it was in vain that the man denied himself many comforts in order to keep himself independent and decent. He was a striving, hard-working, sober man, had a seat in church, therefore must pay the penalty for his uprightness; whilst the drunkards and their degraded wives escaped 'scot-free,' and the same night had a *good fuddle on the strength of it.* This is no isolated case. Any appeal day will furnish facts as pregnant as these to all who are considering how they best can elevate or improve the condition of the labouring classes.

What is the condition of these people now? No. 1 is in London, and when last seen was in a destitute condition. He had to escape from here in consequence of becoming so involved with loans. One loan was obtained to pay another, and ruin was the result. His wife sold things out of the house little by little, and resorted to even worse means for the purpose of obtaining drink, and they are both now habitual drunkards, and thoroughly degraded. No. 2 has become what his wife calls 'a downright wastrel.' He works very little – not at all if he can avoid it – and was seen, a week or two since, in a tattered condition, stopping an old acquaintance and asking for 'the price of a gill.' The wife is supported by the son, who has proved a steady, industrious fellow, and the father is not allowed to come near them. No. 3 is in business for himself, and was noticed last week going up a ladder to look after some of his men, whilst the master he worked for when we first knew him is just now taking the benefit of the act. No. 4 is in Dublin, and doing well; and No. 5 is here, in good circumstances, and fast becoming a wealthy man.

We will now go down the street and notice the inmates of these 'double houses.' Take the first, that next the huxter's shop. Here lived a man who was employed by the dock trust. He had a wife, but no family, and a niece of his wife's resided with them; she was married to a steward in one of the ocean steamers. The cellar was let off to a shoemaker, who had a wife and six children. The proprietor of the house had 21s. per week wages; the niece paid very good rent for the rooms she occupied; there was, in addition, the rent of the cellar; and *yet this man paid no poor rates.* The inmates of the house could turn out in silks and satins when they liked, and the wife could at other times turn into the parish office clothed in rags to appeal against the rates. Out of this large street there were only four persons whose names were on the burgess roll, and these four earned less money than any other persons in the street.[67] But it may be said the collectors ought to see matters of this sort. If all collectors be like the collector of this district, it is utterly impossible for them to see what is the condition of the people, inasmuch as he rarely or never called on them. He sent a man round with the bills, and if he called at all it appeared to be done as a favour; that was all that was ever seen of the collector in this street. Yet he must have been very industrious *somewhere*, for his salary was raised – and this could not have been done unless he deserved it.

Next door to the house first alluded to dwelt a smith. He had a wife and four children. He was in a constant situation, received 26s. per week, but his wife was compelled to take in washing to support her family. The man had 'a canine fancy,' kept a good dog, which he seemed to take a great pride in, for he always took it out with him in his leisure hours. His wife was rarely seen without a bruised face or a black eye, and his children appeared to dread the sight of their father. The man was a cowardly scoundrel, and a great drunkard, whilst his wife was a mild, patient, hard-working, sober, clean woman: she scarcely ever received a penny of the fellow's wages. When he was on the spree he would sometimes come home for cash, bringing with him some companions who all had dogs, and if the money was not immediately forthcoming which he required to gratify his vicious taste, he would take the clean clothes from the line, or from the table, *and throw them in the gutter for spite.* The poor woman was so reduced by want and ill usage at last, that she resolved on taking her husband before the magistrates. He was committed for several months, but came out and was almost as bad as ever. He still visits 'The Canine Tavern,' keeps his dog, and runs it on Sunday mornings; is as ready as ever to 'back his fancy for all he is worth;' and his wife now presents a miserable picture of destitution and abuse. *This man never paid any rates.* His house, when his wife was able to stir about, was always kept particularly clean; therefore, as far as this was concerned, there was nothing to drive the fellow to such a vicious course of life.

At the next house resided a mechanic who earned 28s. a week. He had a wife and child. He turned out respectable, attended a Sunday school in the district, and taught at a ragged school three evenings in each week. He was rated for the support of the poor, paid his rates, and was on the burgess roll, as, we are glad to notice, he is still. The cellar of this house was let off to a mason, in the employ of a large firm, who had a wife and two children; his wages were 27s. per week, and out of this he could scarcely obtain clothes for himself, wife, or children, and he seldom paid any rent. It is a mournful fact, but this man represents a vast number of the operative classes. His wife and the youngest child would sometimes go to meet him on Saturday night when he had obtained his wages, and it would be ten and sometimes eleven o'clock before they reached home. There would be so many places to call at, so many friends with whom they must 'have two penn'orth for luck,' and then they had the marketing to do, which was with them a great matter. The eldest child would be in the house of a neighbour, or a neighbour's child would be in the cellar minding it, until such time as the parents came home – 'muddled,' as they generally did. Some 'toffee' would be brought home for the child; it would then be put to bed unwashed, and the father and mother would set to work preparing their supper. The man would go to the beer-house to pay his week's shot and get a quart of ale for supper, whilst the wife would run about the neighbourhood to borrow a pan to cook the beef-steak! These people spent as much money on their Saturday night's supper as would have obtained for them a comfortable dinner for every day in the week. Saturday night and Sunday were by them devoted entirely to eating and drinking. If any are sceptical as to these practices of the operative class, let them visit their houses, or pass through the streets where they reside, any Saturday evening from ten to twelve o'clock, when the fragrance of beef-steak and onions, roast goose, or the like, will set them at rest on the point. The wife could not be called a drunkard, but she was thriftless and idle. She never washed her clothes until Friday or Saturday, and then she would hang the few rags out on the front railings, much to the annoyance of the landlady of the house, who considered it bad enough of them to pay no rent, but to hang such wretched clothes at the door was much worse. The husband is now dead, having killed himself with drinking, and his wife was last seen in a cellar in Frederick-street – a damp, filthy hole, not fit for human habitation. Can it be possible that the cellars in this street are under the cognizance of the Health Committee?

In one of the cellars in this street, a labourer, an elderly man and his wife resided. The man earned 14s. per week when fully employed, but his work was irregular. The wife was always tidy; the cellar was always clean; and what clothes these people had on were plain and comfortable. This man's mode of living may be best described in his own words – and let it be noticed also that he was altogether uneducated, could neither read nor write, but went for months to a free evening school, and thus became able to do both. During our acquaintance with him, speaking of his mode of life, he said, 'The way of it is, I never spend all I get, be it little or much, and I never spend anything at all in drink. I can labour as hard as any man of my age, and I believe a bit of bread and cheese will do me as much good as a glass of ale. I am not a teetotaller, I don't like them, for they are always talking about it; but I don't drink anything, as I can't see any good in it. When other people, in winter time, are going begging for tickets for soup or bread, we can sit by the fire and boil our own pot, and be independent.' This man wished to be so thoroughly independent, that he pressed the young man who had taught him 'to read and write and do accounts' to accept of some gratuity for his trouble, and when this was declined he found out where his benefactor lived, and whenever there happened to be a fall of snow the old fellow was sure to be at the house early in the morning to clean the snow from the door steps and front of the house. It is cheering to meet with such traits as this in the life of a labourer. Yet this man lived in a cellar, and now lives in a room, and his wages, when fully employed are only 14s. per week.

This district was under the pastoral care of a minister of the Established Church, a young man of active habits, generous disposition, and pleasing manners. He devoted four hours each day to visiting the poor, and during the inclement season of the year his distribution of gifts was not confined to class or creed, but whenever he saw what he believed to be want or woe, his hand was stretched out to relieve the necessities of the people. His church being what is called 'a respectable church' (as if in the matter of religion these distinctions avail anything), few poor attended, and indeed, there was little provision for them until the young minister obtained it. He availed himself of large collections made at the church, and distributed food and clothing with no niggardly hand. His first question on visiting a house was not, 'What place of worship do you go to?' or 'What religion are you?' but, after apologising for intruding on the privacy of a poor man's family, he would ask if they needed any assistance, what earnings were coming in, and then consider what he should do for them. He was often deceived. The people soon found out what a kind, generous nature he had, and were ready enough to impose upon him. We have known this pastor to carry blankets into the cellar where the shoemaker and his family resided, and give them to the wife in order that the children might be made comfortable at night, and the sound of the good man's feet had scarcely left the street before *one of the children was sent to the pawn shop with these blankets*, and the money obtained on them would be consumed in *gin*! The minister's confidence in anything he heard from the people became much weakened, and thus, by the conduct of the deceitful and lying people, the necessitous poor may eventually have suffered. Yet, as long as this young man remained here, he devoted himself very fully in endeavouring to supply the temporal and spiritual necessities of the people, and his labour was not altogether in vain. He held a weekly meeting in the school room for the poor people who could not come to church. Here it was that hypocrisy was fostered. *Women would keep sober on the day of the lecture*, and present themselves – perhaps one or two children with them. The children would be shoeless, and their parents wretchedly clad. The sympathies of the minister would be excited, and a ticket for food would be given; and even loaves or groceries obtained in this way *we have known to be sold for drink*.

In addition to what the church provided for such an extensive district, the Wesleyan body held a prayer meeting in this street on Sunday evening from eight to nine o'clock, a young woman distributed tracts every Sunday afternoon, and occasionally, on fine Sundays, a party of young men would address an assemblage in the open air, 'on the necessity of a new birth.' The audience was frequently more select than numerous. There were two jerry shops in the street, and two more in a street adjoining, together with three spirit vaults, two brothels, and a pawn shop, within a stone's throw of each other; but the church or chapel was a good way off, and the town missionary and scripture reader were engaged in other more destitute districts.

20 'Bagging the Scotchman'[68]

'Why, there they are! Well, if they haven't just all gone into the vaults at the side door.'

The speaker was a stout, slovenly woman, and formed one of a group of women and children, that were assembled at the corner of a court in L_____ street, last Monday week. The words were addressed to a tall, slender man, of florid complexion, who was neatly dressed in a tweed suit, and carried under his arm a square parcel in oilskin wrapper, and held in one hand an oblong memorandum book. He seemed to have been somewhat ruffled in temper, and spoke thickly and fast, and his language was not calculated to conciliate the people by whom he was surrounded.

'Do n't spit your spite at us, Mr. Bilk,' said a lean, sallow, half-naked woman from amidst the throng. 'Do n't spit your spite at us. You thought we were too poor to trust; and you thought you'd got hold of good customers when Mrs. Cain and her set began with you. That's the way with you fellows; them as really would pay you, as never would think of asking you for anythink unless they meant to pay you, you'll turn your nose up at; and now, because she's given you the bag, and has done it for three Mondays hand-running, you're losing your temper, and calling the whole court, as if we had any right to be answerable for other people. We've enough to do for ourselves, haven't we?'

The woman appealed to no one in particular, yet seemed to expect a general response. There was not any shyness manifested by any of them in speaking, for two or three burst out at once in reply.

Just then a little deformed woman, whose covering seemed to consist of a sack thrown over the body, and tied with cord round her waist, came down the court, with a black earthenware dish in one hand, and a wet cloth in the other, and her shrill voice stilled the others.

'So your beauties are off again, Mr. Bilk, are they?' She spoke with biting emphasis, and finished her sentences with a slight hiss. 'After your Christmas treat, and after your standing glasses round for them at the christening, and coming up to see them all the night of the funeral. Yes, Mr. Bilk; it was pleasant of you to pass up the court, and never notice the little things playing about, as had on their backs frocks got from you, and frocks as was paid for; no doubt it was; but it's just as pleasant to me to tell you as we saw your blankets go to the pawnshop afore they had been two hours in the house; and we all said – did n't we, Mrs. Jackson? – as the Cains would be out again on Monday when the Scotchman called.'

There was a hearty smack of satisfaction given to this speech by several of the bystanders. For although the scene described had been enacted in a few moments, there were now more than fifty persons, young and old, present, and all seemed to enjoy the discomfiture of the young Scotchman, except one old man, who came up from an adjoining cellar, and was listened to (the audience considered) with very great respect.

'Oh, here's old Barney!' shouted the boys.

'Listen to wise Barney!' cried the women.

The first manifestation which Barney gave of his wisdom was by stating, in unctuous brogue, and very oracularly, that the devil was in the women, and advising Mr. Bilk, the young Scotchman, to get out of the throng and look after the runaways.

'I told you that they went out into the side door of the vaults,' said the first speaker, as 'the Scotchman' cast a somewhat imploring look around, 'but if you do n't like to hunt 'em out, do n't think as we'll do it for you. A likely thing, indeed; he refused us trust, and now would like us to catch the women as is "bagging" him.'

A loud laugh burst out from the crowd.

'What's to do?' said some fresh comers.

'Oh, only Mrs. Cain and her set bagging the Scotchman,' was the reply.

'I'll see their husbands,' said he, breaking away from the crowd, after talking a few minutes with Barney.

'See their husbands! it's little but broken bones you'll get by seeing them. Not a bit of use in it. Give them chase if you can get on the scent, for if you can run them down to-day you may get a few shillings, but let it go over sundown, and not a copper will you see. Is n't it me that sees them week after week, and day after day. Sure there's not a stitch of clothes they ever got from you that ever was put together, not a stitch put into anything, but just got in and whipped off to the pawn office, and then the bottle set a-going. Oh, it's Barney that knows, and more's the blessing; "the market" suits me for all the clothes I want.'

'I'll go to the vaults,' said the Scotchman, putting his book in his side pocket, and tying his bundle up tightly; 'it's too much to lose,' and away he set off to the corner of the street, followed by several women and a trail of children, which widened and thickened as he got near the striped door-posts of the grog shop.

'Come back and go home with you!' screamed a woman, as she laid her hands heavily upon a little girl, clutching her by the back of the frock with one hand, and thumping her on the side of the head with the other. 'Go home with you! what can you do in hunting for the runaways? Get away home, and none of your squealing.'

With a bitter cry the girl escaped from the clutch and ran down the street, probably towards her home; but she turned to look, time after time, and at length, wiping her eyes with her dirty ragged frock, she sat down upon a doorstep, and gave vent to her grief in loud sobs and with much wailing. A few little children, less than herself, scrambled out of the gutter, where they had been playing with pieces of broken cups, and stared at her; and the stolid sort of sympathy which the girl got from the blear eyes and smeared faces seemed to relieve her, for she was soon silent, and had forgotten, apparently, the treatment of her mother.

'What'll you give us to come in with you?' said a lanky woman, as she twisted her apron round her. 'What'll you give us? say the word. Mrs. Cain would as soon see Ould Harry as me any day, and she's felt my finger ends before to-day.'

She ran up to 'the Scotchman,' and the crowd cheered her on. Some of the women, from their speech, appeared to think that what they called 'a good drink' could be got out of him, if 'Peg' stuck pretty close.

Mr. Bilk did not seem disposed to give anything – did not care to be accompanied into the vaults – wished, so it seemed, to get rid of the crowd which followed him, and hesitated on the threshold. The crowd pressed on, and some rude young girls, shameless in their speech, pushed the young man into the vaults, and with him several of the children, who fell sprawling amidst the soil and sawdust of the floor, from which they were soon removed by being literally flung into the street.

The vaults were long and narrow, but what space there was between the windows and the counter was well filled with men and women, chiefly the latter, in various stages of intoxication. The entrance of 'the Scotchman' did not disturb many. They were far gone, and were talking very confidentially to each other, and swearing eternal fidelity, boundless charity, and 'many happy returns.' At the far end of the vaults a small apartment was boxed off, with seats round the sides, and here the women who had been 'bagging the Scotchman' were gathered.

One of the barmen – a weak young fellow, with a large breast-pin, and a thin long face, straight fair hair, and having a snort in his speech, but very civil withal – soon saw what was wanted, and directed Mr. Bilk to the 'snug,' but distinctly stated that there 'must be no row.'

His entrance to the 'snug' did not in any way discompose the
women who were there enjoying themselves. Mrs. Cain, the
defaulter, did not rise to receive him, but she smiled pleasantly –
at least as pleasantly as any stout woman can smile who has done
two hours' hard work at drinking her husband's earnings. 'You'll
join us, Mr. Bilk,' said one of the women, filling a small cup with
ale, and handing it to him. 'Here's a cousin of mine, just come in
from sea, and he is standing treat for sake of getting home safe,
and for old times.'

The 'cousin' looked very like a striker in a forge or anchor
smithy, and gave an idiotic grin at the speech of his eloquent
relative.

The 'Scotchman' was serious. It was no time for drinking. What
he wanted was money. For three Mondays, he said, the instalments
had been missed, and there must be an end of such work. He spoke
very sharply, and spurned the cup of ale.

'Pop goes the weasel,' says Mrs. Cain, and she tried to rise, but
flobbed into her corner again. 'You're on a high horse, you are; it's
got a switch tail, and it's carrying you where you little expect.'

'Come, Mrs. Cain,' said 'the Scotchman,' his wrath getting the
better of him, 'come, this won't do. You promised me thirty shillings out of the funeral money,[69] and only gave me five; and you
were to give a pound to-day to make up for arrears; and here you
are at work, spending your money on these people. I must see your
husband.'

'There, now, listen to that; to think as a woman has to be talked
to this way of a Monday, and her friends around her, too. My
husband, indeed! Oh, but you'll rue the day as ever you followed
me, that you will.' Mrs. Cain's feelings were fast overcoming her,
and her speech was disjointed. The friends around were indignant
at the rudeness of Mr. Bilk, and what seemed to kindle their ire
more than anything else was the allusion to the 'funeral money.'
The grimy smithy man rose up, whilst the rage smouldered a little,
and having deliberately placed his cup of beer on a particular spot
on the table, and called the Scotchman's attention to the fact, he
hitched up his trowsers, and then held out his huge clenched fist
towards him, saying:

'Luk you here; you may be a very nobby Scotchman, and your
hair may curl nicely, but you're not a man – that's what you're not,
or why would you throw a woman's dead child in her face?'

'Tommy'll give it him,' said one woman, clapping her hands, and
then taking a swig of beer.

'Lave it there,' said Tommy, 'you're name's Bilk. What do I care
for you? Are we going to be disturbed a this road, when we're all
having our drain, just acos you want pay for your ould toggery.

Cut your lucky out o' this, or I'll make you smell what you'd not like to tell.'

This aroused the wrath of the women. They seemed preparing for an attack on the Scotchman, and gave vent to their feelings by shouts, which attracted people from other parts of the vaults. But the barman got in amongst them, and dragged Mr. Bilk away, saying, 'What's the use of wexing people? leave 'em alone; they've no money now. Why do n't you get 'em before they get on so?'

The triumph and defiant shouts which reached the ears of the Scotchman, as he retreated from the snug and vaults into the street, were not likely to be soon forgotten, especially as the crowd outside, who had been waiting to see the result, did not offer any sympathy to him that had been 'bagged.'

Part three
Moral improvement:
housing, health and
local government

21 From 'Recreations' (Town Life)

The rapid advance of manufacturing industry has totally changed the relation of the classes, and the labourers have been left to themselves in a great measure, so far as their recreation is concerned. In rural districts, up to a very recent period, and in many still, the only enjoyment or recreation offered to the working man was the beer shop. This is not so much the case in large towns. There are here some means of rational recreation provided for the people; but the pernicious influence of those amusements which the selfishness or cupidity of men has brought to bear upon the masses causes the former to be despised, whilst the latter meets with ready acceptation. Education, at least scholastic training, does not create all the difference which is seen in the enjoyments of the people. The man with the glossy coat, and the well lined purse, is not a whit better in the choice of amusement than his ill clad, ill fed, illiterate brother. The craving for amusement is common to all. The people, in their eagerness to obtain some, are ever ready to accept any, and, in the absence of anything better, take what they can get with least inconvenience to themselves. In the great majority of cases a want of proper training in early life encourages self-indulgence in practices which become ere long habits, having a direct tendency to debase the mind. In other instances, even when the influence of good precept and example have been brought to bear on the character, the love of amusement leads young men into those snares with which the town is beset. Here continued excess ends in loss of reputation and self-respect. Men abuse their leisure, blast their prospects, and impair their health, morally and physically; but who is to blame?

The English people above all others will not be driven, though they are easily led. Acting on this portion of the character, the plan should be to draw men away from scenes of vice by the counter attraction of innocent and virtuous enjoyment. So far as the working classes are concerned, the depth of social and moral degradation in which a large mass of them are sunk, the depraved taste formed and cultivated thereby, and the active measures in operation to keep the people in this state of thraldom to vicious habits, form the most terrible barriers to their emancipation.

There are people in the world who consider the building of a church in a poverty-stricken and densely populated neighbourhood as the one thing needful to promote moral and social purity, combined with the spread of true Evangelical religion. There are others who consider that the establishment of a society or the founding of a hall for the purpose of providing rational recreation is the main point to be aimed at in order to purify or regenerate the people's pastimes. Of both these classes we desire to speak in terms of the greatest respect. Their sincerity cannot be doubted. They prove it daily by sacrifices of time and money. The ardour of their zeal may cause them to err in judgment, – herein they prove their humanity; but their sense of justice and love of truth ought ever to lead them to *sift* rather than set aside the opinions of those who differ from them.

As to the first, well intentioned men, who have the welfare of their poorer brethren at heart, and are anxious to do something to alleviate their sorrows and sufferings, on the representation of a zealous and enthusiastic district visitor or expectant minister, subscribe their money liberally to build a church. The number of poor families in the district is carefully given. The utter moral and spiritual destitution of the people is painfully pointed out. The church will, it is said, speedily alter this state of things; therefore the church is built. Now in nine cases out of ten, what is the result? By the *modern system of pew-letting* the poor are virtually secluded from the church, and the 'poor man's church' is a hollow sham. Paradoxical as it may seem, the 'poor man's church' is only such whilst it remains a workshop or a warehouse room licensed by the Bishop. Whenever it emerges from this chrysalis state it rises far above the poor man's means: he is a flower from which no sweets can be extracted, and is therefore left to perish in the moral wilderness that surrounds him. As a working man observes, 'Religionists, in our days, are too much like railway companies. They are very anxious to do business, but the main object appears to be that the line should be *made to pay*. They will not take you any portion of the journey unless you first pay the fare; and you can then get any sort of accommodation, according to the class you book!'[70]

We may not go this length, yet will admit that although this sarcasm contains a tincture of severity, nevertheless it contains, also, a sediment of truth. The former may be easily strained off, but the latter ought to undergo a closer inspection. Now, supposing the church, when built in a district such as that alluded to, were to remain, in the fullest sense of the word, a 'poor man's church,' – every seat free – the great result which many expect would not be produced. In the majority of cases the ground has not been prepared, the seed has not been sown. A long course of training and teaching is necessary, and a congregation must be prepared. There is a great work to do before the people are brought up to that standard when regular church or chapel going will have the effect intended. Besides, as it has been again and again put by Non-conformists particularly, and some Episcopalians as well, the church should be the product of the congregation, and not, as many argue, the congregation the product of the church. This is the natural order of things, and we are simple enough to think that, in these matters, the age of miracles is past, – special providences cannot be reasonably expected, and, further, we do not deserve them.

As it is in religion, so it will prove with regard to recreation – the people must be prepared for it. The founding of a hall where amusements of an elevating tendency will be provided, will not, in the first instance, have that marked effect, neither will it meet with all that success which warm-hearted and sanguine men seem to expect. From dissolute habits and degrading pastimes to steady conduct and rational enjoyment is a wide leap, and men must undergo a course of training before they can reasonably be expected to accomplish that feat. As well may you expect the erection of a church to change the character of a district, as to expect the daily visitor to the gin palace, the beerhouse, the canine tavern, or the gambling snug, to become an attendant at the lecture hall, the tennis court, or the chess table without a long course of preparation. These remarks are amply borne out by the history of the Saturday evening concerts at Liverpool. This institution stands proudly as a beacon and guide to all who would successfully endeavour to elevate the character of popular amusements. Here are a few men, with clear heads, and hearts in unison, who make no fuss, waste no time in idle talk, but set to work resolutely with a will to prepare the people for enjoyments of a refined and elevating character. Their beginning is on a humble scale. They hold the meeting in a school room. Their programme is very simple, yet pure. They rise step by step as they find the people prepared to rise with them, and by such means they *educate* for themselves a large congregation, and the crowded Concert-hall, on the Saturday evening, is the result.

There are many men who used, at the school room, to enjoy the simple ballad, the concerted piece, or the recitation of the enthusiastic amateur. These men are now so highly educated that they are competent to judge of, and enjoy music of the highest character, and the committee have, on many occasions, paid immense sums of money to secure the greatest talent, in order that this growing taste of their patrons might be gratified. And further, the taste of the parent or the youth is communicated to other members of the family; hence it is that you see in the Saturday evening audience in the body of the hall such a pleasing and distinctive character, when compared with other places of recreation, where the terms are even higher. The assembling of a large body of people anywhere, for the purpose of general happiness or joy, is a pleasing spectacle. This is more particularly the case when the entertainment is such as to call forth the exercise of the imagination, and thus elevate the mind above mere animal indulgence, which has ever been our experience of the Saturday evening concerts, in Lord Nelson-street. During last winter several other places of similar character were, through the instrumentality of clergymen, brought into operation in other towns, and all were attended with beneficial results. Each of these will, in all probability, be enabled to *educate* a congregation for itself; and if the directors are wise they will, by nicely graduated steps, lead the people upward and onward. By such means the concerts in the school room may lead to the formation of permanent institutions, which will assist in a very important manner to civilize, if not to Christianize, the masses.

The establishment of recreative societies in several of our large towns is very cheering, and their success in some cases highly encouraging. Yet, looking at the giant evils which the true friends of the people have to encounter; at the apathy, if not something worse, of the local legislature; at the total indifference of those who ought to feel most interest in such substantial social advantages, an abundance of patience and faith will have to be brought into exercise. It is worthy of consideration whether the school rooms of every sect and denomination throughout the towns might be made available for recreative purposes; and how could they be more profitably employed? In these, on two or more evenings in each week, something of a simple yet exhilarating character could be brought before parents and children. This would go far to

> Frame the mind to mirth and merriment,
> Which bars a thousand harms and lengthens life.

Instruction might be gradually blended, as the people progressed; but the first thing to be aimed at is to wean them from their degrading habits, and arm them to withstand the allurements of the ginshop. It is a matter of surprise how easily people are amused; and it often happens the more simple the feat the greater the fun. We have seen, in a large assembly, a man take a pipe and balance it on his nose! How the people laughed. Another genius, with inverted ideas of humanity, sings a song whilst standing on his head, and beats time to the tune by knocking his ankles together.

The people roar with laughter, and pitch their pennies at him for fun. Punch, sadly degenerated, and too much given up to those modern accomplishments, friend-killing and wife-beating, yet still the pugnacious Punch of yore, will cause hundreds of people to stop in the daily course of their business, and how heartily they all laugh at the extravagances of the puppet.

Hundreds of people were amused during the summer evenings by watching young men play the game of rounders, in the 'Berkley fields,' and if one of them slipped, or happened to fall over another, the laughter burst forth in peals, the sound of which, under the circumstances, gave indications of what might be, had we a people's park or play-ground. It is said man is the only animal that laughs. How necessary is it, therefore, that these faculties of his nature have opportunity to develop themselves. Certain we are that innocent mirth, provocative of joyous laughter, has much to do with cheering the heart, and lightening the burden of every son of toil. Beyond which, the better feelings of some men can be reached by such means, and, in the first instance, by no other.

It is all very well to talk of a voluntary combination against vice, and to form a society having for its object the suppression of vicious practices; but, if you wish to do men good, the mind and heart must be acted on. Outward compliance, unless it be the result of inward feeling and conviction, will be of no avail – will effect no lasting or permanent result. You can stimulate, nurture, and revivify this inward feeling by a careful, cautious, and very gentle process of education, and by no other means. The germ of good within the man is overgrown with noxious weeds, and has, day by day, all sorts of rubbish thrown over it. In some cases it is almost dead, and you will have to bear on this an influence that will *re-create* it. The terms used, if viewed aright, show the magnitude of that work comprisc l in the word recreation. The condition of the people shows how much they stand in need of this cultivation and preparatory training, in order that they may rightly enjoy and truly appreciate the advantages of rational amusement for their leisure hours.

Most, if not all, the inland manufacturing towns set apart a few days, or a week, at stated periods, during which all labour is suspended, and the labourers have opportunity of enjoying themselves. By means of railways the people have afforded them a cheap and expeditious mode of transit to distant places and towns, and this has been attended with the most important social results. Wants have been created in the minds of the labouring population, at the same time the means have been suggested for gratifying these. Hence you see Liverpool in summer time, day by day crowded with 'cheap trippers' from the region of Cottonopolis and the woollen and hardware districts – thousands of swarthy and hard-handed labourers, decently clad, with their wives, children, or sweethearts. These people fill the museums, inspect the public buildings and shops, assist to wear out the pavement in St. George's-hall, gaze in wonder at the ships, jostle each other and everybody else on the Landing-stage, load the steamers, deluge the Cheshire shores, sail round the Floating-light, carrying with them, in most cases, immense baskets of provisions; and thus, at a cheap cost, and in a rational manner, they enlarge the mind, improve the health, and benefit the town.

After a few short trips of this sort they begin to enlarge their sphere of observation, and, as their means increase, they are found away at the Isle of Man, inhaling the invigorating breezes on 'the head,' sailing about the bays, bathing on the shingle in the creeks, riding over the hills, or roaming through the romantic glens, that abound in Mona's beautiful isle. Others are found in Wales, where the charms of Beaumaris or Bangor, the antiquities of Conway or Carnarvon Castles, the wonders of the Tubular and Suspension Bridges, the sail through the Straits, the ascent of Snowdon, the walk through the Pass of Llanberis, or the more arduous and exciting scramble to the 'Devil's Kitchen,' and the majestic scenery around the entrances to the Pass of Nant Francon, are all brought within the means of the most limited. Steam packets, railroads, and periodic holidays have proved immense levellers, and accomplished much, in a physical and social point of view, by opening up the country to the masses. The aristocracy of travel is past. In these days, with the aid of a few shillings, an inquiring spirit, a cheerful temper, a stout heart, active limbs, and appetites well under control, a working man may see as much in a few days (and enjoy a deal more) as a nobleman could by the outlay of as many pounds, and the expenditure of as many weeks in days gone by.

But, the working people of Liverpool never enjoy themselves in this way.[71] There are, we know, some intelligent artizans and merchants' clerks who lay themselves out, and lay their cash out, for an annual excursion; but the great body of the people never think of such things. They work from week to week, have their Saturday night's spree, their Sunday 'guzzle,' often have to neglect their work on Monday to overcome the Sunday's debauch, and will frequently be heard cursing their fate, whilst, by their conduct, they do all in their power to render it irrevocable. Some of them do find their way to Cheshire on Sunday, but it is more frequently in search of drink than for purposes of rational recreation; and a walk on Sunday through a district inhabited by the working classes is one of the most cheerless and humiliating spectacles that can be imagined. The true object of life seems to be entirely lost sight of.

The chief purpose of man's life, as here seen, appears to be that he may eat, drink, and sleep, – the merest animal gratification. Still, in the matter of periodic holidays, there is hope, – close observation of the efforts working people will make whenever an object is set before them encourages this hope.

Look in the matter of a club anniversary day. This is, in many cases, the only day in the year to which the man looks forward with anything like real interest, and why? He is then expected to appear amongst his fellow workmen, or brother members, in clean and decent attire, and, unless he can go in such wise, he will not go at all. Hence, he makes due provision. By self-denial and frugality he is enabled to accomplish his desire, and he appears on the great day of the feast with good clothes on his back and some 'brass' in his pocket. It is to be lamented that these occasions of social enjoyment are often attended with evil results, and that no better entertainment is offered to the people than indulgence in intoxicating drinks, or listening to the grandiloquent oratory of ambitious aspirants to *select* honours.[72] But what we wish to show is this, if men are found to practice self-denial, frugality, and industry in order that, for one day in the year, they may mingle with their fellows in what is to them social enjoyment, does it not go to prove that, if more opportunities were offered, greater facilities given, a better character of entertainment or enjoyment held out, people would have increased interest in providing for such periods?

By reason of the dock trade and customs' department, in seaport towns, there may be obstacles in the way of setting apart periodic holidays, but, if the matter be viewed aright, and a proper degree of earnestness brought to bear on it, every difficulty would yield, and success would be certain. The talk that is made about a day being no holiday unless the working man has his day's wages paid, is simply good-natured nonsense. Such people would never wish to see a working man truly independent. What ought to be encouraged is to make the working man feel that he has all the means within himself to obtain rational enjoyment and recreation, and that he has only to deny himself of so much drink, and so much carding, and practice more industry, sobriety, and frugality, in order that he may provide for a day of rejoicing, and when it arrives, he is in possession of that which will ensure the most hearty enjoyment of it. We were told by a working man that, by doing without three glasses of rum which he used to get on Saturday night, and placing the money in a box for six months, he had been enabled to visit the Manchester Exhibition, and spend three days at a watering place during the summer. Physically, this abstinence had in no way proved injurious; mentally, the man had elevated himself, and

would, no doubt, return to his home and his labour with a stronger
determination than ever to persevere in a course which was
attended with such excellent and profitable results. What this man
had done and was doing might be done by thousands, and it is just
on this point where the working man requires *direction*, and
nothing more.

On summer evenings the working people who dwell in towns
have opportunity of enjoying outdoor recreation, but there are very
few places where adequate provision is made for this. Magistrates
are frequently heard to stigmatize and condemn the means which
the people adopt for their own recreation, or to which they are
lured by the license allowed for the liquor traffic. Yet they are, in
too many cases, totally indifferent as to the adoption of any plans
which might alter this state of being. When speaking of parks, or
playgrounds, for the people, it has been urged again and again,
'What does a working man want with a playground? If he works
hard, as most have to do, ten, or probably twelve hours a day, he
is so completely tired out when he gets home, that his only walk
will be to the spirit vaults; his only game will be a game at cards
at the beerhouse.' We admit that, to a great extent, this is the case
now. The working man does go too much to the beershop. He has
been trained to do nothing else. He has seen his father do the same
thing, has assisted to get him home on many occasions, and has
been sent out early next morning for drink, so that the night's
debauch might be 'washed down.' But, in the matter of
playgrounds, it will not be the men whose characters are formed
that will be directly acted upon, but the youths whose characters
are in course of formation. These would be by such means withdrawn from the evil influences and vicious practices of the streets.

We noticed one evening, several stalwart men, without coats, but
with clean faces, and enjoying their evening pipe. They had come
to the fields, at the outskirts of the town, to witness the sports of
the youths, and seemed to enjoy themselves most heartily. Some of
their own offspring might be amongst the groups; if so, their
interest in the games was deepened. This is the effect we would be
justified in expecting from the establishment of people's playgrounds. The parents would, in all probability, become spectators
of their children's enjoyment, and by such simple means would
secure their own. We may be certain that in the majority of cases,
each man withdrawn from the corner of the court or street to the
fields or playground, would moreover be withdrawn from the
yawning brazen-faced jaws of the corner ginshop. He would be
withdrawn from the evil companionship which at such places he is
likely to form. He would find, on his return home, that, although
he had smoked 'a dry pipe,' his sleep would be quite as sound as

if he had drank a pot of beer to it, and he would have in the morning as good a relish for his work as he had for his breakfast. With
a few evenings in each week spent in this way, he would find, on
Saturday night, that he had not such large 'shots' to pay; and by
going home sober he would soon be able to see that, in the matter
of order and cleanliness, his house might be improved, his children
might be better clothed, and he would find his means increase to
accomplish this. Hence it is by acting directly on the children we
may, in the most beneficial manner, act indirectly on the parents,
and public playgrounds may be made active agencies in promoting
moral, social, and physical regeneration.

But in most towns there is a large class of men who are rarely
or never considered when speaking of the working classes,
although, in most cases, they work hard enough. They comprise
our merchants' and brokers' clerks and shopkeepers' assistants.
Generally well educated, and compelled to maintain a respectable
appearance on anything but respectable salaries, their position is
worthy of deep consideration. These men, it is said, do not indulge
in the grosser vices. That is, we suppose, they do not support 'fistic
talent.' They do not give 3s. or 4s. a dozen for rats. Neither do
they 'stand a tizzy to draw the browney,'[73] or bet heavily on a
dog fight. We have not seen them at these sports, although some
of their employers set them the example. But they do go to the
dancing rooms, the promenade, and 'the hop.' Respectable men
frequent such places: they are respectable men, therefore, this is the
place for them. They say, 'Now you drive us from these resorts,
what do you expect us to do? We cannot go to the Free Public
Library, and sit in the vitiated atmosphere of that room for an
evening. We do not care about reading. Our occupation during the
day does not involve any great amount of bodily fatigue, and we
need some invigorating exercise to keep us in health and spirits.'
Now, to these young men, a public park and gymnasium would be
a great boon. After a brisk walk, half an hour at pole-climbing, or
an hour spent at jumping, or, if you like, dancing in the open air,
they would be invigorated, and perhaps better able to enjoy a good
book, rational conversation, or a game of chess or draughts with
a friend, and thus prepare themselves properly for the labours of
another day.

Our rulers ought to be more deeply interested in the people's
pleasures than their actions would lead us to suppose they are.
Many noble deeds have been done for the people – amongst the
foremost stand the baths and libraries. But the good here attempted
will be frustrated by the evils that remain to be checked. A short-
sighted policy with reference to popular amusements will entirely
blast all the hopes which have been held out with reference to social

progress. Take this fact:– A new gaol has been erected, costly, but most complete. Everything that science has discovered and philanthropy devised is here put into operation to combine the most effective prison discipline with industrial occupation. This gaol is now filled to overflowing; and, in many cases, the inmates can tell you that *it was in the pursuit of pleasure they became entangled in the meshes of crime.* Some time ago we saw at the Borough Gaol, in all the degradation which the prison garb exhibits, individuals whom a short time since we had noticed indulging in the disgraceful practices and pastimes which we have elsewhere described. It is the duty of rulers and magistrates to see that the enjoyments provided for the people be such as to hold out no temptation to vice in any form – so cheap that all can partake without the necessity of being drawn into crime in order to procure the gratification. To secure recreation of this character all creeds and classes should combine; every political or sectarian obstacle must be cast aside – thus will the greatest happiness be secured for the greatest number.

22 The courts and alleys of Liverpool: introductory

The Courts of Liverpool have in many ways and at various times been rendered unpleasantly notorious. We don't mean the Police courts, nor the Assize courts, nor the County courts, but the 'courts' which form the dwelling-places of a very large portion of the labouring population, and the deeds and doings in which furnish at all times a great proportion of work for all the other courts to do. It was estimated a long time ago that in Liverpool over 50,000 persons lived in courts; but this was before the cellar population was cleared out, and the number must be greatly increased now. But whatever the number may be now, of one thing the public may be assured, and that is – the old dilapidated court houses, with their fetid air and small squalid rooms, still form the only dwellings which are supposed to be within the means of the labouring and casually employed poor. The clearance of the cellars crowded the courts, and, notwithstanding the progress of sanitary operations in Liverpool – notwithstanding the decrease of the death rate, as shown by the returns – the Liverpool courts present scenes of social degradation and misery which it will be almost hopeless to induce people who have no practical acquaintance with the habits of the people to believe.[74]

The prevailing opinion respecting 'courts' amongst those who never entered one in their lives, and who are yet ever ready and well disposed to assist any scheme that aims at the amelioration of human suffering, or the promotion of public health, seems to be that, although they are not cheerful residences, and not particularly healthy, yet, being under the control of the 'Health Committee,' they are well looked after and cared for, and the grosser evils which are known to be attendant upon them are wisely mitigated. But this opinion is not in accordance with the fact; and, moreover, it does the Health Committee an injustice. To a certain extent that committee has control over the courts, but their powers are limited. The Committee do what they can, and no one can judge of what they have done, in the way of promoting cleanliness, except those who have some knowledge of what these places used to be. The evils which now exist, and which we intend to describe, exist in *defiance* of all that the Health Committee can do; hence it is that a strong expression of public opinion is necessary to support that Committee in an effort to obtain still greater powers, as nothing else seems possible.

That the Health Committee are fully alive to the necessity of looking narrowly into the condition of the courts of the town their proceedings from week to week show. Indeed, even on the simple ground of public decency, leaving out morals or health, this would be absolutely necessary. But a committee who simply meet, receive reports, hear statistics, and confirm the minutes of previous meetings, and simply contents itself with that, would not be likely to accomplish any great amount of public good. The real work of any committee scarcely ever comes before the public. The results are seen, but the labour undertaken in order to produce those results is generally overlooked. It is by sub-dividing the labour that the efficiency of the work is increased; hence sub-committees are formed, and, as Mr. Jeffery[75] has very clearly shown, it is in the sub-committees of the Town Council where the work, good or bad, is done. The Health Committee is no exception to this. As a body it never could have dealt with the court and alley inspection, and it was a good idea of Mr. James Crellin to move for the appointment of a Special Committee, to which the duty might be properly entrusted, and who would be responsible for the work done. The idea could only have occurred to a man who had much practical knowledge of the evils which poor people inflicted upon themselves and perpetuated in their families by reason of the habits of life in which they indulged; and the fact that Mr. Newlands, the Borough Engineer, had, in the most marked manner, frequently referred to the pestilential condition of many courts and alleys, in his reports to the Committee, favoured the idea and led to its adoption.

The following extract from the recently published Report of the Borough Engineer, as to the construction of the courts, will be read with interest:–

The houses are generally built back to back, one end of the court, as a rule, is closed either by houses, or, which is worse, by the privies and ashpits; or a worse state of things still, the privies and ashpits are placed at the entrance of the court, and the only air supplied to the inhabitants must pass over their foul contents. But even this miserable state of things can be outdone. There are courts which, by a perverted ingenuity, have been formed in the following manner:- An ordinary street house has had its lobby converted into a common passage leading to the back yard. The passage is of course roofed over, and is, in fact, a tunnel from which the back room of the original house, now converted into a separate dwelling, has its entrance. The back yard has been filled with other houses in such manner as to have only the continuation of the tunnel for access, and from this little area of three feet wide the houses receive their supply of light and air. The passage is generally terminated by the privy and ashpit common to all the wretched dwellings, with its liquid filth oozing through their walls, and its pestiferous gases flowing into the windows of the two last houses. The structural evils of these miserable abodes are aggravated by the filthy habits of the occupants. 'What is everybody's business is nobody's business,' and so the duty of keeping the court and its conveniences clean is neglected. Even when the middens have been filled so as to overflow the court, no one cared to take the trouble to apprize the officers of the Nuisance Department of the fact in order to their being emptied.

To those not conversant with the subject, it may appear that the evils of the court and alley life are exaggerated in the foregoing statement, and that the means taken for their mitigation are excessive. But let any one glance at the analysis which follows this, and then take into consideration the facts as there set forth, and in complete detail in Table No. 11, that in the Borough there are 3,273 courts, containing 18,610 houses; that the average number of houses in a court is 5·86, and the average number of inhabitants to a house is a fraction more than six; and it will be found that upwards of a fifth part of the population of Liverpool is condemned to live in these morally and physically unwholesome dwellings.

There is now a special staff devoted to the inspection of courts, under the supervision of Mr. Newlands. But the Sub-Committee's duty involved the occasional personal inspection of the courts and alleys by the members of the Committee, in company with the Borough Engineer and health officers. This duty, onerous and repulsive as it must frequently be, is, we have good reason to know, very faithfully discharged, and the visits of the Councillors to the courts in the densely populous districts have been attended with the most excellent results. They are by this means brought face to face with the difficulties that the officers have to deal with in carrying out the wholesome provisions of the Health of Town Act; they see in the true light – with their own eyes, and not through the spectrum of a report – what work has really been done, and what there remains still to do; they are prepared to discuss from their own knowledge of the facts any remedial measures which may be proposed with reference to the public health; and, above all, they strengthen the hands of the health officers, and give their visits a moral force and significance which they would never obtain by any other means.

Some time after the committee inspection had been in operation Dr Holland, being in Liverpool, took occasion to accompany the gentlemen during one of their visits to the courts, and the following letter expresses his views relative to the advantages to be derived from such means:

'BURIAL ACTS OFFICE,
OLD PALACE YARD,

'*Westminster, S.W., November 7th*, 1860.

'DEAR SIR, – Permit me to offer my best thanks to you and the Committee for so kindly affording me an opportunity of seeing the great benefits that have resulted from the systematic inspection of the courts and alleys of Liverpool. When I compare their condition now with what I remember it to have been, and with that of similar places in Manchester and elsewhere, I can most cordially congratulate you upon the great success which has hitherto attended the benevolent exertions of your Committee. At the same time, I cannot help regretting that the good work is not even more perfectly performed, as it might be if a few more Inspectors were employed, for it is evident to me that much more can be done by constant supervision than by frequent resort to legal proceedings. In short, the people ought rather to be taught how to preserve their own and their neighbours' health and comfort than to be punished.

'I was pleased to observe the friendliness with which our party of inspection was received. It was clear that your officers were not as much dreaded as welcomed. I did, however, notice several women bustling about, as soon as they saw them, to get matters put right. No doubt the Committee are anxious, and very properly so, to avoid any needless expense; but I am sure I am within bound in saying that every pound spent in enforcing cleanliness saves many pounds in poor-rate, by diminished sickness and mortality, to say nothing of increased comfort, decency, and morality.

'I should be stating only part of the truth if I allowed it to be supposed that I believe that, by enforced cleanliness alone, Liverpool can be made a healthy town. Much may be done by that, but very much more is needed. Large portions of the town have been so badly constructed and arranged, that nothing short of extensive reconstruction will reduce the death-rate to the level of healthy places, and that can only be done by slow degrees. The increase, however, of badly-constructed houses, with insufficient light and ventilation, might and ought to be avoided. All privies with putrefying filth cannot be immediately removed, but their increase may be prevented, and their removal effected gradually and not slowly, as it would be were all alive to the destruction of life and health these abominable poison-pits occasion.

'Believe me, yours faithfully,

'P. H. HOLLAND.

'J. Crellin, Esq., Liverpool.'

There are, in every large town, causes never-ceasingly at work which engender and foster disease and, in some cases, pestilence. This was more particularly the case in Liverpool, from the construction of the courts, – destitute of drainage, and defiant of ventilation. Whole districts have at times fallen prey to raging fever; and even yet there are streets, courts, and alleys where a low, enervating fever holds continual revel, and where the more virulent forms stealthily work. There is found in such districts an indisposition on the part of the people to use those means which are placed within their reach, and which are intended to promote their health and consequent happiness. Whether the physical exhaustion caused by unhealthy dwellings has not something to do with the low state of morals and the craving for exciting drinks known to exist in such districts is a question worth thinking about, but will not now be discussed. The most painful thing that any one meets with in a walk through the over-crowded courts is the indifference of the people to their own degraded condition. To listen to the reports at a Town Missionary meeting – to read the speeches at a Scripture Readers' anniversary – to run over a list of the benevolent societies which are said to be actively at work sowing broadcast the seeds of knowledge – might very well lead any one to suppose that there could hardly be one household or one family but must have had placed before it that instruction which would guide it to adopt ordinary precaution for the preservation of what is so valuable to the poor – health. One might suppose that the motive of self-preservation would serve instead, where nothing higher would or could be appealed to. But it is not so. The stubborn attachment of poor people to foul houses and foul habits is truly marvellous. Where water is given it will be wasted, not used; where courts are flagged, they will not be washed or swept; where lanes or alleys are paved and drained, garbage will be allowed to cover the surface, the gully holes will be choked, and the constant vigilance of the officers fails to secure even regard to the requirements of common decency. It is to overcome this reluctance on the part of the people that the sub-committee have set themselves earnestly to work. They go amongst the people, talk to them, and strive to reason with them, and they have succeeded, in some cases, almost beyond their hopes. The court inspectors, supported by the committee, are gradually forcing upon the people what they so much need, but what they so steadily refuse to take for themselves.

From some facts which came out at a meeting of the Council, we were, some time since, put upon the track of the Courts and Alleys Committee, and, more recently, the Chairman and members of the Committee, together with the Borough Engineer, have been very kind in affording information that will materially assist in laying before the town the social condition of the teeming population of the courts. Just now a deal is heard about 'town improvements,' and there may be some hope that a careful and attentive perusal of the facts which will be set forth in these papers will show the direction which 'town improvements' ought to take. It is one thing to beautify the town, and quite another to promote the health of its inhabitants. The one may be done, and, indeed, frequently is, at the expense of the other. We believe it is quite possible for both to walk hand in hand; and, indeed, that scheme, whatever it may be, which does not aim at moral and social elevation, as well as mere architectural embellishments, even if corner vaults be left out – can hardly be said to be 'town improvement.'

23 Sermons in stones

During the past week, *Porcupine* determined to have another personal inspection of the plague spots of Liverpool, in the shape of defective courts; and the first thing he learned was, that the Sub-committee of the Health Committee, charged with the supervision of these places, had been engaged for many hours upon a similar tour of examination. As on former occasions, *Porcupine* found one feeling uppermost in the minds of the people living in these districts, and that was of something more than respect for the authorities, for the interest shown by them in looking after the condition of their poorer fellow townspeople. Some of the women had had a sharp word or two spoken to them where they had been found wanting in taking their share of the cleansing operations. This had given great satisfaction to the more decent of the women, and appeared to tell famously as the culprit had her dose of reproof administered on the spot, in the presence of her neighbours, with the facts before her eyes not to be gainsayed.

At a nest of wretched hovels in Maguire-street, a singular scene occurred. One of the dames vociferously protested against the hardship of being compelled to bear her turn at cleansing the common convenience, and went so far as to declare, with vehement imprecations, that she would sooner serve three months in prison than submit. An official who was with the sub-committee quietly walked up and asked her if she were really sincere, and was prepared to say seriously that she would prefer being sent to gaol than be clean. The firm and kindly way in which the termagant was met stopped her in a moment, and she evidently had not viewed the question in that light before. A few more words addressed to her in the same spirit effected an entire change in her thoughts and bearing, ending in her admitting that she was bound to do her share of the work, and promising to act accordingly. Promises are sometimes broken, but in this case, if the woman should break her word, she will get into a worse difficulty under a bye-law which is admirably framed to meet such delinquents.

We are here reminded that whilst, in the majority of cases, the tenants are alone to blame for many evils that surround them, yet we have, in our jottings by the way, cases which afford excellent illustrations of what the residents of courts have sometimes to suffer through the inconsideration of landlords. We went the other day, when out on a ramble, into No. 2 Court, Hockenhall-alley, leading from Dale-street. There are three houses here, inhabited by fifteen persons. The entrance is narrow, the court is very much confined, and the privy, which has been converted into a water closet, and the ashpit are fronting the people's doors. Some repairs had been done, either in the yard or houses, and from these a heap of rubbish was left in the corner of the court. The water closet had become choked, the ashpit was filled, and the soil was thrown over the heap of rubbish, causing a stench in the place which was poisonous! *For ten weeks* had these poor people complained of this nuisance without avail. The contractor for the removal of night soil would not clean out this corner because it was *rubbish*, and his contract did not include the removal of that. The top dressing of night soil which had been given to the rubbish made it somewhat tempting to the men; but, as it was said, 'when they dug in they got among the stones and rubbish, and then they dropped it quick enough.' It seems, from what we could learn, that it was clearly the landlord's duty to have this rubbish removed; and yet, although he was not unmindful to secure his rent regularly, he condemned these tenants of his to breathe this tainted atmosphere, and even the pleading of the women of behalf of their little children failed to move him. In many cases the filthiness of courts is to be attributed in a great measure to the residents; but in this case, both externally and internally, the people seemed to have done what they could, and it was grievous to see that their efforts were not better supported.

Going a little further, an illustration of a different class was met. The keeper of a provision shop called the attention of the inspector who accompanied us to the condition of her cellar. There were courts at the back of her premises, and the drainage from one of the privies in these percolated through the cellar wall, making the air very offensive throughout the whole of her house. What made the case worse was, that this cellar formed the storehouse for her goods. Here she kept her pans of milk, piles of cabbages, &c.; and it can be very well understood that the air of such a place would not improve the flavour of any of these articles. In many instances that have been met with in the poorer districts of the town, it is surprising how negligent or ignorant people are regarding the effect which foul air has upon food; but the shopkeeper here, much to her credit, seemed to be somewhat alive to the deleterious effect which the noxious gases from the midden must necessarily have upon the milk, and she does use some precautions for protecting it, but these are of little avail. The whole atmosphere of the place was impregnated with the odour, and one could not help but think of the families around who had to live in such confined places, and who, in addition to the evils consequent upon this, had to use the milk and vegetables which were thus stored.

But to return to our last walk through the courts. We met with the ever-recurring broken flag-stones destroyed by the chip-choppers,[76] and with the poor little children who seem to have scarcely any other home than such as these stones afford. The more comfortable portion of the public of Liverpool do not know the town they live in. Probably not one in a hundred of them has ever been in one of these places, much less noted, as *Porcupine* has, the regular attention from lowest depths to lower still, by which the children living in the worst of the courts sink below the condition of the children living in places a shade better. To such of the public as are strangers to all this misery, *Porcupine* communicates the sermon which was preached to him by the stones on which the neglected little ones were seen.

These children are mostly allowed to wander up and down the alley, and the street into which it runs, from morn till night. The stones and the gutter are to them what green fields, the mountain side, and silvery streams are to peasants' children in the country. They see nothing of Nature except what is loathsome – hear nothing but what is debasing – learn nothing but what is ruinous. Many of them have all the elements for making fine men and women, but it is almost inevitable that they should become burdens on society, and a large portion in the most loathsome form. Well conducted parents know that, after they have set their offspring the best example, – sought to keep all injurious influences away from them, made them intelligent, watched over them, prayed for them, – still, when they come in contact with the world, they will often go wrong. From the days of poor Adam's sorrow for his son's misdeeds, where there could have been no bad example, till the end of time, we fear this misfortune will continue. If this be true of those who are tenderly nurtured, what can be hoped for the poor creatures reared in the alleys of the town? We are not discoursing about the clothes they wear, or rather do not wear; the food they eat, or rather scarcely eat; or the shelter from the weather which they find: we are speaking of their moral condition. We put it to every mother and father in Liverpool what must be the fate of people whose infancy is passed under the conditions of the poor children we refer to. What a dreary life is theirs! The everlasting piles of brick and mortar – the surroundings of mud and stench – the habitual indifference to soap and water – the early impressions of life all wretchedness – no cheerful strolls with decent parents – no innocent fun with proper playmates – no friends' houses to be taken to and be petted – 'tip' unknown – everything good unknown – everything bad daily instilled.

Look at that grog shop at the corner of Maguire-street. Look at that pale, shrivelled, dirty, ragged woman just leaving the door. Notice how her lips are parched – how her eyes glare – how her cheek is cut – and the way in which the few rags are made to hang upon her emaciated form. Now she lunges into the middle of the street, and, holding a quart bottle half filled with ale in one hand and a jug in the other, she waves a triumphant defiance at some one up the street. But look by the kerb-stone. See that little creature with curly hair, and its face and legs so caked with dirt that the flesh is not discernible. Hear how piteously it cries, because *Mother* is leaving it. The little hands, fresh from the gutter, are pressed against its eyes as it strives to cross the street and reach its mother, who is still waving the bottle and hurling imprecations on all sides. Poor little toddler – what a life is opening up for thee!

You grown-up men and women who are going on rightly! *Porcupine* asks you why are you as you are? How much of anything about you that is good have you done for yourselves? We must all confess that if there be any part of one's conduct that has ripened out satisfactorily, the seed was sown in days long gone by. The Apostle is a great philosopher when, passing in review such reflections as the above, he declares – 'By the grace of God I am what I am.' We are all agreed upon the difficulty of reclaiming people who have become confirmed in badness, and therefore *Porcupine* invites such of his readers as believe they owe a duty to their fellow creatures to lose no time in becoming acquainted with the real truth as regards the inmates of the courts and alleys, and to lend a helping hand in preventing thousands of little children from being lost.

24   What Mr. Stitt might see if he would

The representatives of the ratepayers in the Town Council don't intend to take any steps towards improving the health of the town by opening up the filthy courts and destroying the pestiferous alleys which day by day send forth disease and death on all around. We judge this from the proceedings at last Council. £23,000 of the surplus fund was taken towards reduction of rates, but not a word was heard of expending such a like sum in real, not fanciful, town improvements. Well, the rates will have to be paid one way or other; and any persons looking at the rate of mortality in Liverpool will see that, notwithstanding all our expenditure for sanitary purposes, the town is becoming more unhealthy.[77] And this can hardly be otherwise when the evils which have been pointed out in these pages are permitted not only to exist, but are encouraged to thrive and flourish.

Our illustrations to-day shall be taken close at hand. We will suppose Mr. Stitt[78] to have attended a meeting of the Health Committee, at the Town-hall. He has been talking (to the reporters) about the interest he takes in promoting the social prosperity of the town, and, as he knows that his speech will be in to-morrow's paper, he now goes off, as his manner is, to see for himself whether these things be really so. He finds himself in Preston-street, and, before turning into the courts, he stands to admire the progress which the new Public Offices are making. He knows much money has been *saved* by this land being laid waste for so many years, and he adds this to the money that he is sure will be saved when the offices are all brought together, and, having found what a nice round sum this is, he throws back his head with an air of self-satisfaction and settles down to his work of court inspection, in order that he may be properly aware of what best to do when the time comes. Yes; 'When the time comes,' he says, as his hat is dinged by the court entrance.

In No. 1 Court, Preston-street, Mr. Stitt finds six houses, very dirty, very close, with children (squalid, ragged, and filthy) staring at him or trying to play in the gutter. The midden-steads of the

front houses *are close to the doors of these houses in the court*, and
the odours arising from these not being considered pleasant, the
people keep all their windows shut.[79] There are lodging houses in
the court, and when the number of people who are allowed to sleep
in such places is looked at, no wonder need be manifested at the
signs of moral degradation and physical decay which meet you at
every door.

Coming out of the court, and very likely being glad to get out,
Mr. Stitt finds in the open street that matters, in some respects, are
no better, and, in other respects, much worse. There are twelve
front houses in Preston-street, that have no conveniences whatever
attached to them. There is a court of eighteen houses in Shawhill-
street behind, and *for the use of these and the twelve front houses,
seven water closets are crammed into a corner of the court.* The
characters met with in the houses in Preston-street are as
demoralized and depraved as anything that can be seen in Liverpool, and there is no attempt made to conceal the means by which
they are supported. Bloated girls, in all states of undress, loll about,
and the walls of the houses are covered with portraits of celebrated
pugilists, alternating with the most obscene French prints. The
people complain of the rent charged, (5s. per week,) but, as to the
inconvenience attending the houses, by reason of the water closets
being in another street, nothing is heard about that. They seem to
be altogether indifferent to such trifling matters.

Passing from Preston-street to Shawhill-street Mr. Stitt has an
opportunity of inspecting 'the Liverpool Street Railway' in operation, and will doubtless admire the way in which the paving of the
street has been treated. 'The railway is very handy though,' as many
of Mr. Rankin's men will explain.[80] There are eighteen houses in
this court, in Shawhill-street. It is tolerably open, and flagged, but
the nuisance caused by the seven water closets in the corner cannot
be described. They are rarely in working order; sometimes they *are
days without water*, and generally the stench from them is over-
powering to a stranger. The inspector says that, although they are
visited every day, or nearly so, it is utterly impossible to get the
people to keep them clean. They are fouled and choked almost
immediately; and, to see little girls and boys running about dabbl-
ing in the filth, as we did, or Mr. Stitt might, is enough to settle
the question as to the social progress we are making, and the
educational advantages which the children in these days possess
over those of a past generation. The people here to not seem, on
the whole, to be so utterly degraded as those in Preston-street, and
some of the houses give evidence of tolerably successful attempts at
cleanliness. From what we have seen, not only here but in several
districts of the town, of the action of water closets, and their effect

upon the air of the court, we are disposed to pronounce entirely against them, and feel surprised that the Health Officers do not speak out on this question. After being in this court it did not surprise us to hear that a man close by was '*laid up in a bad fever!*' This was a natural consequence – was it not, Mr. Stitt?

Turning on Shawhill-street, and passing Rankin's Foundry, Mr. Stitt would reach Spitalfields. Now, this is a nice, lively place any time of day or night. There is a little show of work made by the bonnet-box makers; but this doesn't go far, and you are not many minutes in the street before half a dozen thick necks with shock heads on the top are before you, and a dozen piggish eyes glance at you defiantly. There are three courts here, with eight houses in each. The privy and ashpit are at the top of the courts, in the true Liverpool fashion, and there is not the remotest chance of the houses being in any way ventilated. Courts 3 and 5 are apparently given up to prostitutes and their parasites, and the houses are let for 3s 6d per week. In No. 1 Court there is said to be no prostitutes, and the rent here is 4s per week. Seeing that the houses were similar in construction, we were led to inquire why the difference was made in the rent. An intelligent woman, who spoke with a Scotch accent, and whom we met with in No. 1 Court, explained the matter in these words:

'In this court we are all trying to keep ourselves decent, and there are no prostitutes amongst us, and on this account we have to pay sixpence a week more for our houses. In the other courts there are nothing but prostitutes and their followers, and we cannot sleep at nights for their brawls and carryings on. We have to pay sixpence a week as a tax for trying to live decently.'

The owner of this property is said to be a most devout man, and one who is disposed to 'fear God and work righteousness,' and this may account for his not seeking to draw extra profit, as other men do, from the vicious purposes for which his houses are rented. It is a pity he does not carry his scruples a little further, and clear out Courts Nos. 3 and 5. For our part, we don't think that it is anything to the credit of parents who wish to bring their children up in a proper manner to be found in such a neighbourhood, when better houses, better neighbours, and better air might be had elsewhere at less cost.

But Mr. Stitt will not likely feel tired or jaded yet, and, therefore, leaving the broad-set girls in bedgowns to air themselves and 'chaff' each other or passers-by, on the house steps or court corners in Spitalfields, he will pass on to that large court, in the Haymarket. It used to be called Vaughan's-buildings, but is now called No. 1 Court, Albion-place. There are here thirty-two houses, and the only convenience for the large multitude of people which the place contains *are seven privies – four behind, near to Pooley's Foundry, and three opposite the doors in the far corner of the court.* The people here are all industrious and striving, and as such deserve some consideration at the hands of those who are supposed to have some charge of health or some influence upon morals. Mr. Stitt will see here in a quarter of an hour more than he could learn by a couple of years' reading or the consumption of a few tuns of 'midnight oil' how it is that, in spite of education grants and improved tuition, our boys and girls grow up, in densely populated neighbourhoods, perfectly ignorant of the first principles of morality and utter strangers to the common decency of civilized life. Having seen this he is sure to talk about it at committee, and we will be forced to read his speeches.

25 The vagrant sheds

Vagrancy and its treatment ought to excite general attention; and to this end the weekly reports read at the Workhouse Committee, are suggestive.[81] They mean more than they express, and express more than can be understood by 'the general reader,' – the man who takes reports or ought else, just as they come, asking no questions. It will excite no surprise to hear that destitute persons abound, or that they are, by the proper authorities 'relieved and accommodated.' The fundamental principle of the poor law declares that destitution shall constitute a title to relief; and our object is now to show what is the nature of the relief, and what the character of the accommodation given to the destitute poor at the vagrant shed in Brownlow Hill. This is done simply as a matter of justice to the ratepayers, whose 'pennies,' it will be seen in this case, are so grudgingly given, and whose 'pounds,' in other cases, are so unsparingly squandered. It is right that all should know what is done at the vagrant sheds and it is believed that the harrowing facts need no comment.

Take the case of a houseless and homeless wanderer which has come under observation. Wretched and wearied after a toilsome walk, as day fails he has reached this great town of Liverpool. If his present position be the result of his misconduct or misfortune, or a combination of both, it is now clearly beside the question. Here he is, without food, almost without clothing, has no friends and no money. He is perhaps not ashamed to beg, but *he does not steal.* He has not yet reached that point when the law can take hold of him, and thus make 'his bread certain and his water very sure.' No, tempted sorely as he must have been, the germ of good within the man is not yet destroyed. He tells you that he has sought for work and failed to find it; he has asked for food and it has been denied him: he is almost famished and would gladly lie down anywhere to rest – it 'may be sleep would take the hunger off.' Why, there are the vagrant sheds – that is the place where such a poor creature will be 'relieved and accommodated;' and he is directed thither, or a policeman will take him, for in many cases of this sort the police evince much consideration and display good feeling. The old porter at the workhouse gate will direct the wanderer up the yard to the receiving office. At the door of this, he is met by a police officer, who takes him to the clerk, a mild-spoken old man in pauper garb, who has charge of the record book.[82] Name, age, place of birth, and other particulars are all enquired into, and the entries duly made. Whilst this is being done the scrutinizing glance of the officer is directed to the appearance and manner of the applicant for relief; and if it be certified that he has 'not been here three times before,' he is handed over to 'the searcher.' It may happen that he has nothing about his person but an old black pipe, but this is very carefully examined, taken from him and laid aside, and he is then shewn through the door into the first compartment of the sheds and requested to take a bath. But he is hungry; yes, that is understood, but the rules of 'the house' compel him to take a bath, he may enjoy his food all the better after it! Well, the man takes a bath, and what then? Why, his supper is handed to him, and he will be shewn to what is to be his resting-place, you will say. Nothing of the sort, simple hearted reader. You are thinking of some scheme of unpuffed private benevolence, such as the *old* 'refuge for the destitute,' with which the revered name of 'Old Egerton Smith' will ever be associated. Philanthropy has made great progress since his days, and *comforts* are here in store for this well-nigh worn-out brother of yours, which you fail even to dream of.

Immediately on the man leaving the bath he is met by the official who has charge of 'the mills,' and is shown his work. Yes, startle not at this. He is shown to his work, for philanthropy here is pre-eminently practical, and the man must earn his supper before he gets it. He is directed to a hand corn mill, at this he is expected to grind thirty pounds of flour; this labour will occupy two hours or more, his payment for which is a tin of gruel and a hunch of bread; then he may go up stairs to rest for the night. Like thousands more in this town, it was on this point that we were incredulous; but, having visited the place and seen what is described, our incredulity has been removed at the expense of feelings which are difficult to repress.

When 'at the mills' the men are in a sort of alley turning the handles. This is the only portion of the mill with which they have to do, and it is the only portion they are permitted to see. 'The hopper,' containing the allotted quantity of grain which they have to grind is at the other side of the wall, in the store house. Besides being anything but light, the labour is extremely monotonous; and this is increased, and the labour rendered doubly severe, by the fact of the worker being unable to see how his work is progressing. Hope, which renders labour light and is in many ways so cheering, is here shut out; and there is nothing for it but to turn on and grind away in dogged sullenness, as some do, or give vent to the bitterness of their lot, as others do, in blasphemous mutterings, or ribald scribbling on the white-washed wall.

The task having been in some way got through, the tin of gruel and the hunch of bread are earned, and therefore given. The gruel is very good, so is the bread; and surely they ought to be, seeing what the man has paid for them, who has ground at a hand corn mill thirty pounds of flour. Supper over, 'the vagrant' is shown up to the sleeping apartment – a large room, dimly lighted, the walls of which being blackened with coal tar, gives to the place an air of gloom and misery. Here, on a large iron frame, are stretched strips of canvas, in hammock fashion, according to the number of wretched men who seek accommodation, and thereon, with wood for their pillows and no coverings but their own rags, are laid the vagrants who have done their work and have earned this rest. Poor, foot-sore creatures, their blistered feet bare, meet you on your passage round the room, and fierce features scowl, large eyes gleam upon you from off those wooden pillows, and heavy sighs escape from the wretched forms on which you gaze. Young and old, companions in misery lie side by side: and if you stand at the entrance of this dreary vault-like apartment, listening to the deep breathing of those who are fortunate enough to have found a temporary refuge from their woes in sleep, you will be constrained to contrast the position of these men, who have not the brand of felony on them, with the very different position of them that have.

In the morning, if these vagrants should have the misfortune to be hungry they have to earn their breakfast by 'winnowing,' or some other labour. Female vagrants are treated precisely in the same way – the bath – the mill – the bread and gruel – the same sort of resting place. They are separated from the males by a large yard. We found women working at the mills at eleven o'clock at night, and one of them seemed so feeble that her punishment for being poor and keeping herself honest, seemed great indeed.

Without entering on the discussion of the 'labour test,' what concerns the Ratepayers of Liverpool is this fact. The parochial authorities pay able-bodied labourers for grinding thirty pounds of flour, *threepence*; and it is boasted loudly in a Social Science publication, that women, 'can, at the mills, earn one shilling per day.' Look then, at the case of a vagrant who grinds thirty pounds of corn at night and 'winnows' next morning. The cost of what the poor creature receives is calculated by the workhouse authorities as 'rather over a penny,' whilst the value of the labour done is estimated by the same authorities as *'about fourpence!'* Does not this shew the progress of our age? Vagrancy is not only 'self-supporting,' but profitable to the parish. After such facts, this extract, shewing 'one week's business,' will be significant:-

Mr. Carr, the governor of the workhouse, reported that during the week 302 destitute persons were relieved and accommodated at the vagrant sheds, being 155 men, 107 women, and 40 children, being a decrease of 130 persons during the week, but an increase of 52 persons as compared with the same week of last year.

Has it then come to this, with a Churchwarden, bearing the respected name of 'Cropper,'[83] and a Select Vestry[84] composed of 'eminent philanthropists,' that Liverpool is to punish poverty, whilst crime is pampered. Are female visitors to the workhouse of greater moment than righteous supervision at the vagrant sheds?[85] Are the results of cabdrivers' soirées to be at all compared with the results of driving vagrants to be something worse?

26 Mr. William Bennett

Mr. Alderman William Bennett is a tradesman of great respectability. He succeeded his father as an ironfounder and grate manufacturer, in Sir Thomas's Buildings, and under his careful management the establishment has progressed till it has become one of the largest in the town, employing a great number of workmen.

Mr. Bennett first entered the Council as the representative of St. Anne's Ward, and had not long been a member before he was made an Alderman. He is very quiet and urbane in his manner and deportment, and very constant in his attendance. He has been more remarkable for his persevering opposition to the 'Pike scheme'[86] than for any legislative talent he has displayed. Many a weary hour have the Council sat listening to his formidable speeches against the Pike and its engineer – to his direful prognostications of its bursting pipes, the absence of water at Rivington to supply or fill the reservoirs, and his hundred-times-repeated asseveration that the whole scheme would prove a lamentable failure, and ruin the ratepayers. Not one-tenth of his lengthy speeches has ever been given to the public, for nothing could be more monotonous than the worthy Alderman's immeasurable orations on this interminable subject. That he is sincere there can be no doubt; but he has dwelt so long upon 'the Pike' that a phantasmagorial spectre of it must haunt him by day and night. At times he appears to be unconscious of the existence of anything else; and if he had been engaged in a cause in which foresight, boldness of conception, judgment, and true economy were combined in his favour, instead of being on the side of his opponents, his unflinching and pertinacious spirit would have made him one of the greatest of local heroes instead of one of the greatest of bores. Under the circumstances, however, his opposition declined into absurdity, and detracted from his general usefulness. There is a time for all things. When the measure was under consideration it was competent for him – and, thinking as he does, it was his duty – to give his most strenuous opposition to the scheme; but after the works had been commenced, and the decision of a majority of the Council had pledged the town to the scheme, Mr. Bennett would have acted more wisely if he had followed the example of other members of the Council who also disapproved of going to Rivington for water, but who have, since the scheme became an established fact, laid aside their prejudices, and given every aid to the committee in carrying out the plan economically and successfully.

Mr. Bennett is an amiable man; and although the course he has pursued has subjected him to many hard knocks, he has never lost his temper, nor retorted in any other than a courteous manner. Members have sometimes been very severe upon him, but he has borne their sharp assaults with such constant and enviable equanimity that we have sometimes been puzzled whether to attribute it to philosophy or indifference, to good nature or to the want of appreciation, or to a combination of all these qualities.

Mr. Bennett is a well informed man on many subjects, and was for a session chairman of the Polytechnic Society, where he displayed considerable ability. He is systematic, and it is with pleasure we add that, although his speeches are very heavy, owing to his slow and solemn delivery, they are generally consecutive in their arrangement and logical in their matter. That the worthy Alderman prepared his speeches on the water question we make no doubt, and it was amusing to watch the countenances of the members when he took out of his pocket a large bundle of documents, and began systematically to arrange them before speaking. Had the Town Hall been on fire, and the members of the Council had been doomed to sit in their chamber whilst the engines played on the burning building, there could scarcely have been greater consternation and shivering. With a more than hydropathic devotion to water himself, he created in his hearers an aversion to it almost amounting to hydrophobia. Mr. Bennett does not speak much on other subjects. Occasionally, however, he does so; but his slow utterance, his solemn manner, and his apparent disregard of the value of time, cause him to be listened to with weak and divided attention. In fact, being desirous in these slight sketches to do strict justice to all, while we freely comment upon all, we are constrained to admit that the worthy Alderman is one of the members whom the reporters consider to be 'rather a bore,' and he has himself only to blame for that opinion. Nevertheless, we frankly and cheerfully acknowledge that as a private individual all must admire Mr. Bennett. His amiable disposition, his well-known benevolence, his kindness to his workmen, his admirable and consistent conduct, are beyond all praise; and if he made a mistake when he ventured upon the arena of public life, for which his disposition and the turn of his mind seem to unfit him, he made a mistake which has been committed by hundreds who had not a tithe of his sterling qualities to redeem their misconception. A desire to serve the public is a pardonable fault; and Mr. Bennett's amiability and rectitude make one regret that nature has not cast him in the mould of public men. Persevering he may be; but his round, happy, tranquil face indicates a lack of firmness, decision, penetration, and alertness of intellect. Like David, he is 'ruddy and well-favoured,' but he could not, like the shepherd youth, sling the stone and bring down the giant. Mr. Bennett is respected for his conscientiousness and good nature; and, from the little that we know on the subject, we are inclined to believe that his business qualifications on the committees of the Council are of a respectable order. Seated on his chair, and in momentary forgetfulness of Rivington and oratorical solemnity, Mr. Bennett speaks like a man and a gentleman; but we sincerely trust that he has made his last speech on the one great topic of his public thoughts.

27 Mr. John C. Fernihough

Mr. John Charles Fernihough is one of the active, bustling spirits of the Council. Mr. Quicksilver, in Warren's novel, was not of a more energetic, restless disposition; indeed, he may be designated 'the fiery Tybalt' of the elective body to which he belongs. He is a tall, sharp-eyed man, in the prime of his life, just 40 years of age, possessing volubility of speech, rapidity of thought, and a power of utterance possessed by few. Mr. Fernihough was till lately extensively engaged in business as a tobacco manufacturer (if such a term is not a misnomer), having succeeded his father in an old and respectable firm, which has existed over half a century.

In the year 1849, on the retirement of Mr. J. A. Tinne[87] from the Council, Mr. Fernihough became a candidate for the representation of St. Peter's ward, and beat his opponent, Mr. Thos. Clarke, by a majority of 43 votes. He has since been twice re-elected without opposition. From his entry into public life Mr. Fernihough became a favourite. Like his friend Mr. Alderman Parker, he directed his earliest efforts against 'the extravagances of the Finance Committee,' and many and severe were the attacks which he made upon the proceedings of that body. His onslaughts were better directed and more sustainedly vigourous than those of the bustling Alderman, and the consequence was that by the time Mr. Fernihough had been in the Council twelve months a seat in the 'Select Committee' was offered to him, and accepted. This was, we believe, the first instance in which so young a member had been placed on the most important committee of the Corporation, and proved one of three things – that Mr. Fernihough had early obtained the confidence of his brother members, that he had inspired them with a wholesome and overwhelming dread of his acute criticisms, or that they were determined to silence his censures by permitting him to participate in the transactions of their business. The result was in accordance with established precedent. The critical castigator became the steadiest supporter, and Mr. Fernihough is now ready on the shortest notice to scatter hand grenades and Congreve rockets amongst those who impugn the proceedings of the Finance Committee or any member thereof. To this feeling may in some measure be attributed the support which he gave at the last election to Mr. J. B. Lloyd[88] (an old Finance Committeeman), in Lime Street Ward, in opposition to the candidate of Liberal views. Mr. Fernihough stands well to his guns, and fires with precision and effect. He is the warmest tempered man in the room. He might have been born on the side of Mount Etna, and learned when a child to play with the burning lava, so very fiery is his temperament; and the natural consequence is that he occasionally 'gets into scrapes.' About three years ago he made some remarks on the chairman of the Health Committee which were considered so offensive that Mr. Gladstone[89] procured from the committee a vote of confidence in their chairman. On the bringing up of the proceedings a second scene took place. Mr. Fernihough displayed more obstinacy than discretion, and finally succeeded in defeating a motion which he thought might compromise his inflexibility. On a recent occasion some very warm words took place between him and Mr. Robertson Gladstone; but the storm passed off without doing any damage. There is determination in Mr. Fernihough's look, and he is not the man to give way nor to be put down when he thinks he is in the right. When he first entered the Council he spoke fluently but wanderingly. He has, however, much improved during the last year or two; and, while he pours out a torrent of words with such rapidity that the reporters can scarcely follow him, he concentrates his ideas and is consecutive in the chain of his argument. Even when he is denunciatory and declamatory his reasoning is cogent, and his off-hand speeches show that he is naturally a discriminating and clever man. He is also grammatical, is devoid of Lancashireisms, and puts that most abused letter 'h' in its proper place of aspirations or abeyance, as the case may be.

Mr. Fernihough uses violent action when he speaks, and the muscles of his face work with excitement. His 'dander' is soon raised; his nervous excitable temperament makes him quick in retort; and he displays a restlessness of manner which gives indication both of high temper and ability. It requires a good constitution to withstand so much nervous excitement. Mr. Fernihough is *toujours prêt*. Like the warrior who fought under the Black Prince, and who when his spear was broken was left surrounded by enemies, yet plied the remnants of the shaft so vigorously as to come off victorious and win his spurs on the field, so Mr. Fernihough would fight even if he were disarmed, and, unless his enemy were keen and vigilant, he would be victorious too. Nevertheless, Mr. Fernihough might take a higher position in the Council and in the town than he does, and it is his own fault he does not do so. He 'reasons well,' and appears to be familiar with the various subjects that come under discussion. He incurred some censure from his constituents a few years ago, in reference to a subject which was not then popular; but as he acted on the occasion independently and from conviction, the dissatisfaction subsided.

He is, we are told, regular and punctual in his attendance at the meetings of the Finance Committee. At the Baths Committee he is looked upon as 'the presiding genius.' In fact, so great is the interest he takes in the progress of the baths and wash-houses in Cornwallis Street, which are near his residence, that he is almost a daily visitor, and can tell exactly the number of bathers and the receipts every day, and the number and receipts on the corresponding day every year since the establishment was first opened. He can give the most minute particulars as to the length of the piping in the building, the depth of water in the plunge baths, the quantity of water used; and nothing affords him greater pleasure than to conduct his friends or strangers over the baths, and explain to them the accommodation given and the benefits conferred thereby upon the inhabitants of his native town. In fact, on all matters connected with baths and bathers, wash-houses and washers, he is a sort of living encyclopædia; and no one, therefore, need be surprised to learn that, by precept and example, he is a warm advocate for the hydropathic treatment.

During the time he was a member of the Watch Committee he was in the habit of visiting all parts of the town at night, and whenever a fire occurred in any street he was usually one of the first on the spot, and one of the most efficient in his endeavours to extinguish the flames. He was an amateur police inspector of the first order, and, *con amore*, a vigilant superintendent of the fire brigade.

Mr. Fernihough is cavalier in manner, and has a somewhat haughty air. He does not forget that he is a 'public man,' and will not be dragooned. If he be not one of the 'leaders' of the corporate body he is assuredly not one of the followers. Whilst announcing himself a Liberal, he appears to have great pleasure in coqueting with the Tories of the higher rank, and yet he is independent in mind and in action; and from the experience he has had of municipal affairs must be a very useful member of our local legislature. It requires a bold man to attack him, and an able man to defeat him. He has his peculiarities, but they do not detract from his usefulness. He is generous to a fault, is a faithful, painstaking ally, but a bitter opponent, and you need expect no mercy at his hands if you thwart him in his views, or oppose or severely criticise the proceedings of his two favourite committees, the members of which appear to him to combine in their own persons the concentrated essence of municipal wisdom. He is of a social and genial nature, is fond of company, has fascinating conversational powers, is good at rapartee, and one of those municipalists who often pass a pleasant evening in snug quarters, talking over Council matters, when the absence of reporters leaves them unrestrained. Mr. Fernihough is one of those who can enjoy 'the feast of reason and the flow of soul,'; and few can give more eloquently the 'Hip, hip, hurrah.' If he were a country squire he would be a keen sportsman, and a preserver of his game. It is said that he was at one time passionately fond of the sports of the field, that he is a good judge of horses, and that in several steeple chases he was not the last at the winning posts. He has been for some time a member of the Royal Mersey Yacht Club, and is a constant and active attendant at its meetings and matches. He is one of the few men in the Council who stand out from the mass, and while it cannot be said that his talent is first-rate, it is very far above the average; and the confidence which he possesses, his aptitude for business, the knowledge he has obtained, and his great readiness in adapting it to the question at issue, have created for him a position which ought to induce him to make still greater efforts. He has been a diligent representative of the ward he represents, and there is not much danger of his losing his seat so long as he continues to display the independence, zeal, and ability which have ever characterised him.

28 Cornwallis Street Baths

It is with feelings of great pleasure that we now turn to another phase of Liverpool Life. We have not by any means exhausted the materials collected for exposing the abominable resorts and vicious haunts which deprave our youth and degrade our town; but as we proceed, and by way of contrast and relief to ourselves, and no doubt to our readers, we intend to introduce occasionally a paper or two to show what is being done *for* the people – what is being done to humanise and elevate the masses. It is not surprising that in some quarters our matter, manner, and motives have been misrepresented or condemned. By the young fop, with quizzing glass to his eye, and who could only exclaim 'disguesting,' *our* aim would not be seen, neither was *our* end desired. The hoary-headed sinner, dreading our exposure of his haunts and habits, has, in unmeasured terms, denounced both end and aim; the young libertine has actually worked himself into a frenzy on the subject; and in almost every taproom the voice that has been loudest raised against exposure had been that of the greatest scapegrace. Even where the object was professedly appreciated, the means adopted for its accomplishment have in some instances been questioned – the mode tabooed. To attempt the cure of social evils by gently covering them over with 'the fig leaves of decent reticence,' is nothing new; were the attempt ever to succeed, a novelty would be the result. That public exposure of ill doings not unfrequently leads to amendment and well doing, many believe; and recent events which are now the subject of history testify to the truth of this opinion. In all cases purification may be expected from publicity. There are ever to be found mawkish sentimentalists ready to cry out against, or cry down, the wholesome exposure of corrupting influences which silently work into and destroy the best features of our social life. Their profession is make-believe to lament, their practice studiously to conceal. To another class, *deeply interested*, such exposure suggests the cry, as of old, 'our craft is in danger;' and they of course entertain the worst possible fears as to the result. Deeply as every well-wisher of his species should regret the *cause* which led to the publication of this series of papers, we feel cheered in our task by hopes for the consequence, by the expressions of approval which crowd upon us, especially from clergymen and ministers, by the fact that one of the dens of iniquity has been closed since our exposure; and so leave all sentimental croakers, objectors, and their objections, to their inevitable fate.

We have seen what the authorities permit individuals to provide for the recreation of the masses; we will now see what the authorities themselves provide for this purpose. First, and above all, we class the Public Baths and Washhouses established by the Town Council. These institutions, extensively as they are known, and largely as they are taken advantage of by those for whom they were intended, are, notwithstanding, by many thousands totally uncared for and neglected. It may, perhaps, excite surprise that some members of our local legislature know nothing more of these life-invigorating and body-cleansing establishments than they may be supposed to learn from hearing the proceedings of the baths committee read from time to time in the council chamber. Yet the public baths reflect honour on the town, bestow abundant credit on the council, are model sanitary purifiers, and are hourly bestowing blessings, cheap, pure, and healthful, on the toiling masses of this great community. A few statistics will bear out this statement. The weekly bath returns are made up each Wednesday. During last week, nearly 25,000 persons bathed at the public baths, at a cost to themselves of more than £500. At Cornwallis-street baths, the daily receipts range from 4s. 6d. to £53 6s. 5d. Last week, at that establishment alone, 10,516 persons bathed, the receipts being upwards of £179. In the corresponding week of last year, the receipts were £53, and the number of bathers 3,678. On Saturday, throughout the year, the number of bathers is generally double that on any other day of the week.

The Corporation Baths, as is well known, are situated in Cornwallis-street, Paul-street, and George's Pierhead. Paul-street baths have attached to them washhouses, and for the south end of the town there are washhouses in Upper Frederick-street. The latter were originally the public baths – the first of the kind established in this town or country – and were opened fourteen years ago, principally through the instrumentality of that friend of the poor, William Rathbone.[90] It is to the baths in Cornwallis-street that we now wish to draw particular attention. They are the largest, most modern, best frequented, and contain the most recent improvements. The foundation stone was laid in 1849, by Mr. J. A. Tinne, the then chairman of the health committee. The edifice was designed by and erected under the superintendence of the borough engineer, Mr. James Newlands; and well do the baths deserve the high encomiums which have been passed upon them by celebrated and professional men who have visited them. The building contains

three large plunge baths – first, second, and third class; sixty
private warm baths of similar classes; together with shower,
vapour, and sitz baths; the whole being under the management of
Mr. Andrew Clarke, the superintendent.

The first thing that strikes the visitor to these baths is the
scrupulous cleanliness everywhere observable, the order and
regularity with which business is transacted, and the highly trained
and systematic manner in which all the servants appear to discharge
their duties – no unnecessary noise, no bustle, even when business
is brisk, and bathers are waiting for the bath rooms. 'The system'
here seen in operation is not only commendable, but worthy of
imitation. This opinion is formed after having frequently visited all
the public baths in Liverpool during the whole time they have been
in operation. That all the arrangements are brought into such a
state of efficiency is to be attributed in a great measure to the long
experience and firm yet respectful demeanour of the superintendent,
who is zealously supported in all his plans and arrangements by the
present chairman and vice-chairman, Messrs. Wagstaff and
Fernihough, and some of the other members of the baths committee. If it be a good quality in a servant to take a deep interest in
his work, and display zeal and assiduity in the discharge of his
duties, the town council are fortunate in securing the services of
Mr. Clarke. He thoroughly identifies himself with the place by all
he does and says; and as we walk through the various departments
accompanied by him, and listen to the continuous flow of common-
sense observations, given, as they are, with a rich smack of the true
Milesian[91] brogue, the fact is still further impressed upon us. He is
a tall, powerful, well-built man. In early life he was engaged in
constructing the wooden walls of old England, and in middle age
he assisted to man them. He has been in all quarters of the globe,
and picked up a variety of information, and thus profited by his
travels. He is not possessed of showy or shining qualities, but, like
a good, old-fashioned craft, carries a good cargo without making
much display. Age is fast telling on him, and he has undergone
much change since he 'mixed a nice comfortable bath' for us, fourteen years ago, in Frederick-street. He is yet hale, hearty, and obliging, and we hope he may long remain so, and that speedily the
great wish of his heart may be granted him – 'a regular supply of
water from Rivington, when I can keep my fountain in play, and
my place in the order it should be.'[92]

In the old-fashioned way, and in order to convey an idea of the
baths to our readers, we will begin at the bottom, and look at the
third-class plunge bath, or, as it is commonly called, the
'twopenny.' We are now at the entrance, talking with the
superintendent. It is Saturday evening, about eight o'clock; half a

dozen dirty-looking little fellows, shoeblacks and others, are coming up the steps. Cash in hand, they walk up to the money taker, and demand 'a twopenny'un.' They receive for the twopence a ticket and a clean coarse towel. There is no doubt of their having been here before, for as soon as they obtain the ticket and towel they run down the flight of steps leading to the baths, screaming with delight in anticipation of their enjoyment. We follow them, the superintendent observing as we descend, 'These pay me the best; they are my best customers.' The noise of boys out of the water, the splashing and shouting of those in, prepared us to some extent for the scene that awaits us. On entering the bath we find upwards of a hundred boys, most of them in a state of nudity, ducking, diving, floundering, plunging, dousing, sousing, rolling, sprawling, tossing and tumbling in the water. The turmoil in the water, the tumult of voices out, are for the first few moments positively stupifying. Mr. Clarke notices our consternation, and quietly chuckles at the sight. The bath is forty-one feet long by twenty-seven wide; the water is five feet deep at one end, two and a half at the other; the floor is of ashphalte, the sides of stone; there is a 'springboard' placed at the deep end to assist the lads in diving. There are twenty-four rooms, or receiving boxes, around the bath, all being destitute of doors. In these the bathers place their clothes, and as many as ten or twelve boys at one time deposit their habiliments in one of these boxes. As our conductor feelingly remarks, 'Poor little fellows! their clothes in most cases occupy little room, and what I give them is the only clean covering they ever get.'

In the good old days of good old Egerton Smith,[93] who, as is well known, took an active part in promoting a knowledge of the useful art of swimming, it was our practice and privilege to visit the Floating Bath. On one occasion a young man unacquainted with the bath, jumped into the 'deep end,' and, as he could not swim, was in some danger. We assisted him into shallow water, and afterwards in the bath became very friendly; both being destitute of clothes, an equality was constituted. We returned to our respective dressing rooms and again met on the deck whilst 'waiting for the boat.' Much to our surprise, the young man did not speak. He was dressed in the height of fashion, considered himself no doubt a gentleman, and could not condescend to notice or look upon plebeians. 'Old Egerton,' as he was familiarly and affectionately called, saw this, very likely knew what we *felt*, and quietly walking up, he took hold of our jacket, and rubbing the cloth, he said, 'Never mind him: *this* is the difference between you; and though you will now have to be two people, the same boat will carry you both ashore.' This was our first lesson in 'the philosophy of clothes.' It made a deep impression, and we felt it in full force whilst looking at the crowd of boys and young men disporting themselves so boisterously, yet innocently, in the twopenny plunge bath. As old Sandy Mackay remarks, 'There, ye're a' brithers noo, on the one broad, gran' fundamental principle o' want o' breeks!'

Many gentlemen visiting this bath are impressed with the good appearance of the boys when destitute of clothes. Lord Alfred Paget, who visited it a short time since, in company with the Earl of Derby, expressed his great surprise and astonishment when looking at the clear skins, well knitted frames, and in some instances wonderfully developed muscles of the boys. 'They might,' he said, 'be all noblemen's sons.' What an admission! He could have gone further than this, and yet have spoken the truth.

Many of the boys not having any regular employment stay a long time in the water. The keeper tells us that he notices the boys who bring a little bread with them; they will stay in the water two or three hours, going out occasionally into the box to eat a little food, and then dash into the water again. Many of them are very expert swimmers, and they all appear to be excellent divers. A deal of amusement, of a very profitable character to the boys, is frequently witnessed by visitors throwing money into the water, in order that the boys may dive for it. The vice-chairman of the committee (Mr. J. C. Fernihough) is well known by the boys for his enjoyment of this sport, and his presence with a few friends is generally the signal for a display of diving diversion. The gentlemen cast their coin upon the waters, and it is found, after a lapse of a few moments, in the possession of some of the boys, who swim about in great glee, holding the much-prized coin between their teeth. Their dexterity in diving and bringing up the smallest coin is remarkable; and although in many cases they not unfrequently jump on each other, we witness no display of ill temper. On remarking this to our guide, he says, 'I had many a hard turn with them before I got them to this order; but now most of them know that so long as they behave decently they will be permitted to remain, and no longer; and as soon as I see or hear of any act of violence, they have me down on them.' Mr. Clarke seems to take an interest in the lads learning to swim, and says, 'the next generation will be a generation of swimmers, and in a great seaport like this it ought to be so: the great majority will be indebted to my baths for that.'

There are some strange scenes to be met with at 'the twopenny.' On one occasion a swimming match had been determined on between two boys, one of whom had lost an arm; the other was destitute of a leg. With that love of fair play which is and we hope ever will be the distinguishing characteristic of true Britons, the whole of the boys, to the number of eighty or ninety, left the bath, and stood, naked, shouting, huzzaing, and rollicking, on the brink.

By this means they secured for the contending swimmers a 'clear course and no favour.' The distance was once round, starting from the shallow end. The excitement of the spectators was very great, and the cries most comical. 'Now legs,' 'Bravo, arms,' 'Go it, pegleg,' 'Pitch into it, stumpy,' resounded on all sides. More fun of an innocent character amongst boys of such a class we never saw. Many of the lads laughed until they fell into the water; others fell over them for fun; even the grave face of the bath-keeper relaxed into a genial smile, and all were uproariously mirthful. It soon became evident that legs had the advantage. He with the two propellers gained speedily on his opponent, and came in an easy victor. He was speedily surrounded by his companions, one of whom, clapping him on the back, observed, 'I knew very well you could soon take slates out of stumpy.' In a few minutes they were all in the bath again, kicking, splashing, and tossing about, and enjoying themselves in the water as only boys can.

We leave the 'twopenny' and pass on to the fourpenny plunge bath. This is similar in appearance to that noticed, but, not being so much used, the place has not such a dingy appearance. The rooms here have a looking-glass and door attached to each. They are twenty-six in number. This bath is frequented more by middle-aged and young men, who find it hard to stand the rollicking fun of the boys, and therefore pay the additional twopence for the additional comfort. Seeing the crowded state of the twopenny bath, we learn with great satisfaction that the committee have resolved to reduce the price of the fourpenny to twopence. This will likely have the effect of inducing more to go into the first-class bath, whilst it will be conferring a great boon on those of the humbler class, to whom twopence is a great consideration, and a good bath a positive necessity. It is very pleasing to observe here the young and middle-aged mechanic laying out a few pence so judiciously on a Saturday evening. Contrast what may be obtained here for fourpence or for twopence, with what may be obtained for a like amount at the gorgeous and glaring palaces that are fast adorning every corner of our streets; and reflect also which mode of expenditure constitutes the best preparation for the Sabbath. It is said that cleanliness is next to godliness, that health of mind is in a great measure dependent upon that of the body, and that cleanliness of the one will induce to purity of the other. These things, it may be supposed, savour too much of the earth for our ministers to notice in the present day, or we might hear more of washings and purifications, and less of religious rancour, than we do now. That filthiness of person and viciousness of disposition are closely allied, all must admit; and all must admire, even in its present limited extent, the means which our local governors take to purify the bodies of the people. Every ward in the town ought to have its public baths. Baths would be much cheaper than gaols – the more cleansing the less crime; and if the price of the plunge baths could be reduced to a penny for the poorest class the change would be glorious.

We pass on now to the first-class plunge bath, which is a very beautiful building. The style and decoration are purely Egyptian; the colouring is in exquisite harmony, displays good taste and sound judgement, and is altogether the best display of ornamentation we have seen in Liverpool. The bath is fifty-seven feet long by forty-one wide; the sides are of tiles, the floor of Yorkshire flag stone; the bath is emptied and the floor is thoroughly scoured with sandstone twice a week. The water is three feet deep at one end; and seven at the other. By reason of the floor being lighter in colour than the other baths, the water here has a beautifully clean appearance. There are thirty-three dressing rooms round the bath, each of which contains a looking-glass and bootjack. This bath is not frequented as much as we might expect. There are now twenty persons in it, chiefly young or middle-aged men. We notice one youth who is an excellent swimmer, and the bath-keeper informs us that this youth on one occasion swam round the bath forty-five times, thus performing a distance of upwards of two miles in one hour and three-quarters. In the centre of the bath stands a fountain, in the form of a vase, from the edge of which the jets send forth the water. When this is in play with two-thirds of the pressure on, the form is very beautiful. It is a source of regret to the superintendent that he cannot keep the fountain continually in play, by reasons of the scarcity of water; 'but,' he says, 'when Rivington is all right, and I get my proper supply, I will keep it going, for, besides moderating the temperature of the bath, it is beautiful and refreshing to the eye.'

We now visit the department of the building devoted to private warm baths. The charges for these are – First-class, one shilling; second class, sixpence; third class, twopence. It is very interesting to observe the distinction which is made between the classes. In the first we find a carpet, two chairs, a bootjack, boothooks, shoehorn, fleshbrush, hairbrush, and comb, a large looking-glass, hand ewer and soap, and three towels. We notice further the fleshbrush has a long handle. There is also a tap by which the bather can regulate the temperature of the bath. In the second class we find a carpet, a chair, a small looking-glass, a fleshbrush without a handle, a tap for regulating the temperature, and two towels. In the third class we see no carpet, no fleshbrush, no tap, one towel, and no looking-glass. Thus it would appear, as was suggested by a gruff-looking mechanic – probably a Chartist – 'That a poor fellow who can only pay twopence is not worth looking at, and it would do him no good to be allowed to see himself! and as to a fleshbrush, it's the swells as needs all that sort of thing.' In one respect the baths are all alike – they are exquisitely clean. The warm baths are frequented chiefly by mechanics and persons engaged in sedentary occupations. All that we had an opportunity of conversing with expressed themselves in the strongest manner and in grateful terms as to the good which the establishment had conferred on them physically and socially. Our conversation with the superintendent showed this in a much stronger and clearer light.

'I have men coming to me now,' said he, 'who used to come to my place in Frederick-street fourteen years ago. I noticed them week after week, and now look for them as regularly as I do for my meals. At first they were content with merely bathing; after a few weeks I noticed them bringing small bundles under their arms, which I soon discovered to contain a change of linen, or probably, in addition, a clean singlet and stockings. They then brought a piece of soap with them, and gave themselves a thorough cleaning and brushing. And many a Saturday night, after I have closed my place and gone to take a walk through the market, I have met some of those customers of mine, nicely cleaned up, their wives with them, sober and respectable, making their little purchases for the week. Such sights, I assure you, do my heart good to see; and what I often say, the Corporation never have done, nor will they ever, lay money out to a better advantage than in building baths for the people.'

In addition to the first, second, and third class private warm and plunge baths, the charges for which range from a shilling to twopence, private cold shower baths may be had in the third class for a penny. We are glad to learn that many a working man on his way to his daily toil steps into the baths at Cornwallis-street, pays his penny, gets a clean towel, and, entering the third class bath room, refreshes himself by a cold ablution in the morning.

The warm baths are more in requisition on Saturday evenings and Sunday mornings, and for this purpose the committee wisely keep them open until ten o'clock on Saturday, and from six to nine on Sunday morning. We confess that the visit to these baths on a Sunday morning has given us more unfeigned pleasure, and awakened within us more cheering hopes for the elevation of the people, than anything we have ever seen. The attendance here, and the characters of those who attend, are a further proof that if pure and wholesome recreations be provided for the people, at a cost within their reach, they will be so well appreciated as to become remunerative to the promoters – a fact that Mr. Clarke again and again insisted on when pointing to the crowds of youths and men pouring in on the Sabbath morning. Persons who thus commence the day by purifying their bodies will not be found at the 'cat hunt' or 'dog race' as the day advances. Their enjoyments will be of a purer, loftier, and more pleasing character; and from all we have seen and all we have heard, we know of no institution here or elsewhere, that is in a quiet, unobtrusive way bestrewing the pathway of the labourer with such rich, lasting, inexpensive and abundant blessings as the Corporation baths.[94]

Part four
Moral improvement: the institutions of improvement

29 'Our church'

'Now you'll be sure to come to "our church"? Come next Sunday; our curate will preach; and he has such an affectionate and endearing manner, you'll be quite cheered with him. I'll expect you.'

The young woman who thus spoke was tastefully, but rather showily, dressed, and was engaged in visiting 'her district.'[95] She had been observed now ducking into a cellar, then coming up smiling to tap at a house door; now plunging into a court, then floating out gaily into the street, just in time to give a tract to 'the coal man,' who was resting on the shaft of his barrow, wiping the sweat and dust from his brow. She was altogether a lively, affable, merry-voiced little body; and as we were somewhat desirous of seeing 'our church,' and hearing 'our curate,' whose style and manner were spoken of as likely to have such a cheering effect upon a 'coal man,' we, without receiving any invitation, on the following Sunday visited 'our church.'

Externally, there was nothing either attractive or particularly repulsive about 'our church.' Tufts of lank grass studded the walk; the steps had been recently washed by the rain. The notices of rates to be levied, which were *nailed* on the doors, were ragged; and the comments, in pencil, were not flattering to the gentlemen whose names were attached. A short-necked, broad-faced, wide-mouthed man, who had a plaid handkerchief tied tightly round his neck, was dressed in soiled clothes, and who smelled of rum, stood at the entrance to 'our church.' On asking him for a seat, he looked shrewdly, as if taking our measure, or 'social standing,' and then led on up the aisle, opened a door, and left us to edge our way into a narrow pew, something like an uncleaned 'twopenny bath.' The atmosphere of 'our church' was not refreshing; a close, moist, mouldy smell prevailed. The seat was of the hardest wood we ever sat upon; the back of the pew was straight and high. The dust had not been disturbed hereabouts for some time; yet it was of an affectionate character, for it stuck to coat and hands admirably.

Some pews, a good distance from where we were, had curtains closely drawn all round the top of them. Into these, after a little time, tall hirsute men led broad swaying forms of women; and after a few swirls of the feathers in the head-gear of these, and after the men had peered perseveringly for a few minutes into the crowns of their hats, they sat down, and were lost to sight. The bell now began to ring faster, and people walked up the aisle with quicker steps – some not at all serious, but light and tripping rather. It was very difficult for many of the women to get into the pews. 'Our church' had been constructed before such proportions in the female form were considered in good taste. Cushions were lifted up, books were knocked down, buffets were kicked and jerked, and there was considerable bustle in the place for a few minutes, before the congregation got properly seated.

Very few persons who had the air of 'working people' were present. Two young men sneaked in – yes, on consideration, that is the correct term – they 'sneaked' in, as if ashamed of themselves or the place, and sat down upon a form which ran along the side aisle. They hid their faces in their hats for a second or two, and then looked around wiping their brows as if refreshed or relieved. A young woman, who looked very like somebody's 'our girl,' came dashing up the aisle with a large book in her hand, and a white handkerchief folded around it; she stared very hard at the mildewed pew in which we sat and then bounced in, giving her book a tilt out of the handkerchief on to the form, and swagging herself down with an indecorous plop.

The organ now pealed forth, and, after a few discordant twitches, settled down to a decent fugue. Perhaps the organist would have played better if he had known anything of the instrument; but he quarrelled with it at the outset, and got badly on in consequence.

We noticed 'our district visitor.' She was in good time, and looked round approvingly at almost every person who entered. Two meek young men, with long light hair, faint whiskers, unhealthy looks, narrow shoulders, and a stoop in their gait, received from this pleasant woman a most friendly recognition. There was a tall young man who grew a beard, and had his hair divided down the centre, who 'shambled' into church, and was some time before he could get his expression up to what he thought it ought to be; he was noticed by many persons, male and female. Then came a handsome young fellow, with a very long, very light, fancifully curled moustache, and he, for a few minutes, attracted all eyes by the 'evolutions' which he went through, in order to get a young woman who accompanied him into the pew. She made two attempts and failed; eventually, two boys who had effected a lodgment in the pew were ordered to retire, which they did in single file, and then the mass of drapery was crushed through the narrow door, and the moustache followed.

The vestry door now opened, and two clergymen, followed by

the clerk, walked solemnly towards the desk. Taking a sharp turn, one of them, when he had reached the centre of the church, made off rather hastily (as it seemed) towards the communion table; and it did not add to the dignity of the man, or his profession, to see him holding up, at each side, a soiled and creased surplice, which was very loose about the neck, and evidently 'fit him too much.' The other clergyman, who seemed what the *Record* calls 'a new hand,' wore spectacles, and appeared to be near-sighted, and had to feel his way to the desk. He was a tall, sallow, whiskerless man, of a very serious cast, and his appearance and reverential bearing impressed you with the sincerity and earnestness of his character. The clerk lost no time in giving out a hymn, and the service began.

It was not an impressive sight when the congregation rose. For the first five minutes everybody turned round to look at everybody else; and those who were in the high curtained square pews, and who commanded a view of all sides, lost no opportunity of enjoying it. Stragglers kept coming in, and shoes 'creaked,' and silks rustled. In vain the singers did their best; in vain the organ pealed; seriousness did not prevail. Then began the service of the Church, which, if read with judgment and effect, is every way worthy of being called 'a grand old form of sound words.' But although the reading was distinct in the main, it was not good. There was a nasal twang, a hasty jerk, and then a sudden, unaccountable fall, which were perplexing to a stranger. The reader, no doubt, felt the force of all he read – showed himself to be in earnest – still, his waving himself to and fro; his lurching, now on this side, now on that, gazing vacantly the while, and slowly rolling out sharp short passages into long ones, was not pleasant, neither was it calculated to excite devotional ardour.

The singing was confined strictly to the choir, and was hearty rather than good – methodistical rather than cathedral-like. The responses were given by the clerk. No one even dared to interfere with him; he reigned alone, and felt, evidently, the responsibility of his position. When the communion service began we had an opportunity of seeing 'our curate,' who had been so warmly commended by 'the district visitor.' He was a short, stiff man, with a weak voice, and an affected manner. He was on good terms with himself, and seemed somewhat pragmatical. He allowed the book to lie negligently on the corner of the table, whilst he read the commandments, and held his hands clasped before him, turning round occasionally to refresh his memory. There was in this something at variance with the usage of the church – something so contrary to what we had been accustomed – something so indicative of self-sufficiency, and in the minister such an air of idleness and indifference that the effect which this service, when properly discharged, often has, was completely destroyed. Bad as were the responses of the choir – inharmonious and grating as they were – they were made worse by 'our curate's' languor and affection.

We had now been in 'our church' an hour and a half. The air had not improved. There seemed to be no means of ventilation. The sun was shining brightly outside; but means were adopted to hide its brightness from all within. Birds now and then fluttered against the windows, and the chirpings of the sparrows had in them something joyous. But before and around us, every one looked tired and flagging. Even the women's bonnets did not look so bright as formerly, and several of the women themselves had to fall back upon not the most fashionable means of fanning themselves. Men tried how a change of position would relieve them – others resigned themselves hopelessly to dozing. One elderly man, in the pew adjoining ours, who had two very ruddy-faced stout young women with him, had been asleep during the litany, and his snoring had attracted the attention of his daughter, who pushed their prayer books against his side and so awoke him.

We looked around to see if the 'interesting coal man' had been courageous enough to come to church, but he was no where to be seen in the small space allotted 'for the poor,' and it was by no means likely that the sexton would have accommodated *him* with a pew, empty as many, and dusty as they all were. Whilst the hymn before the sermon was being sung 'our church' presented a very drooping appearance. The grimed, rain-stained walls – the long rows of narrow pews, with a bonnet or a head jutting up here and there – the small-paned windows, the corners of which were festooned by the spider, and the frames of which were thickly coated with dust and dirt – the glass globes surrounding the gas jets well smoked and finger-marked – the paint on the pew sides and doors dark, damp, and sticky – the cushion of the pulpit and reading desk faded and soiled, the fringe draggled, the tassels hanging, in one instance, by a thread; add to these what had been endured by reason of bad reading, worse singing, foul air, and somnolent neighbours, and then will be seen the inducement which people have offered to them to spend here two and a half hours on a Sunday morning.

Such was the 'state and condition' of the congregation at 'our church,' when 'our curate' ascended the pulpit, to preach in his 'affectionate and endearing manner.'

It has been either said or written, by some shrewd observer, that there are certain looks of simple subtlety, in which whim and sense, seriousness and nonsense, affectation and anxiety, are so blended, that all the languages of Babel, let loose together, could not describe them; and it was a look of this character which 'our curate' set on, when he laid aside the little prayer book, from which he had been reading a short collect, as the 'prayer before the sermon.'

Intense mental effort manifests itself, outwardly, in a variety of ways. The consequential air of 'our curate' underwent no change; there were the shoulders well thrown back, the head moved affectedly, a very slight attempt at coughing indulged in, the congregation blandly overlooked, whilst the Bible was being slowly lifted to the necessary angle; all this carefully, studiously gone through. Yet there might be observed a nervous twitching about the sides of the mouth, a compression of the lips, a gathering up of the brow, which betokened anxiety. And no one could be surprised at seeing a young minister anxious under such circumstances. Granted that all the members of the congregation had conducted themselves with becoming seriousness and gravity up to this moment; that many were desirous of listening to, and profiting by, the discourse about to be delivered; that 'our curate' had in nowise checked their devotional ardour; that the reading had been excellent, the singing and responses effective; still, there were the length of the service and the vitiated atmosphere of 'our church' to contend against – and these had visibly told upon all present – so that it was almost physically impossible for them to give that attention which the serious and solemn character of the service, in every way, now required. 'Our curate's' anxiety might therefore be considered, under the circumstances, most becoming, and the very peculiar manifestation of it be charitably passed over.

The deep responsibility of the young man's position was enough to create anxiety; and as he looked around and saw what he knew to be the proud, the mean, the tyrannical, the slothful, the crafty money-grubber, side by side with the reckless and vicious spendthrift; the meek and unpretending worshiper by the side of the self-righteous Pharisee, the man who had but just now left the pursuit of some interesting branch of human knowledge; and others who had devoted their early morning to reading their business letters; he might well and deeply consider, 'believing all that my position indicates, what can I do to awaken the interest of these people in the great truths which Christianity proclaims? How can I best set before them what will mitigate the jealousies, bickerings, disappointments, cares, and sorrows, which inevitably surround their life?'

Well: what he thought on these, or whether such things were considered altogether beneath his notice – whether, like the Irish prelate, he ascended the pulpit to preach *himself*, or, like Paul, to preach his great Master, cannot be judged of; but he gave out the text in a weak faltering voice, and having read it to both sides of the church, threw his body well back, and addressed himself to his introduction.

His text was taken from – but it is of no use quoting the passage,

seeing that it had little or nothing to do with the sermon, was only
mentioned in it twice, and was simply a dislocated joint of a
sentence, selected as a striking head or a taking title. Nothing,
either doctrinal or practical, was suggested by it; and if it had any
application at all, the day, object, and circumstances considered, it
was to 'our curate' himself.

From his introduction we gathered this. Some men, who went to
church regularly, had got into the habit of judging for themselves
as to the truth or force of what the preacher taught; this was 'a
frame of mind to be guarded against.' Moreover, it was dangerous.
It was calculated to puff men up, and destroy their reliance on the
simplicity of gospel truth. There was a deal more in this strain, 'our
curate' insisting strongly upon the necessity of men 'hearing the
church,' and throwing overboard their own wills and judgments.
Those who did not do this were stigmatised, satirised, their tempers
slandered, their 'so-called philosophy' sneered at and
misrepresented; and all this done with a heartiness and honesty that
was forcibly rendered by a concluding smack of the lips! 'Our
curate' did not suppose that any of the characters to whom he
alluded were present! no, he said, as we took it down, that he
'could not, for one moment, entertain the degrading thought of
such persons being present.' It would from this appear, therefore,
that he enjoyed the opportunity for 'smiting people behind their
backs;' but it should be borne in mind that he was not now
engaged in preaching against 'bearing false witness.'

Thirteen minutes of smart fire effected a breach, and he entered
upon his sermon. Now he had to take a comprehensive view of what
man was – what he is – what he should be – what he must be –
what it was originally intended that he should be – and 'what he *will*
be inevitably.' For this purpose, he 'deemed it more in accordance
with the true spirit of Biblical teaching' that he should 'begin at the
beginning.' In flowery language Eden was described – 'the
characteristics of the foliage,' 'the glories of the sunsets,' 'the
plumage of the feathered tribes,' 'the *symphonies* of the meandering
streams.' 'The voice of the Lord in the garden' was transcendentally
dwelt upon, 'its startling tones' spoken of. Then came the fall, and
Milton was quoted. Then a neat stroke at the rise of husbandry, and
the blessings which result from hard work at farm labour – if the
labourers are true Protestants. Now Noah comes on the scene, the
building of the ark, 'the stocking of it,' with a pleasant reference to
the 'Great Eastern'. Then the flood and its termination, winding up
with these words, very deliberately, and as 'our curate' thought,
impressively delivered: 'Noah – stepped – forth – from – the – ark
– upon – the – still – deeply – saturated – earth, – whilst – the –
sound – of – the – receding surges – reverberated – in – his – ears.'

Thinking that 'our curate' had not the authority of Scripture to bear him out in this extremely 'elegant extract' and poetical description, we referred to Genesis; and, by what is there stated as 'the facts of the case,' our interest in the sermon was not heightened. Indeed, nothing could be much further from the truth, than the statement so deliberately made. But, on, on, he goes through the Patriarchal age – the Levitical – the Prophetical. Then he lands us in Greece, then in Rome; and it is attempted to be shewn, that progress in the arts and sciences is always indicative of the moral or religious retrogression of a nation. Here, an opening occurs for a wholesale condemnation of the present age; and this is taken advantage of to show that unless true Protestantism – which alone is that one thing – is 'the righteousness' that exalteth a nation – unless this be clung to, England is lost; and Macaulay's New Zealander – who, by the way, was put into peculiar costume for the occasion – 'would take his stand on the ruins of London Bridge at a much earlier date than might, in all probability, be expected.'

The last burst, and, for 'our curate,' it really was a burst, had the effect of completely turning our attention from the sermon. Again and again was an effort made to trace any connection between the rhapsodical utterances of the preacher and the great and serious purpose for which the men and women around had been gathered together. It did not surprise us in the least to hear some people rustling, others coughing; to see others looking about and relaxing themselves by a quiet yawn. We were in hopes that 'our curate' would take the audible hints which were given, and bring to a close a discourse, than which any thing more unreasonable, incoherent, illogical, unpractical, or uselessly suggestive, it has never been our misfortune to listen to.

But he did no such thing. He looked warm, and seemed to think that he was making an impression. His sermon was written out (the leaves, as he turned them over, seemed well thumbed, too) and he must empty upon us the cup of his rhodomontade to the very dregs. For three-quarters of an hour did this young man continue to pour forth crudities that were a disgrace to his very name; indulge in sneers which were unbecoming his position; and give expression to ideas which we hoped had long ceased to exist in the minds of Christian professors, and the simple utterance of which cast a scalding sarcasm upon the Church of which he is a member.

Such was the service and sermon to which the 'coal man' had been invited, and which were thought to be well calculated to cast a cheering ray upon his murky life of toil. Such are the services to which thousands of men and women are invited, and which thousands attend. It is pleasant to think that all ministers do not waste precious hours and insult the intelligence of their hearers to the same extent as 'our curate;' but he represents sadly too large a class, and the sooner these men are put in their right place the better for morality and religion. There is just now a vigorous effort being made to build 'free churches' – 'working men's churches;' but if any men, more particularly those of the artizan class, are to be induced to spend their Sundays in church, they must not have heaped upon them the dreary platitudes of 'our curate.'

Those ministers who have been most successful in attracting working men, are just those who, in their addresses, study simplicity and talk common sense in plain English. It has been our pleasure to hear, again and again, one of the greatest preachers of the Church of England; and nothing has struck us more than his logical accuracy, his clearness, his plain nervous English, and the great facility which the right use of these give him in riveting the attention of the people, and causing them to think for themselves. Even if a man have a well grounded affection for the services, and a wholesome reverence for the forms, of the church, these are not sufficient to cloak the wretched exhibitions of vanity and self-conceit which are too frequently made by 'our curates' in the pulpit.[96]

30 The model district

Still continuing our glimpses at life as it surrounds us, we turn now to a comparatively modern district of the town. In this only three courts are found. The streets, all formed within a few years, are well laid out; the houses are chiefly what are termed 'two-story cottages;' and in point of convenience, comfort, ventilation, and appearance, they will bear comparison with any in the surrounding districts. The population is large, and consists almost entirely of the labouring classes. The rents of the houses vary from 3s. to 6s. per week, and in some cases are so arranged as to include all rates. The church provides for the people two curates, two scripture readers, what has been called 'a devoted band' of district visitors, and day and Sunday schools. The Dissenters are here very active, and they provide day and Sunday schools, tract distributors, and Sunday and week-day services; and the Town Mission has an agent who devotes a considerable portion of his time to this locality. Taking it for granted that these agencies are calculated to promote or perform the work of social and moral regeneration in such a manner and to such an extent as many good men believe, we may expect to find in a district so well provided for and watched over very important results, in support of the views frequently advanced on behalf of these 'philanthropic efforts.' We ought, however, further to state, that amongst the important influences brought to bear on the moral and social life of the people, here are ten beer-houses, five spirit vaults, two skittle alleys, and one pawn-shop.

There is here one street of cottages which is looked upon by all who understand the wants, wishes, and requirements of working men as models of neatness and convenience, combined with a cheap rent, a good supply of water, and abundance of good air. They contain four apartments – a front living room; a back kitchen, with sink stone, boiler for washing, and all conveniences; a good yard capable of storing a couple of tons of coal; and upstairs are two good bed-rooms. The rent, which includes all rates, is 3s. 10d. per week. They were built by a man who had 'risen from the ranks.' When he earned 24s. per week as journeyman, *he lived on 10s., and saved the balance.* He well knew the value of money, and also had experienced the value of a comfortable home. He made no pretensions to philanthropy in the building of these cottages, but built them with the object of making them 'pay.' At the same time he gave, at a very moderate cost, a comfortable compact home to the working man; and we have not seen either in this or other towns any thing at all to compare with these cottages, either as regards character or cost. Such are the houses. What or who are the inhabitants?

In one dwells a man who is in constant employment, at 30s. per week. He has a wife and three children. The husband has not lost a day's work for many years – is a sober, industrious man; yet he is poor, and his children are ill clothed. The house evinces the husband's taste in decoration, and his wife's neglect in point of cleanliness. She is not a drunkard, yet the earnings of the husband are squandered, and his hard labour lost. Everything is got on credit – the groceries, the vegetables, coals; clothes from the 'Scotchman;' and sometimes money is borrowed 'to make the week out,' and, as the woman says, 'the wages are all eaten up before she gets them;' yet will she persist in her ruinous course; and all this, to a great extent, is carried on unknown to the husband. The district visitor will inquire kindly after the children when she calls, and will exchange the tract, and hope to see both husband and wife at church, but they rarely or never go. The man 'does not believe in the Church.' He thinks 'chapels are all alike,' and religion 'all a sham.' When he gets a new suit of clothes he intends to go to church and chapel too, to show them. His wife has more respect for religion and its teachers, but in her present embarrassed state how can she think of anything but the present life and its wants and woes? What might the town missionary do when he meets with such a case?

Next door dwells a man who holds a good situation at 28s. per week. He has a wife and two children, and is professedly a Churchman – indeed, a testimonial from a minister was required before he obtained his present situation. He is said to be in the possession of sound Protestant principles; is a member of a lodge, and on the anniversary day walks in procession, decorated with party-coloured ribbons. His wife and children, with many more like them, bring up the rear of the display in spring carts. These sound Protestants are now compelled to confine their display to the rural districts; and fearing lest they should not have an opportunity of displaying their principles, they have on recent occasions taken with them a cart filled with barrels of ale, and their close and unremitting attention to that part of their duty has been the subject of general remark.[97] There is a skittle alley close by the houses now under notice, and here this man's evenings are generally spent. As to reading, or spending his leisure hours with his family, these seem to form no portion of his religion, therefore he never practises such things; but he can appreciate fully a running match or a rabbit race, on Sunday morning, and if a pugilistic encounter should result from the former, which is frequently the case, it seems not in any way to clash with his principles. His wife is an industrious woman, and has to take in washing to help support the family; but there seems a lack of true independence about the people. They will take advantage of 'the clothing fund' at the church, receive anything that is offered to the poor during an inclement season, and *a spirit of mendicancy is gradually being cultivated by them*, than which nothing exerts a more baneful influence on the social standing of the people. Here is a man with ample means to preserve himself and family in comfort and independence, and a rightly balanced mind would scorn to accept of that which, by his own industry and frugality, he might earn and enjoy. The cases of this description, met with in this and other districts of the town, cause one to blush for the moral training the people receive, and if rigidly inquired into and reported would shame ministers and teachers into something like practical usefulness – unless, indeed, as many suppose, teaching and preaching have become moth-eaten with the sordid views and worldly feelings which are said too frequently to characterise the modern professors of religion.

As a contrast to the foregoing, there is in this street a man engaged in out-door employment, whose wages are 27s. per week; but in bad weather he loses a deal of time, which limits his income considerably. He has a wife and three children; neither he nor his wife is a strong person, and for a long time the wife has been in a bad state of health. Their house is the picture of comfort and cleanliness: the children are neatly clothed; the parents have a seat at church, and contribute a little to the various funds for religious or philanthropic purposes. The home training of the children is very carefully attended to – which, after all, is the main point in education, and the parents even now reap the reward of their labour, in the obedience and good behaviour of their children. There are no clothing-fund tickets taken in this house; indeed the district visitors rarely think of speaking on the subject *where they find a house clean and the people comfortable*. In winter time we have known this house, with its cleanliness, to be the abode of poverty, but it was not abject. The people bore their sorrows without a murmur; and if the good nature or kind offices of friendship brought them any relief, oh, how feelingly was it accepted, and how fully and faithfully returned. This man has not spent a penny in intoxicating drink for fourteen years; and to see him and his family on their way to church causes one ardently to long for the 'good time coming,' when multitudes of working men will be like him.

A case has come under our notice during the last few weeks which reveals social evils of such a nature as to call for special attention. In a room 8 feet by 9 (not in the street of which we have been speaking) dwell a working man, his wife, and two children. They have nothing but this room for living and sleeping. There is no bed in the place, but a bundle of shavings and straw thrown on the floor answers the purpose. Two of this man's children died of fever a short time since, and the two remaining present a very unhealthy appearance. *The man is in constant employment, earns good wages, and the wife goes out washing and charing.* Both parents are drunkards, and neither themselves nor children have any change of clothing. To use the man's own words – 'We have a good blow-out on Saturday night and Sunday, and then we put the screw on,' which, being interpreted, means they eat and drink almost the whole of the week's earnings on Saturday night and Sunday, and have in consequence to starve themselves and children the remaining days. There are several washerwomen in the neighbourhood, and this woman works for some of them occasionally. She also resorts to a scheme for raising money during the week which we understand is becoming very common; and fraught as it is with the greatest dangers, the public cannot be made acquainted with it too soon. It is called *'borrowing a pledge.'* She will go to some of the washerwomen, who, for a consideration, lend her some dirty clothes. These she takes to her pestilential home, and washes as the convenience there will best admit. They are hurriedly dried, ironed, or mangled, and taken to the pawn-shop, where she is well known. The money received on these enables herself and husband to drink and eat until Saturday night, when with his wages she releases the clothes, and takes them from the pawn-shop to the washerwoman who has so kindly lent them. They are placed in the basket and taken home, and, as the woman says, 'what harm is done to the owner of the togs, and what if his name was read at the pawn-shop?' Last week, we know, three shirts and a pair of light trowsers were pledged for 4s., and for several weeks past this woman has obtained clothes by such means, on which she had procured sums varying from 8s. to 12s. The pawnbrokers must be aware that the pledges offered are not the woman's own property, and why not check the evil?[98]

Passing now into one of the courts, we find four houses, which, although not old, appear in a dilapidated condition. In one resides a mechanic, who earns 28s. per week regularly, and has a wife and three children. The woman and children are in a filthy state, and the house as wretched as the inmates are degraded. This man never enters a place of worship, and boasts that he has only been once in church since he was christened, and that was to get married. He does not lose any time from work for purposes of drunkenness, yet he consumes an enormous quantity of ale. He will frequently drink two gallons of ale on Sunday morning before his breakfast, sleep that off, eat as much food as ought to serve him a couple of days, and then set to work drinking again. His wife has no knowledge of household affairs, having served her time to a trade. She understands that, and nothing more. This leads to domestic broils, which often result in blows, but the wife has in this respect clearly the best of it. She is of an ungovernable temper, and highly combative. On one occasion she, with a child in her arms, was passing a neighbourhood where they used to reside, when the keeper of a little shop stopped her and asked for the settlement of a small account. Some words ensued; she passed her infant to a companion to hold, then, throwing off her shawl, and turning up her sleeves, she proceeded, in true British style, to settle the account, by giving the creditor what she calls 'a good belting.' And so with differences at home. They are settled in like manner: on one occasion recently *she tore the front out of her husband's shirt whilst they sat at meat*, merely because he questioned her qualifications as cook, and threw the pudding against the wall. These people never dwell long in one place, The weekly wages do little more than keep them in drink, and for food they 'get trust in the shops about,' and for clothes 'get all from the Scotchman.' When they are pretty deep in everybody's books about, they are said to have 'sold the plant,' and therefore look out for another residence, adopt the same plan here, and move off again. The man amuses his companions and shopmates by telling of the tricks he and his wife resort to in order to cheat people out of food and clothing, and relates with great glee a story showing how he is training his children to habits of lying and all manner of deceit and hypocrisy. This man and his family have lived in all districts of the town, and in all kinds of houses; yet neither air nor habitation seems to have in any way improved his character, which would lead some people to think that all real improvement, mental, moral, or social, must proceed *from within a man*, and is not dependent on external circumstances to any great extent.

One of the Scripture readers in this district holds meetings at some of the houses, where the poor and infirm, or those who may be otherwise prevented from attending the church, have an opportunity of hearing the Scriptures read and explained. He goes round and informs the people of the time of the meeting, and invites attendance; but his other duties must be of an extraordinary or harassing nature, for on several occasions, after calling the people together, *he has forgotten or neglected to come himself.* On a very recent occasion, a number of poor people waited at the appointed

house *two hours*, and he never appeared. On another day he kept
them waiting an hour and a half, and then appeared to lament his
being so much behind time, but it had in the multiplicity of his
other engagements quite escaped his memory.* The recent report of
the Scripture Readers' Society laments the fact that they have not
the means to employ more labourers. The fact of a man being
worked so hard that he forgets what his duty really is, shows the
necessity that exists for *other labourers* being appointed, in order
that such men may be relieved. Without wishing in any way to
undervalue the service which these men render or the good they
accomplish, we doubt the policy of spending large sums of money
for such purpose, unless a foundation is laid upon which a
superstructure of religious teaching may be judiciously and
permanently built.

'House-to-house visitation' is highly spoken of in some districts
where it is practised. Whether anything of the sort prevails here we
are not in a position to state; but this much is known. At a house
within a stone's throw of the church resides an old woman, who
'has been bought up to the church,' as it is termed, and who had
a near relative who filled a pastoral office in a rural district. This
old woman is now infirm, and cannot get to church. The minister
of the district was written to respecting her case, and the result is,
that the curates have visited her *three times in seven years*! It is true
her children attend to her, and in a pecuniary or physical view she
wants for nothing; but she is one of those people who for very
many years of her life was in the habit of seeing and conversing
with 'the parson.' She also likes this intercourse, and believes it does
her good. When she resided in the country, and the parson had
sometimes a great distance to come, where there was neither district
visitor nor Scripture reader, the spiritual consolation which she
derived from the pastor's visit was regularly obtained. But now,
with the shadow of almost a century upon her – with a body
enfeebled, and yet the mind comparatively vigorous, tottering under
the weight of years – she has to travel the remaining portion of her
journey unheeded, uncared for, so far as these ministers and
teachers are concerned – this, too, in a district which, within the
last month, has been held up before a large, influential, and
wealthy congregation as 'a model district.'

It was our intention to notice at some length the effort which has
been made by a body of gentlemen in this town to construct model
houses for the operative classes. The subject has, however, been
entered upon by other hands, and we therefore leave it to them,

---

* It is right to state that the person alluded to is not employed by the Church of
England Scripture Readers' Society, but is supported from a separate fund.

contenting ourselves by saying that, however much the mode may be questioned, the object and motive are worthy of all praise. The houses erected in Frederick-street, and called the Albert Cottages, are neat and cheerful in appearance. Those erected in Northumberland-street, by 'The Liverpool Labourers' Dwelling Company,' cannot be considered either neat or cheerful in appearance, whatever be the conveniences they contain.[99] Beyond this, the rents are, in the main, too high for a labouring man to pay. A man with a wife and five or six children, whose wages weekly are 26s. or 28s., cannot feed and clothe his family and pay rent of 5s. or 6s. per week. Whilst visiting these houses we met with a man and his wife who were looking out for a house, and having heard of these they had come to look at them. It would have done the committee of this company and all concerned great good to hear the criticism of this working man and his wife on the appearance and construction of these model houses. The man had read that an Englishman's house was his castle, and he liked to consider it such, and thought it ought not to be made to appear quite the reverse. The woman had notions of cleanliness and privacy which she could not reconcile with the construction of these dwellings, or the regulations drawn up by the committee for the guidance of the tenants. That the company are actuated by the best and purest motives, the names of several gentlemen on the committee abundantly testify; but there is a practical man wanted amongst them. If people are to be drawn from the foul and filthy courts into which they now crowd – and it is desirable in every way, socially, and physically, that they should be – houses should be so constructed that the rents would fall within the means of these poor people, or how can they be expected to avail themselves of the desirable change? There are some of the houses in Northumberland-street at a rental of 3s. 9d. This for a comfortable house is moderate. But any man, more particularly an Englishman, who can pay 6s. per week, will locate himself in a neat cottage house, where he can have that independent action and domestic privacy which, to some extent, cannot be obtained in large blocks of dwellings with a common entrance. The company have started the work, and public attention being now directed to it, we may expect in this as in other cases that publicity will be the true cure of social evils, and that whatever defects are discovered in the construction or arrangement of these dwellings will be remedied, when this or another company erects another block of model houses for the working classes.[100]

31 The Street Boys' Concert Admission, One Penny

It has often been said that any one who could devise a scheme for amusing the poor, which would be at once cheap, wholesome, and attractive, would thereby promote public morality.[101] Working people have made several efforts to establish for themselves recreation for their leisure hours apart from the destructive influences of the public house; but they have never succeeded very well. In one instance, at Bond Street, some well-intentioned men undertook to provide what they supposed the people required, and professed to infuse a strong solution of the 'working-class element' into the committee. They did not succeed in their endeavours. The intention of philanthropists is one thing, the manner in which they carry their intentions out – the way in which they meet and mingle with those whom they wish to benefit – is quite another. Working people have peculiar notions, strong prejudices, stubborn wills and an earnest and emphatic manner of expressing themselves. They have not received that character of education which teaches them how to conceal their thoughts, consequently their bluntness is often mistaken for impertinence, their earnestness looked upon as vulgarity, and their demeanour spoken of as not being at all 'gentlemanly.' It is, therefore, not at all surprising to find that in the matter of amusements there should arise a difference of opinion between the classes.

To counteract the pernicious influence of the minor theatres and cheap singing saloons on youth, various schemes have been tried with varied success. Our attention was directed to an effort of this nature which is being made at the Stanley Hall in Richmond Row. Last year, the concerts, &c., given here were to a certain extent under the auspices of the Temperance Society, which holds its meetings in this room on Sunday and Tuesday evenings. The committee were working men, and had faith enough in their work, and were so earnest in their endeavour as to subscribe a small sum each week in order to defray the expenses. The hall is now taken as a private speculation, but the same principle is adopted as to the nature and carrying out of the entertainment.

We visited the room on a Saturday evening, and found an

audience of about 180 persons, chiefly boys – very few were over 16 or 17 years of age. There is a stage at one end of the room and a coffee stall at the other. The admission is one penny; the charge for a cup of coffee is one penny; buns, cakes, fruit, &c., on terms equally reasonable. Over the stage is the motto 'Sobriety leads to Domestic Happiness,' and the decorations of the room in any particular cannot be said to be extravagant. But then as we were told, 'what can you expect for the price?' The entertainment consists of singing and dancing by amateurs, and on special occasions an attempt is made at a dramatic performance, but it is on a very limited scale, as the stage and its properties readily suggest. The audience were well behaved, considering the class of life from whence they were gathered, and the majority of them seemed to take great interest in the singing, joining in the choruses with a heartiness which bespoke strength of lung, rather than knowledge of the music.

The manager of the room very judiciously blends patriotic, sentimental, and comic singing with recitations and dancing. 'The talent' would appear to be concealed by a small curtain at the side of the stage, and at the other side is the piano, a wretched instrument, which is presided at by a professional. There is no time lost, for no sooner is one song or recitation ended, than the manager announces the next, and the name of the performer. The young men and boys seem to enjoy their pipes, and but few indulge in the luxury of coffee. To prevent any interruption to the performance, the manager is ever on the alert to hand a youth, or boy, a light for his pipe, and has also a good supply of water, which he liberally dispenses to poor, thirsty, little fellows. During three-quarters of an hour we hear (*for a penny*) two sentimental, two Irish, and two comic songs, together with a recitation, exhibiting the horrors of drink. Besides, the pianist gave the 'Gambler's Wife,' and a young man, said to be a 'butcher's boy,' danced an Irish jig in character. It would be unfair to criticise the singing – it was of no great merit; but the dancing was excellent. There is considerable freedom taken with the original music of the songs, as may be expected, and to hear 'Larboard Watch' sung as a solo, had an air of novelty about it, yet this did not compensate for the lack of taste on the part of the singers.

There were two thoughts forced upon our attention whilst we stood in this crowded hall. The great number of very young boys amongst the audience, and the dirty state in which all appeared – at least 100 boys must have been under fourteen years of age, and the wan faces, sunken cheeks, and tattered garments, told a tale of parental negligence and indifference. They seemed to be little fellows who had but just left their work, and it was painful to think that it was perhaps on the whole better that they should be under shelter here, than exposed to the temptations of the streets, or corrupted by the evil example to be found at their homes. What a view does it give of the social life of the people, to find such a number of little boys cast upon their own resources so soon.

An incident which occurred whilst we were present is very characteristic of the coolness of English boys. The night was very wet – the sky-light of the room had been opened for purposes of ventilation, and as the rain began to beat in, the manager thought it advisable to close it. He began to work the cords for that purpose, but the frame slipped in, fell, and the glass in large pieces came tumbling down on the heads of the boys. They never flinched – there was not the slightest disturbance – in fact the chorus was never for a moment interrupted. Those who had been hit, rubbed their heads, and others behind suppressed a titter; and so the accident passed off. In some audiences an accident of this sort would have caused injury to many, and perhaps death to a few.

It is well known that there are in Liverpool as elsewhere, many men blessed with the will and means to help any humble effort. Let them see the way and their work is well nigh done. All that we would suggest on behalf of this very humble 'Saturday Evening Concert,' is that some good Samaritan would step forth and hire these poor fellows a decent piano; and further, that they might occasionally be supplied with a really good singer. To go further might be thought interference and so lead to a 'smash up' of the concern. It appears that in order to insure a supply of singers, &c., for the evening, some amateurs have to be paid a trifle; and in these cases, the manager might very properly insist upon personal cleanliness being acted upon. If these lads were accustomed to see even a few of their fellows with clean hands and faces, and decently patched clothes, it would have an educational effect upon the mass. It seems very clear that if the boys who composed this audience are ever to be taught habits of cleanliness, this must be taught *from home.*[102] There might be a move, a very gentle one it must be, made towards this object, by the adoption of the hint which we have thrown out.

32 An hour in a Co-operative store

Last week the improvidence of working men was illustrated by describing 'An hour in a Grog Shop,'[103] the aim is now to shew the providence of working men by a visit to the Co-operative Store. Dick Stubbs with his stout cheerful little wife, and what he calls his 'big little family', live in a neat cottage house in Toxteth Park. It is a picture of domestic happiness to see Dick, after he has had his tea, rolling about the floor playing with his children. Of course his wife 'fairly dies' with laughing at them, and of course his wife, children, and home are all the world to Dick. But Dick was once 'a wastrel,' he was not a great drunkard, but he took 'a good sup,' and this made him indifferent to home joys, reckless, and improvident. Dick likes to tell how 'his eyes were opened,' and on this point a week or two ago we heard him in very plain terms declare how much working men might do to help themselves, if they would only practice a little self-denial, and said he, 'Come to the Store any Saturday night and see for yourself. We make no bounce. We spend no money in advertising; we don't *palm* the papers to report even our annual meeting at length. We work hard, but don't *talk* much; and you'll not be likely to know much about us, unless you come and see.'

Such were the concluding remarks of Dick Stubbs, with whom we had been conversing on work men's savings and work men's earnings. Co-operation was his great panacea for the healing of the nation's social wounds; and he was zealous and truthful in his advocacy of it. Being thoroughly convinced, by practical experience, that anything which will tend to the formation of provident habits amongst working people, must ultimately prove extremely beneficial, we readily accepted the invitation to spend an hour on a Saturday evening in the Co-operative Store, in Camden-street.

Most people have heard of the Co-operative Associations of Rochdale, of Leeds, and of other manufacturing towns; but with reference to Liverpool, it is much as our friend says, the mere existence of the society is little known, certainly not as much as it ought to be.[104] What the association aims at is, 'The improvement of the social and domestic condition of the members, by raising a sufficient amount of capital to establish a store for the sale of provisions, clothing, &c., to the members only.'

The Liverpool Co-operative Provident Society has, for the convenience of its members, branches in different parts of the town. In the South, Warwick-street; in the North, Virgil-street; and in the East, Lord-street, Edge-hill. These branches are open on stated nights in each week, and are supplied with goods packed up and ready for delivery, from the Central Store, Camden-street.

The capital is raised by shares of £1 each; and each member is required to take not less than five, nor permitted to hold more than £100. The payment is brought within the means of any working man, being not less than threepence per week for every five shares. There is an entrance fee of one shilling. Thus, *any who can pay this entrance fee, and who can contrive to save threepence per week, may become a member*, and is at once entitled to the advantages which the store offers for the purchase of good, and, so far as the vigilance of the officers can secure, unadulterated groceries, clothing, &c., with honest measure and weight, at a fair and reasonable price.

To shew the progress made by the association, a few figures only are necessary. In 1851 there were 34 members, the capital was £60, and the receipts on sales amounted to £317. In 1860, there were 1200 members, the capital was £2200, and the receipts £15,000. The magnitude of the operations involves the employment of a manager and permanent staff in the Central Store; and it is gratifying to learn, that after defraying the cost of management, and paying five per cent. per annum to the members upon their accumulated capital, a sum has always been left to be divided amongst the members to the extent of their purchases, the average profit being about 1*s*. 4*d*. in the pound.

But, we can fancy a working man saying on reading this, 'It may be all very well, but instead of a dry yarn why don't you tell us how the system works, that's what I want to know.' Well, have patience, my hearty. Here is Dick Stubbs and his wife coming along Lime Street, with the intention of getting the weeks supply of groceries, and some 'extra goods' at the Central Store in Camden Street, let us join them and Dick or his wife (she is the talker) will soon show how the system works.

To reach this Central Store Dick and his wife have walked from Toxteth Park, and they have on their way passed the doors and flaming lights of *forty-three* public houses! No small temptation for a working man, on a bitter cold night, with money in his pocket and not very thickly clad. But Dick has found that he cannot eat a cake and have it, and he is so far on the right track as to forego present pleasure for future good. He could easily have spent three or four weekly subscriptions to the Store fund whilst walking this distance. Three two pennorths of rum for himself and wife would have amounted to four weeks' subscription, and this would be considered a very 'small Saturday night allowance' by hundreds of men and women.

Business is brisk at the Store – the manager and assistants seem hard at work supplying the wants of working people in the way of groceries and provisions. The place is not very well lighted, neither are the fittings of the recognised fancy class. Whilst setting themselves boldly against any useless expenditure in this way, it would be a great mistake if the committee should go to the other extreme. Utility and neatness may be combined without extravagance and there *is* an educational effect to be secured by this means whatever people may say to the contrary. The gradual expansion of the business has something to do with the awkward appearance of the shelves and the mode in which they are 'pieced out' sets all conventionality at defiance. On the one side, butter, bacon, cheese, &c., are being disposed of, at the other tea, coffee, sugar, &c.

Here is Dick's stout little wife; she brings with her a list of articles which she requires, this she hands to one of the assistants, together with her pass book, and her goods will be looked out. Some of them, (such as butter, cheese, &c.,) she selects – the amount will be entered in her book, and her list be filed as a check on the storekeepers. The list of articles is printed and supplied by the society, and the working man or his wife can fill in the quantity of each article they require at their leisure and at home. Cash is paid for all groceries.

But whilst we have been looking about this lower room of the Store, we have observed women, most of them very neatly and comfortably dressed, leave their orders and pass up stairs. We learn that they are bent on a supply of 'extra goods,' and we follow them. Here is a really fine room, well fitted, neatly arranged, the goods tastefully displayed, and an air of solid comfort and substantiality, which is very pleasing and suggestive. This is the drapery department, and women seem very much at home here. Husbands are standing by, whilst the home comforts for wives and children are being measured and chosen. The stock comprises everything in the way of clothing which working people require, and the go-to-meeting suits for both sexes seem to have received due consideration. This department was set on foot to counteract the rapacity of 'Scotchmen,' whose dealing with working men's wives have earned for them such unenviable notoriety.[105] In a few weeks these co-operatives will have, in the rooms above the drapery department, shoemakers at work, and will manufacture their shoes on the premises; indeed there seems to be hardly any limit to the extent to which they may push their operations, if they be conducted with the same sagacity and prudential foresight, which would appear to have secured their progress thus far.

But the term 'extra goods' requires explanation. In most Co-operative Stores cash payment is required for every article, and purchases may be made by the general public. In this, the sales are confined to members, and *credit is given on 'extra goods.'* That is, articles of clothing or coals. Here is our friend Dick. He has paid up five shares, of one pound each, and is therefore in a position to obtain four pounds worth of extra goods on credit. His wife may have a good shawl, frocks and flannel for the children, and he may have a pair of shoes or whatever he stands most in need of; or he may have a couple of tons of coals, and his repayments must be made at the rate of one shilling per week. And mark, there is no interest charged for this; if he pays up his instalments regularly he receives his full share at the division of profits. This is a feature novel in Co-operative Societies, and if it can be successfully worked, may, in many cases prove extremely useful.

But as we see it, the great advantages of a society of this nature, beyond the obtaining provisions of good quality, weight, and measure, is to be found in the facilities which it offers for *saving*. It requires a great effort on the part of a working man or his wife to save at all. Now here is a fulcrum which gives the *start* and makes the progress steady and easy. When a man has five pounds in, he feels a degree of independence to which thousands are strangers; and besides, should any misfortune occur, the cash is always attainable for use; indeed it is not an unusual thing, as the manager told us, to find workmen at pressing periods withdrawing their money to meet extra demands made upon them. It may be that many members of the society could be steady, frugal, and industrious without any such aids, but numerous cases were given which go to show the Co-operative Association has been mainly instrumental in *raising men and their families*, socially and morally, and this from what has been shewn can be easily understood.[106]

From reflection on the hour spent in this store we are firmly of opinion that if all working men could be induced to concern themselves about the *right use* of wages as much as some are led to concern themselves about the *rate*, they would be placed in a more manly, honourable, and independent position, and might then *possess* what now they in many cases only *talk* about.

But if all have not learned true wisdom on this matter, it is pleasant to know that some have. The Tortoise clumsily built, awkward in its movements, perseveringly travelled on whilst the Hare, its boastful opponent, slept. In like manner, whilst Social Science philosophers after their boastful talk, are sleeping, a few working men – men with little to say, and 'small very' to look at, have passed them by, and so far as solving what is termed the great problem of Social Economy is concerned – have won the race. All honor to such men, and success to the Camden-street Co-operatives!

Notes on the text

1. The magistrates' policy with regard to licensing public houses and places of entertainment was a source of long-running conflict in Victorian Liverpool. In 1862 the licensing justices angered Shimmin still further by ceasing to take account of the notional needs of the neighbourhood when considering new applications, and heeding only the suitability of the premises and the character of the applicant. (See Winskill and Thomas, 1887, p. 65; Cockcroft, 1974, pp. 155–7; Hull, 1979, pp. 20–1.)

2. 'Cavendish' is tobacco which has been pressed and formed into rectangular shapes. (*OED.*)

3. Cf. P. Bailey, *Leisure and class in Victorian England* (London: Routledge, 1978), chapters 1, 7; R. Poole, *Popular leisure and the music-hall in nineteenth-century Bolton* (Lancaster: Centre for North West Regional Studies, 1982); P. Bailey, *Music hall: the business of pleasure* (Milton Keynes: Open University Press, 1986), pp. 2–5, 20–2; and for a Manchester free-and-easy at about this time, *Free Lance*, 2 March 1867. But they do not discuss the kind of up-market 'free-and-easy' which is the main target of Shimmin's criticism.

4. Brown bess is the older type of breech-loading rifle, which was being displaced by new muzzle-loaders, including (from 1852) the Minié. (H. Strachan, *The reform of the British army, 1830–54*, Manchester: Manchester University Press, 1984, p. 157.)

5. An allusion to the Crimean War battle of that name.

6. A 'shade' in this context was a wine or beer vault with a bar: the term seems to have originated in Brighton (*OED*). The identification with oysters in this brothel-related setting is appropriate: one of the slang uses of 'oyster' meant 'the female pudenda'. (E. Partridge, *A dictionary of slang and unconventional English*, ed. Paul Beale, London: Routledge 1989 edition).

7. Prostitutes were listed as such by the census enumerators in this part of Liverpool in 1851, but not in 1871. The label 'milliner' was clearly a popular disguise.

8. See also the description of a Liverpool free concert room in Razzell and Wainwright, 1973, pp. 281–2. The *Morning Chronicle* correspondent, writing in 1850, stressed the ubiquity of such places, and remarked on the large attendance of noisy teenage boys along with the foreign sailors. He also found some of the entertainment to be lewd and indecent.

9. Dickens, 1978, and *Free Lance*, 22 December 1866, 2 February 1867,

are two of many other observers who identify occupations as well as social status at sight. This is clearly aided by the large number of men who went straight off for a night out in their working clothes, and often in their working dirt. (Cf. Dagmar Höher, 'The composition of music hall attendances, 1850–1900', in Bailey, 1986, pp. 73–92.)

10. A dark mark on the face. It is not clear from the context whether it is a mole or natural blemish, or something else. (Partridge, 1989.)

11. Since at least 1835 a 'blue' had been a policeman, so this is clearly a plain-clothes policeman; and as Shimmin recognises him, he presumably also knows Shimmin. (Partridge, 1989.)

12. A classic example of 'the observer observed': Shimmin's presence on this occasion alters the character of what he has to report. We are left wondering whether this may have occurred more subtly, or gone unreported, on other occasions.

13. For background to this see D. Brailsford, *Bareknuckles: a social history of prize-fighting* (Cambridge, 1988). But this event involved gloves, and it had counterparts in more elevated places by this time. See 'Cuthbert Bede', *The adventures of Mr Verdant Green* (London: Blackwood, n.d.), Part I, pp. 105–6, for Oxford undergraduates (who also became involved with 'the fancy' by way of ratting). We owe this reference to Judith Rowbotham.

14. This disregard of punctuality is another clear demonstration of the immorality of pugilism.

15. The term is presumably derived from cock-fighting, though we have found no evidence for this.

16. Another boxing pub. (Partridge, 1989.)

17. Shoes. (Partridge, 1989.)

18. This addresses one of the great sporting debates of the period, from an unusual angle. See R. Holt, *Sport and the British* (Oxford: Oxford University Press, 1990 edition), chapter 2.

19. This evidence adds to Holt's short account. (Holt, 1990, pp. 58–9.)

20. An allusion to the limited powers of regulation provided by the 1830 Beer Act. See B. Harrison, *Drink and the Victorians* (London: Faber, 1971), pp. 81–6.

21. The analogy is with the speculative activities of Liverpool merchants, who met on 'the Flags' to transact business.

22. As the next sentence makes clear, this comment is, of course, ironical.

23. 'Beaks' in this setting are magistrates. (Partridge, 1989.)

24. These issues are developed by J. J. Tobias, *Crime and industrial society in the nineteenth century* (London: Penguin, 1967), p. 82.

25. See R. Poole, 'The Lancashire wakes', Ph.D. thesis, Lancaster University, 1985, for confirmation and documentation; or J. K. Walton and R. Poole, 'The Lancashire wakes in the nineteenth century', in R. Storch, ed., *Popular culture and custom in nineteenth-century Britain* (London: Croom Helm, 1982), pp. 100–24.

26. This is true of Liverpool itself, but Shimmin himself, in *Town life*, describes the influx of town dwellers to Hale and Tranmere wakes, which had been effectively taken over by the Liverpool working class.

27. A 'float' according to *OED*, was 'a low-bodied, crank-axled cart, used

for carrying heavy articles, livestock, etc.'. A spring cart was altogether faster and more manoeuvrable, and became almost an inevitable, even symbolic accompaniment of the Liverpool 'rough' on a spree.

28. Partridge, 1989, tells us that 'Palmer's twister' was a strychnine pill, named after the infamous Rugeley poisoner of that name.

29. Sunburn was, of course, a sign of outdoor manual work, or vagabondage, and low status at this time.

30. Aintree racecourse was owned by the Topham family.

31. In this context 'the talent' were the backers of horses, in league against the bookmakers: 'Clever because they make a horse a favourite.' (Partridge, 1989.)

32. To come off 'crabs': to be a failure, be unfortunate. (Partridge, 1989.)

33. This and the previous chapter are particularly notable for their documentation of a raffish, pleasure-seeking Liverpool middle class who seem a world away from the enduring belief in a predominant work ethic. (See also Taine, 1957, pp. 32–8, for London.)

34. Fashionable head- and neckwear, although Partridge confuses the issue by telling us that the pork-pie was a woman's style between 1855 and 1865, and the name was applied to male headgear only from 1920 or so. See also p. 43 for a public-house waiter wearing a pork-pie hat, possibly in this case a second-hand one?

35. For child prostitution cf. K. Chesney, *The Victorian underworld* (London, 1970), p. 325.

36. The commercial use of the terminology of rational recreation shows how necessary it was to claim 'improving' or educational attributes if at all possible, and it is also a reminder of how the notion of 'rational recreation' could be appropriated and subverted. (Cf. Bailey, 1978, and R. Poole, *Popular leisure and the music hall in nineteenth century Bolton* (Lancaster: Centre for North-West Regional Studies, 1982, p. 48.) A parallel, though more up-market, instance is the lecture on 'craniology and phrenology and mesmerism' which Francis Kilvert and his mother attended in Weston-super-Mare in 1872, where the entertainment was of much more account than the 'science'. (W. Plomer, ed., *Kilvert's diary*, London: Penguin edition, 1977, pp. 210–12.)

37. The pleasurable properties of nitrous oxide, or 'laughing gas', had been discovered by Humphry Davy at the end of the eighteenth century. Southey and Coleridge were among those who tried it out in the early 1820s, and it was being offered as commercial entertainment in the United States in 1844, though with ostensible pretensions to gentility and decorum which could not be sustained in Shimmin's Liverpool. See A. J. Youngson, *The scientific revolution in Victorian medicine* (London: Croom Helm, 1979), pp. 45–50.

38. James Newlands was Liverpool's borough engineer. The context suggests that he had devised and introduced a form of public urinal.

39. For charity bazaars, F. K. Prochaska, *Women and philanthropy in nineteenth-century England* (Oxford: Clarendon Press, 1980), pp. 47–72.

40. Shimmin's critical perspective on these activities does not surface in Prochaska, 1980, pp. 73–94, which looks at children and charities.

41. The theme of the beerhouse as the start of the slippery slope that leads inexorably to prison was common among social reformers: see Harrison, 1971, pp. 81-6, and J. M. Fraser, 'The grim crusader', M.A. dissertation, Lancaster University, 1983, for the Preston prison chaplain, Rev. John Clay.

42. These comparisons are presumably based on indignation rather than on comparative empirical research.

43. The best general introduction to this theme is M. J. Daunton, *House and home in the Victorian city, 1850-1914* (London: Edward Arnold, 1985).

44. For the origins of the Liverpool courts, I. C. Taylor, 'The court and cellar dwelling: the eighteenth century origin of the Liverpool slum', *Historic Society of Lancashire and Cheshire* 122 (1970); and Treble, 1971, pp. 167-220.

45. This evidence indicates that slum dwellers did not become so inured to their surroundings that they ceased to notice evil smells.

46. These are unusually explicit references to incest: usually the subject is veiled in allusion. See A. S. Wohl, 'Sex and the single room', in Wohl, ed., *The Victorian family* (London: Croom Helm, 1978).

47. This was clearly an extremely unfeminine activity.

48. An interesting example of the female observance of 'St Monday', which is usually treated in terms of male craft workers and miners rather than housewives. See D. A. Reid, 'The decline of St Monday, 1766-1876', *Past and Present* 71 (1976), and Wright, 1867, 'Saint Monday – its worship and worshippers', pp. 108-30.

49. A comic actor, then at the height of his fame, who commanded high fees in the provinces. (M. Baker, *The rise of the Victorian actor*, London: Croom Helm, 1978, pp. 53, 75, 117, 118, 166.)

50. An allusion to the provision of escape routes for malefactors, as in the London rookeries. (Tobias, 1967.)

51. Head Constable of Liverpool, 1852-81.

52. J. J. Stitt, an American merchant, was an active Liberal municipal politician, first elected to the corporation in 1856. His obsession with the cleanliness of his person, and especially his boots, was both an asset and a liability from the sanitary reform perspective. (Obituary in *Liverpool Citizen*, 16 January 1889.)

53. The offices of the municipal Health Department.

54. Cf. Thomas Wright's version. (Wright, 1867, 184-203.)

55. Almost certainly Godfrey's, or a near relative: a mixture of sassafras, treacle and tincture of opium.

56. A trip across the Mersey to Eastham or New Brighton was a popular outing for Liverpool working-class families when in funds, especially as the ferries were very cheap.

57. 'Scotchmen' or 'Scotch drapers' sold patterns and materials for clothing on credit from door to door. (M. Tebbutt, *Making ends meet: pawnbroking and working-class credit*, Leicester: Leicester University Press, 1983, pp. 21, 176-7; and see below, chapter 20.)

58. A payment to a friendly society for insurance, usually made in a pub. See P. H. J. H. Gosden, *The friendly societies in England, 1815-75*

(Manchester: Manchester University Press, 1961), and *Self-help* (London: Batsford, 1973), chapters 2–4.

59. An absolutely standard comment. For domestic servants generally, P. Horn, *The rise and fall of the Victorian domestic servant* (Dublin: Gill & Macmillan, 1975).

60. The state of the labour market in Liverpool made domestic servants more readily affordable here than in most towns. The story-line of *Harry Birkett* suggests that Shimmin's sisters went into service (p. 276).

61. For Brown see Caine, 1887. In the appendix Henry Young noted that the people at the lectures were 'nearly all unmistakably of the working class, all decently dressed'. Ironically, in the light of the tale of Jem Burns, Young was told by a listener, 'It's best to bring a cap here that it's hard sitting so long.'

62. A pub which acted as a trade union headquarters and labour exchange for members of the trade.

63. The unprepossessing man is collecting money, ostensibly for the benefit of a prizefighter.

64. The work of the translator is nicely described by Hopkinson, 1968, pp. 101–2.

65. Note the continuing recourse to cellars, in spite of the attempts to clear them in the 1840s. See Treble, 1971, pp. 194–9.

66. For a critical discussion of these loan societies see also *Porcupine*, 22 June 1861.

67. There may well be significant implications for local politics here.

68. See above, n. 57. Bagging: deceiving. (J. O. Halliwell, ed., *Dictionary of archaic words*, (1850; reprinted London: Bracken Books, 1989, p. 132.)

69. Insurance money from a friendly society or burial club, probably received to pay for a child's funeral.

70. K. S. Inglis, *Churches and the working classes in Victorian England* (London: Routledge, 1963), pp. 48–57, discusses this theme.

71. Cf. J. K. Walton, 'The demand for working-class seaside holidays in Victorian England', *Economic History Review*, second series, 34 (1981), pp. 249–65.

72. For a vivid description of such an occasion, Wright, 1867, pp. 67–82.

73. A tizzy was sixpence, a browney a copper coin. (Partridge, 1989.)

74. See above, n. 44.

75. For Jeffery see White, 1951, pp. 82, 85.

76. Chopping wood for kindling was one of the staple ways of making ends meet among the Liverpool poor, as in London. (Ayers and Lambertz, 1986; Stedman Jones, 1976, pp. 61, 91.)

77. McCabe, 1975, p. 27, confirms this.

78. For Mr Stitt see above, n. 52.

79. See above, n. 45.

80. The Liverpool Street Railway was a pioneering horse tramway which began operations in July 1861 but seems to have been removed in the following year because 'it was badly constructed and the rails were considered dangerous to other traffic which crossed them obliquely'.

See J. B. Horne and T. B. Maund, *Liverpool transport, I (1830–1900)* (Hanwell: Light Railway Transport League, 1975), chapter 2, for the full complex story.

81. For vagrancy and the poor law in general, M. A. Crowther, *The workhouse system, 1834–1929* (London: Batsford, 1981), pp. 248–52.
82. Crowther, 1981, p. 124, says that workhouse masters might *surreptitiously* (our italics) employ literate paupers to do clerical work. But Liverpool was a special case within the poor-law system. (Midwinter, 1971, chapter 4.)
83. Cropper was a churchwarden in Hugh Stowell Brown's parish, a leading member of the temperance movement, and a campaigner against dancing rooms.
84. For the special status of Liverpool's Select Vestry see Midwinter, 1971, chapter 4, and Feehan, 1988.
85. Simey, 1951, chapter 5, provides a context for these digs at female workhouse visitors.
86. For this great water supply controversy see White, 1951, pp. 55–8; Midwinter, 1971, pp. 103–6.
87. See Shimmin, *Pen-and-ink sketches*, pp. 114–16.
88. Ibid., pp. 84–6.
89. Ibid., pp. 67–74: a very eminent Liverpool figure, and brother of W. E. Gladstone.
90. One of Liverpool's leading citizens, a member of its merchant patriciate, the leading light in its charitable circles, and a Liberal M.P. in 1868–95. (Waller, 1981, p.507.)
91. Irish.
92. See above, n. 86.
93. Founder of the *Liverpool Mercury*. (Biography in Liverpool Library, H920.SMI.)
94. For the baths see also J. Newland, *The establishment and present condition of the public baths and wash-houses in Liverpool* (1856).
95. For district visitors, Prochaska, 1980, chapter 4.
96. On these themes see also chapter 21, above, and n. 70.
97. For a similar gloss on popular Protestantism and the Orange Order see Ingram, 1988.
98. Tebbutt, 1983, p. 73, has further instances of this practice.
99. Taylor, 1974, pp. 65–70, provides the background to these schemes.
100. This was a common, perhaps a universal, set of problems with philanthropic housing schemes of this type, and recurs throughout the literature.
101. Bailey, 1978, develops this theme.
102. That is, *away* from home.
103. See above, chapter 1.
104. Brown, 1929, pp. 51–62, shows that three Co-operative societies were flourishing in Liverpool in the early 1860s; but their success was to be short-lived, and in 1867 the Central Store in Camden Street was rented out as a music hall after a startling drop in trade and turnover.

105. See above, n. 57.
106. These ideas about the results of co-operation were widespread at the time. (Gosden, 1973, 189–90.)

Index